the

private death

of **PUBLIC** DISCOURSE

Other books by Barry Sanders

Sudden Glory: Laughter as Subversive History

A Is for Ox: Violence, Electronic Media, and the Silencing of the Written Word

ABC: The Alphabetization of the Popular Mind

The Sacred Paw: The Bear in Nature, Myth, and Literature

BARRY SANDERS

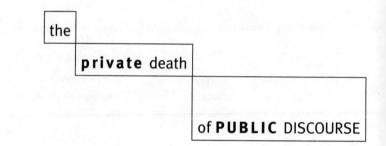

the
private death
of **PUBLIC** DISCOURSE

BEACON PRESS Boston

Grateful acknowledgment is made to the following for permission to reprint: "First Grade—Standing in the Hall," from *Dirt Road Home* by Cheryl Savageau, published by Curbstone Press, 1995. Reprinted by permission of Curbstone Press.

Postscript from "Prologue: The Birth of Architecture," from *W. H. Auden: Collected Poems* by W. H. Auden. Copyright © 1965 by W. H. Auden. Reprinted by permission of Random House, Inc.

Beacon Press
25 Beacon Street
Boston, Massachusetts
02108–2892
http://www.beacon.org

Beacon Press books are published under the auspices of the Unitarian Universalist Association of Congregations.

© 1998 by Barry Sanders
All rights reserved
Printed in the United States of America

03 02 01 00 99 98
8 7 6 5 4 3 2 1

Text design by Diane Jaroch
Composition by Wilsted & Taylor Publishing Services

Library of Congress Cataloging-in-Publication Data

Sanders, Barry, 1938–
The private death of public discourse / Barry Sanders.
p.   cm.
Includes bibliographical references and index.
ISBN 0-8070-0434-0
1. United States—Civilization—20th century. 2. Popular culture—United States—History—20th century.   3. Rhetoric—Political aspects—United States.   4. Rhetoric—Social aspects—United States.
5. Freedom of Speech—United States.   6. Public speaking—United States.   7. Mass media—United States.   I. Title.
E169.1.S242   1998
306.2'0973'09045—dc21
97–24485

GRACE

Nothing is at last sacred

but the integrity of your own mind.—

EMERSON, ''SELF-RELIANCE''

Contents

the
private death
of **PUBLIC** DISCOURSE

The truth of this book lies in the telling. If I were talking to you—my face looking directly at your face—instead of writing to you, you could ask me what I mean by "lies." How can I bring truth and lie so dangerously close together, you might ask, in one sentence? Do I mean to be mean? Am I lying? Deliberately? But of course you can't ask me anything. And even if I were to respond, you couldn't hear me. Marcel Proust catches the differences between conversation and reading in the delightful essay "On Reading," which he planned as the introduction to his translation of John Ruskin's *Sesame and Lilies*:

Reading cannot be assimilated . . . to a conversation, even with the wisest of men; that the essential difference between a book and a friend is not their greater or lesser wisdom, but the manner in which we communicate with them, reading being the exact opposite of conversation in consisting for each one of us in having another's thought communicated to us while remaining on our own, that is while continuing to enjoy the intellectual authority we have in solitude and which conversation dispels instantly, while continuing to be open to inspiration, with our mind yet working hard and fruitfully on itself.*

Although this is a book about discourse, I simply cannot talk to you. So I have tried to compensate by making the telling of the book resemble, as much as possible, the way stories get told in oral cultures. I want to provide a sense of narrative flow quite distinct, that is, from the patterns of literacy.

In oral storytelling, the teller does not usually move in a straight line, first one subject then the next, in an orderly progression, but wanders

---

*Marcel Proust, *On Reading*, trans. John Sturrock (New York: Viking Penguin, 1995), p. 26.

back periodically, picking up earlier threads and weaving them into the action. The teller repeats, adds details, twists and turns, remembers and adjusts. In that way, the story accretes; details begin to arrange themselves, like metal filings, around a central theme or themes, the pattern looking more like reflection, or thought in process, than revised, polished prose.

This book takes as its theme the death of private, interior space—what Proust called the *moi profond*, the "deep self" uncovered in reading. This book is always heading in its tiny odyssey toward regeneration and reinvigoration. In significant ways, then, the discussion leads to a climactic celebration of the human spirit and then traces a journey away from that celebratory moment. I have chosen as the key event July 4—not, however, July 4, 1776. Instead, I have settled on another, slightly more obscure but more personally demanding July 4: the publication of Walt Whitman's *Leaves of Grass* on Independence Day 1855.*

In the Declaration of Independence, a document for the liberation of the country, prose moves at the slow, stately pace of reasoned argument—"When in the course of human events, it becomes necessary for one people to dissolve the political bands which have connected them with another"—and though it advertises itself as a statement, a spoken utterance (for that is what *declaration* means, after all), it clearly derives from literacy.† The Declaration must be read. Its opening grammatical construction, a subordinate clause—not a short one at close to fifty words long—followed by an independent sentence, hardly ever appears in oral cultures. The independent sentence—"They should declare the causes which impel them to separation"—arrives with force, and mandates utterance—some significant discourse.‡ Probably unconsciously, the framers manage to

---

*Scholars have a difficult time dating the poem; Whitman does not help. I use Malcolm Cowley's date.

†"When in the course of human events" does not merely refer to time, but to space as well. A "course" only takes up time because it moves through space. This intimate tie between space and time I explore later in the book.

‡Orality does not accommodate complex sentences because, by the time audiences get to hear the independent sentence, they have already forgotten what depended on it. Listeners have a difficult time holding fifty words in their heads. It's much easier for a reader to turn back to the dependent clause, as often as necessary—a luxury that literacy affords—to retrieve total meaning.

express their own political ambitions for the nation through grammar—to move from dependence to an anticipated independence. "The Unanimous Declaration of the thirteen United States of America" assumes, through its repeated use of the coercive *we*, that everyone else shares in that great literate transaction—or at the very least, should share in it by becoming a national subject. Even though the General Congress adopted an oral form, a *declaration*, for their document, they wanted to have it both ways, "to solemnly publish *and* declare." In the end, though, they created a legal instrument, giving the states "full power to levy War, Conclude Peace, contract Alliances, establish Commerce, and to do all other Acts and Things which Independent States may of right do."

The Declaration frees people; it breaks bands in the creation of "Free and Independent States." The fifty-seven signators bear witness to the birth of the body politic as an amalgam, as the eighteenth-century word has it, of *Americans*. Not a pen that day, though, for a single woman, or black, or Native American. The instrument has holes. The Declaration may have insisted, finally, too heavily on independence.

Less than eighty years later, on July 4, 1855, Walt Whitman aimed to fill those holes by embracing all America's people—every gender, color, class, sexual leaning—and bringing every last one into his poem. He relates himself—in the sense of kinship connections—to everyone around him. Whitman's liberation, his independence, is the declaration of an individual—the birth of a powerful and unique self. Whitman took the Declaration of Independence more seriously than most citizens. In his poem, he has become the country itself. We take *him* to be self-evident, self-reliant. He smiles, and the sun shines. Whitman owns nothing and everything. Embarrassment, frustration, shame, envy, even anger—the emotions seem to have vanished from his life. Only love remains. And he wears it loose and easy, loafing and inviting friends and strangers to rest their heads on his bosom.

Whitman sings; he is all voice. Put your ear close to the page and hear him breathing. But *Leaves of Grass* arrives just as the great gears of industry grind at near full speed. The pursuit was on—for wealth and success, for happiness. People had to scream above the din of a million machines to be heard. Two ideas collide head-on: happiness and mechanization; or, more flatly stated, life, liberty, and the pursuit of happiness with what Whitman calls the "cast-iron, civilized life."*

This country, stretching like a giant from one coast all the way to the other, should be able to accommodate both liberty and, these days, technology. Shouldn't it? Whitman took a breath and inhaled all of it, all of us. Somehow, some way, however, the country has grown smaller. And that means we, too, have shrunk. Think about the several images of Independence Day we have seen in the past year or two. The producers of the blockbuster, special-effects movie of 1996—a film that stars computer-generated images rather than human beings—chose to title their study in violence *Independence Day*. The action culminates on July 4, and includes, smack in the faces of every viewer, the fiery explosion of the White House. What an image of horror: the president of the United States a victim of homelessness.

A superior force from outer space—the Other—like some powerful virus, has attacked America, and there, in one mighty megabyte event, the aliens eradicate "unalienable Rights." The thought is intended to chill: We are not alone. Space takes up more room than we ever imagined. All the majesty and might of America, called into doubt by our failure in Vietnam, come crashing down in nightmarish detail in *Independence Day*.

In another, more intelligent *Independence Day*, the compelling novel by Richard Ford, for which he won the Pulitzer Prize in 1995, we hear the story of Frank Bascombe, who plans to commemorate July 4 by taking his son, who lives with Frank's divorced wife, on a trip from Haddam, New Jersey, to Cooperstown, New York, to visit the Baseball Hall of Fame. Bascombe has a weird premonition about the undertaking:

---

*W. E. B. Du Bois comes to mind here: "There are no truer exponents of the pure human spirit of the Declaration of Independence than the American Negroes. . . . We black men seem to be the sole oasis of simple faith and reverence in a dusty desert of dollars and smartness" (*The Souls of Black Folk* [New York: Dodd Mead, 1961], p. 15).

There is, in fact, an odd feeling of *lasts*, to this excursion, as if some signal period in life—mine *and* his—is coming, if not to a full close, then at least toward some tightening, transforming twist in the kaleidoscope, a change I'd be foolish to take lightly and don't. (The impulse to read *Self-Reliance* is significant here, as if the holiday itself—my favorite secular one for being public and for its implicit goal of leaving us only as it found us: free.)*

The most notable detail of Frank's nervous life is his profession: he is a real-estate agent. Bascombe's job is to see that every person in America owns a house. America—the solid fact of America, measured in its clods of dirt—has been sold off, piece by piece. In Ford's novel, America has been parceled out and exchanged in countless transactions, over countless years, for cash. As Richard Ford has said, someday, everybody in America will be a real-estate broker.

For Frank Bascombe, everything has fallen apart—he has lost a child, endured a divorce, given up his career as a sportswriter, and been forced out of his own house. He has a hard time talking to anyone but himself. And he doesn't know how to fix his broken life. Inside, Frank feels dried up; but he is trying, desperately trying, with the help of his new girlfriend, Sally Caldwell, to relearn how to love. Worried about his impending trip with his son, he talks it over with Sally by phone, the dad suddenly a founding (and foundering) father:

Last night sometime after midnight, when I'd already slept for an hour, waked up twice twisting my pillow and fretting about Paul's and my journey, downed a glass of milk, watched the Weather Channel, then settled back to read a chapter of *The Declaration of Independence*—Carl Becker's classic, which, along with *Self-Reliance*, I plan to use as key "texts" for communicating with my troubled son and thereby transmitting to him important info—Sally called. . . .

"Hi, hi. What's new?" she said, a tone of uneasy restraint in her usually silky voice, as if midnight calls were not our regular practice, which they aren't.

"I was just reading Carl Becker, who's terrific," I said, though on alert. "He thought that the whole Declaration of Independence was an attempt to prove rebellion was the wrong word for what the founding fathers were up to. It was a war over a word choice. That's pretty amazing."

---

*Richard Ford, *Independence Day* (New York: Alfred A. Knopf, 1995), p. 7.

She sighed. "What was the right word?"

"Oh. Common sense. Nature. Progress. God's will. Karma. Nirvana. It pretty much all meant the same thing to Jefferson and Adams and those guys. They were smarter than we are."*

Ford has done something remarkable. He has written a novel less *about* America than *for* America, a book that speaks for the country, for the desperation of its plight. With plain talk difficult to come by, *Independence Day* provides voice for all those people who have lost their own. Ford has gone for the "Big Book," what we call jokingly, in cocktail conversation, the Great American Novel—*great*, that is, in size and great in impact. It is a book full of talk, and attempts to talk. Ford makes his narrator, Frank Bascombe, intentionally wordy. He needs the companionship of language. For Bascombe knows, instinctively, that only words, only palaver, will carry him back to health.

I offer *The Private Death of Public Discourse* as a road map, not to Cooperstown—the home of America's heroes, of its national pastime, a home on which no bank can ever foreclose—but a road map, a tourist guide, to America before it got so small. I recognize the irony here, that electronic technology promises to expand my world, that with a PC and a modum I can theoretically hook up with anyone I choose anywhere on the globe. I can retrieve any piece of datum—no matter its age or location: The world expands and expands.

I don't believe it. I argue in these pages that the more we move on-line the more our internal worlds shrink. And as our interior space begins to diminish, so our range of experience grows smaller. The two—inside and outside—depend on each other. Maybe, on reflection, independence needs tempering. Maybe, as Walt Whitman and, more recently, Frank Bascombe make clear, we have to emphasize what I term *contingency*—an openness to chance, to surprise, to change, in our meetings with each other. We've had more than two hundred years of independence. It's time, per-

---

*Ibid., pp. 8–9.

haps, to focus on the subordinate clause, on the dependent part of the Declaration of Independence. In a time as fragile as ours, we connect with each other through the slimmest, the most evanescent, elements—words. Every sentence is a lifeline. "In the desert," Emerson observes, "life hangs on the contingency of a skin of water."

Public discourse is a web, a complicated, variegated net of language that can capture the shadow truth—the ambiguous nature—of a problem, in stark contrast to the way that numbers and statistics bypass and cancel the flesh and bone of experience. The Dutch novelist Abel Herzberg, a survivor of Bergen-Belsen, makes the point that the Nazis did not exterminate six million Jews. Rather, he says, the Nazis killed one Jew, and then another, and another, over and over six million times. Protests and demonstrations, with people braced at the barricades delivering speeches and offering solutions—wrongheaded at times, but fiery, personal—those goodwilled demands for change have nearly become relics. Polls and interviews have replaced them. We fill out forms to indicate what we think about the most potent political issues. We mail in our views or paste them on our bumpers. We have only to look at poverty statistics in this country to demonstrate the barrenness of virtual vision.

According to a December 1996 report released by the National Center for Children in Poverty, at the Columbia School of Public Health, the number of children under six years of age living in poverty jumped from 3.5 million to 6.1 million between 1979 and 1995. During that same period, the rate of poverty also expanded, from 18 to 25 percent. The numbers translate into something shocking: one out of every four children under six years of age lives in poverty, in the midst of what is still, by almost every indicator, a nation of extraordinary wealth. Those numbers about young children baffle and confuse. Surely, they describe, not the United States of America, but some other, impoverished and constricted country. But those children have not become a topic of national debate or even of much concern. In fact, the Urban Institute estimates that with the cuts in guarantees of cash welfare for poor children passed by Congress in 1996, 1 million more children will probably move into deep poverty and out onto the streets by 1998.* The streets can only grow more crowded.

Those desperate youngsters have not become part of our public conversation because there's no story there. The kids remain mostly invisible. They have no voice. They do not vote. But we should not doubt that, day by day, hour by hour, each of them fades a bit more. In debate, politicians talk about them, around them, over them—use them as an issue—while out on the mean streets, young children, known to few but their broken families, die a mean death. How do we save them? How do we rescue them from a ghostly and pale existence as virtualized human beings?

As adults, as a nation, we depend on our children, and the god-awful conditions on the street are a damning reflection of our own blasted interiors. Nature writers like Gary Snyder, Wendell Berry, and Richard Nelson suggest that we cannot truly feel at home without a spirit of place—without knowing, say, the watershed we inhabit. Continue the metaphor and imagine, now, our interior landscapes as deforested, denuded, ravaged by one electronic medium or another statistic. In this double disorientation of external and internal landscapes, what chance, then, for celebration or community?

The most radical answer to this question involves a return to one of the most basic and unruly (without rules) of human interactions—the seemingly lost art of conversation. We have to *talk* those stricken kids back into fleshy, palpable existence. We have to retrieve them from columns of numbers and percentages, from bar graphs and bell curves, and try to see them and hear them and smell their poverty. By getting them to course through our discourse, maybe we can take them into our hearts. Grab those kids away from politicians, even the most liberal of whom tend to talk about them without comprehending the bleakness of their daily lives: "Lib-

---

*The Department of Health and Human Services, using the Urban Institute's statistical model, reached the same conclusion. This country, by the way, already has one of the highest poverty rates among children of any developed country.

erals were never prepared to counter the inversion of rhetoric that's taken place—this way of saying, 'We're [cutting welfare payments] to help the children.' . . . The country has come to mistake the symptoms of social breakdown for the causes, and for that, I'm afraid, there's plenty of blame to go around."*

Emerson demands of his fellow citizens nothing less than a commitment to the integrity of the mind, and he goads us with words, words, and more words.† I have tried to shake some loose here with this talking book. Right now, those kids in the street don't have much of a chance. For talk—talk unfettered by politics and formulas—has all but dissolved. Frank Bascombe can't do it. On Independence Day, he desperately wants to talk to the son he has not seen in so long, talk man to man, father to son, but he has to fall back for help not even on the Declaration of Independence itself, but on a book *about* the Declaration of Independence. For want of talk, Frank uses words like "text," "communicating," "transmitting," "info." He needs a script. Frank Bascombe's dislocation from the original—from his own "flesh and blood"—speaks to our own disorientation. Millions of Americans dial up talk radio, or turn on Oprah and Geraldo, or latch onto some piece of propaganda. They boot up or go on-line. They hook into the Web or a chat room.

What they do not do, however, is talk very much. The words that users scroll onto the PC monitor pass for speech. Frank Bascombe's answer to Sally Caldwell's question about the right word is telling—he answers with a long list and concludes, in the most general way, "It pretty much all meant the same thing." It doesn't, of course, all mean the same thing, *karma* a far cry from *progress, nature* radically different from *nirvana.* And Frank can't be bothered to find—or, rather, in his state, he can't get at—the right word. Finally, most dramatically, Frank and Sally don't talk it over,

---

*Daniel Patrick Moynihan, quoted in John Heilemann, "Washington's Last Loud Liberal," *New Yorker*, August 5, 1996, p. 24.

†Ralph Waldo Emerson, "Self-Reliance," in *Essays and Lectures*, ed. Joel Porte (New York: Library Classics of the United States, 1983), p. 261.

don't reason it out. It's a telephone call, after all, not face to face, not conversation. It's midnight: the day's over. The two lovers have only a phone line to connect them. The scene peters out in an unstrung series of words.

Too often talk devolves into paired monologues that by accident, fatigue, indifference collapse into lukewarm agreement. Conversely, when each side holds fast to an agenda, very little can flow back and forth. Real conversation arises from a single location—from deep inside a person. This thing called conversation is an art that takes enormous practice and patience, requires real concern for and interest in the one you talk to. It works best when you can see each other's face, notice expressions, observe bodily stances and gestures. Pacing back and forth works well; laughter too. Touching helps. Erotic stuff, the passing of ideas. We sometimes forget its old name: social intercourse.

I draw here on *The University in Ruins* by Bill Readings, a remarkable little book never really completed, because of the death of its author. Readings' understanding of teaching is directly translatable to the idea of discourse. The character of conversation—the discipline of discourse— derives a good deal of its strength from *thinking*. With that in mind, Readings could be describing conversation when he reframes teaching as "sites of *obligation*, as loci of *ethical* practices, rather than as means for the transmission of scientific knowledge. Teaching thus becomes answerable to the *question of justice* rather than to the criteria of truth."* Too often the desire to be right, to stake a claim on truth, destroys all chance for conversation. When that happens, we need to remember those guides: the questions of justice and our obligations to each other.

Readings goes on to dismiss Ferdinand de Saussure's description of discourse, in which a sender delivers a sentence to a receiver who chooses to remain silent, so that "a message is passed from a sender (full vessel emptied) to a receiver (empty vessel filled). Dialogue [thus becomes] merely the

---

*Bill Readings, *The University in Ruins* (Cambridge: Harvard University Press, 1996), p. 154.

exchange of ideas between two persons, so that the sender becomes in turn the empty receiver, and so on."*

Saussure's scheme for the transmission of information—communication, really—resembles the user's interactive interface with a computer: full vessel (machine) to empty vessel (user), full vessel to empty vessel, again and again, until the operator turns off the machine in satisfaction or disgust. We might all be lulled, in this time of electronic fallout, to hold to such a model, especially if we learn the habit of discourse on the Internet, in chat rooms, through e-mail, or on the Web. The operator may feel like the sender but is in fact always the receiver—of one program or another—and is never really in control of the transmission, though it all looks so neat and simple in its virtual chumminess.

I prefer the truly messy, truly dynamic model described with deliberate care and urgency by Mikhail Bakhtin, who asserts that both receiver and sender have been crammed full of words and sentences over the years, with ideas and habits, soaked in multiple layers of meanings. The language of one person meets the language of another, and in that entanglement of understanding and misunderstanding, with a good deal of work and some luck, glimmerings of meanings struggle into focus. What I call discourse Bakhtin calls heteroglossia or dialogism: "Word comes into contact with word." Echoing Bakhtin, Bill Readings concludes that speaking must "respect what might be called the *abyssal space* of reading by the other."† In the chase after meaning, discourse may offer its own end. Truth may finally elude us.

Discourse thus resembles the heart of experience, unfolding little by little, surprising in its twists and turns, frustrating and also delighting with its great arc to the infinite. At times, discourse may not seem to get any real work done, to move anywhere—merely rolling on and on aimlessly, a mythical river emptying, far off and unseen, in the sea. At other times, like

---

*Ibid., p. 155.
†Ibid.

still water, it may appear murky and cloudy, incapable of ever providing refreshment. Nothing makes it flow quite like play, nothing keeps it on course quite like goodwill and the recognition that the lives of those you talk to inhere, most powerfully and most intimately—and very often, with great fragility—in their inner speech.

In moving through this book, I ask the reader to keep in mind the Bakhtinian pulse of dialogue, which I hold out as a goal for the book's conclusion. Dialogue—discourse—may be the fulcrum for lifting from America its heavy burden of nastiness so that we can move to compassion and understanding. My narration *has* to lie in the telling, for I can only hint at, vaguely point to, the full horror of the problem; I can only try to uncover its outlines with the written word as I wander down the path of our pathology. To arrive at any real solutions to our gravest problems—problems now masked by meanspirited and outrageous acts, by anger, even hatred, and mindless violence—we all must rededicate ourselves to an enormous undertaking: to the goodwilled and vigorous exchange of ideas, to that tired but terribly reliable old dog just waiting for the word to come alive again—to public discourse.

1

Open the dictionary to any page and you lay bare a compelling collection of mysteries. Take the word *mean*. That four-letter word reveals a truth about the English language so deeply puzzling it seems almost impossible to believe. *Mean* derives from three separate sources, one late Latin (*medianus*, "in the middle"), and the other two Teutonic (*gamaini*, "possessed jointly," "belonging equally to a number of people"; and *meinen*, "to have in mind," "to signify"). These three streams ran together some time in the eighth or ninth century to create a remarkable set of paradoxical definitions, all of them current by the late fourteenth century. Since this book turns on that single word, on the way *meanness* has replaced *meaning* in contemporary life, I take some time here explaining its history and behavior.

First, the word *mean* reaches deep into the language, into its most basic function—to understanding itself. What does this word mean? This sentence? This paragraph? Or even this entire book? During recent years, these questions have become harder and harder to answer—and more and more absurd, in fact, to ask—as critical theories have slowly drained meaning out of literature, history, and the sciences. In the introduction to his collection of essays *No Passion Spent*, George Steiner notes the difficulty of trying to get at meaning, particularly in the wake of postmodern theorizing: " 'Post-structuralism,' 'deconstruction,' and 'post-modernism,' have diversely put in doubt the relations, as these were classically conceived, between words and meaning. . . . 'Meaning' is no more than a momentary play of interpretive possibilities, dissolving into self-subversion in the very moment of illusory decipherment."* Steiner charges the nineteenth-century poet Stephane Mallarmé with breaking the connection between word and world and thus exposing as a futile pursuit our attempts to describe reality with nothing but a set of arbitrary signs. After the Symbolist poets—Mallarmé, Rimbaud, Baudelaire—people could no longer expect to make sense out of language. If that fissure marks our entry into the modern period, as Steiner argues, then perhaps the deeper ruptures of meaning caused by the electronic media mark the beginning of the postmodern period. The most deliberate notions of *meaning*, to define, denote, and delineate have, over the past few decades, seeped out of all things familiar. Everything—from sports, to politics, to everyday events like the weather—comes to us packaged and produced, stripped clean of the ambiguity that can surround even the most mundane occurrences. You can download an avalanche of data off the Internet, but how does anyone make sense of such an array of information? To search for meaning is to dance with ghosts.

Some thirty-five years ago, commenting on the Kennedy-Nixon debates, Daniel J. Boorstin, in his book *The Image*, predicted the inevitability of staged events, of crucial political debates, for instance, reduced to TV docu-dramas or, even worse, insufferable sit-coms. The 1996 Republican National Convention bears Boorstin out. It came across as such a tightly scripted affair that Ted Koppel and his *Nightline* staff abandoned the convention after the second day, declaring the proceedings no more interesting than an infomercial. How could it have been anything else when its producers demanded preapproved, meticulously rehearsed speeches, applause on cue, scheduled interruptions of enthusiasm, and most damaging of all to the idea of public discourse, the total eradication of all dissent, opposition, or even criticism? Network officials have said that they may not cover the conventions—Republican or Democratic—in the year 2000.

The Republican National Convention attracted 1,990 delegates,

---

*George Steiner, *No Passion Spent* (Chicago: University of Chicago Press, 1996), p. ix.

and a whopping 15,000 more members of the press. Most of those 15,000 watched the proceedings, not in front of the podium, but in front of television screens. So thoroughly devoid of any spark of dramatic life, let alone real conversation or discourse, the convention received miserable ratings. The total number of viewers on all three networks fell from 1992, a convention already down from 1988. Even protests had to follow strict guidelines laid down by Haley Barbour, chairman of the Republican National Committee: Barbour restricted demonstrations to a parking lot across the trolley tracks from the convention center, limiting them to no more than fifty-five minutes, after which the microphones went dead. Plain and simple the message: No electricity means no power.

In a second sense, the word *meaning* insinuates itself deep inside one's interior life, in the form of the penetrating question, the simple but direct "What do you mean?" In this regard, *mean* forces the speaker to take a stand, to adopt a position and articulate it—for best results, without equivocation or hesitation. To satisfy the demands of this sense of the word requires time, effort, and, above all, concentration. Here, too, as I hope to show, because of the effects of electronic technology, trying to find meaning has become more and more difficult.

Nevertheless, *meaning* offers the possibility of answering the question "What do you mean?" by providing the right "means," a pathway, or a method for solving problems, including even a sufficiency of money (the "means") to buy one's way out of a tight squeeze. These means can sometimes *justify* the ends by forcing the conclusions of arguments into neat and orderly patterns, into sentences that not only sound but look convincing. This sense of *justification*, then, orders and aligns the margins of a page so that the reader confronts the text as a solid and unified block of prose. Thus, the means have a natural affinity with the dignity of borders: tidy margins and orderly edges.

But *mean* does not in every instance require a speaker to adopt a position and find a way of defending that position. True to its contrary nature, *mean* can also ask a person to abandon a commitment to secure positions in favor of a space that offends no particular camp—a movement to the middle, the *mean*. The ancient Greeks called this space "the happy mean" or "the golden mean," an enviable position of conscious restraint, a tempered response that avoids the extremes both of excess and deficiency.* Here the word recalls the eighteenth-century British *middling*, average and common. Indeed, over the following one hundred years or so, it became so common that it descended into downright inferiority and turned out to be nothing more than coarse, or just plain "mean," in the final sense denoting an inferior moral disposition, meanness of spirit, or more accurately, a paucity of spirit, that often compensates for its lack of substance in increased stridency.†

Thus the word that straddles the middle—a term born out of conscientious restraint—further demonstrates its contrary nature by moving from a happy medium right back to the very edge. Meanness—true meanness—works most effectively at the extreme called excess. Middle-of-the-road meanness comes off namby-pamby and sniveling: a sham. Out at the edges, the fringes—the borders of behavior, really, where acts command attention through their boldness and strength—meanness flexes and fulminates. That's where anger and vitriol erupt. That's where you get your point across. And that's how the argument gets forced, many times, across the border—through mean-spirited and vicious outbursts.

At the borders, then, meaning and meanness merge solidly together. Or, more to the point of this book, in extremes meanness has a tendency to supplant or stand in for meaning. That tendency seems more true today than at any other time, making the world a scary place. One can see it everywhere. Young kids who want respect take on something called "attitude"—or, to use the slang, "cop a 'tude." A bumper sticker warns, "This Car Protected by Smith and Wesson," while another, a bit more funny, perhaps, but still downright nasty, advises, "Save the Planet, Kill

---

*The French called the nineteenth-century, liberal politics of Louis-Philippe, the *juste-milieu*—literally, "the happy medium."

†While *demean* comes from a different Latin root, *minare*, "to lead" or "to conduct," and comes into French as *demener*, "to conduct oneself" (Modern English *demeanor*), the word *demean*, on the model of *mean* as "common," takes on the sense "to debase." This ability to debase oneself is acquired just as seventeenth-century philosophers begin to explore the self. I take up this topic in chapter three.

Yourself." A T-shirt proclaims, "Fuck Everything!" A psychologist named Daniel Goleman writes an entire book, *Emotional Intelligence*, to address what he describes as a most vexing question: "What might account for the disintegration of civility and safety in this country?"

Louis Farrakhan levels the meanest of charges against "bloodsucking Jews and Koreans" and "diseased faggots." Bill Clinton addresses the National Rainbow Convention and chastises Sister Souljah, the rap singer, for suggesting (even humorously) that blacks take "a week and kill white people." In the O. J. Simpson double murder trial, millions of viewers listen in shock to the horrific racial epithets of L.A.P.D. officer Mark Fuhrman, repeated by Simpson's entire battalion of defense attorneys. College newspapers, like the *Dartmouth Review*, print articles supporting gay bashing and carry ads denouncing blacks. The Simon Wiesenthal Center requests America Online, CompuServe, Prodigy, the Microsoft Network, and dozens of other Internet service providers to refuse to carry "messages that promote racism, anti-Semitism, mayhem, and violence." The issue of electronically delivered hate worldwide has prompted into being Net Hate, a World Wide Web page based in Montreal, that seeks to expose hate speech on the Internet.

A wall at Pomona College, in Claremont, California, makes the *New York Times*. For years and years, students have written their opinions on a wide range of topics on that wall. The administration has generally allowed the writing to remain, permitting other students to write over past messages, in layer upon layer of friendly give and take. The wall has become one of the school's most enduring traditions. Recently, however, antiblack and anti-Asian scribblings have prompted college officials to monitor the wall and to erase the hate, and they have proposed doing away with the wall altogether.

In politics and public life, in education and the arts, in virtually every domain one can mention, the way a good many people express their ideas sounds more and more hateful and feels more and more mean-spirited. Users get "flamed" on the information highway; youngsters get shot on the streets; children get abused at home. Athletic competition, too, has moved to the edge, with "Extreme Sports" attracting enthusiasts like street luges, who skate down the pavement at speeds over sixty miles per hour, sky surfers, and downhill mountain bike racers. Even architecture, a profession that must adhere to the narrow tolerances of safety and precise limits of engineering— "the art of putting an ordered public face on things," as Herbert Muschamp, one of the architecture critics of the *New York Times*, defines the profession—even architecture stalks the borders by designing fear and revulsion into some of its most prominent public buildings. Muschamp places such contemporary architects as Emilio Ambasz, James Wines, Aldo Rossi, Peter Eisenman, the Miami firm Arquitectonica, Bernard Tschumi, Frank Gehry, and Rem Koolhaas in that "extreme" category; but he singles out Raimund Abraham and his proposed design for the Austrian Cultural Institute in Manhattan for special consideration: "The building will be clad on the street side by three overlapping planes of glass that jut out sharply, like blades, on their lower edges. Mr. Abraham has compared the facade to a guillotine, a comment that has provoked the displeasure of those who see something uncivil in such a violent image."*

People expect—even demand—safe cities. Here, the architect has memorialized a classic instrument of torture, the guillotine, in the heart of one of America's biggest cities. Anyone strolling past the facade of the Austrian Cultural Institute must confront that image of capital punishment. In an earlier time, aesthetics would have demanded that the facade—the whole design, really—reveal the business of the building. But Abraham has moved well beyond what the architecture critic Christopher Jencks calls "form follows fiasco." The postmodern gargoyle, the architectural decoration, has become in the contemporary period a machine of death. One can only long for architecture that embraces Le Corbusier's definition of a building—a machine for living.

Perhaps we should not be so scandalized by Abraham, given the recent turn in our criminal justice system. In many states, for instance,

---

*Herbert Muschamp, "Buildings Born of Dreams and Demons," *New York Times*, January 7, 1996, sec. H, p. 27.

youngsters twelve years of age or younger, who have been charged with violent crimes, can be tried as adults. New York has lowered the age all the way down to seven. America has also shown a desire to punish the already-punished, in the so-called three strikes legislation, as well as a renewed passion for capital punishment. In 1995, according to the Bureau of Justice Statistics, state governors signed execution orders for 56 murderers, nearly double the number (31) in 1994, and the highest since 1957. Moreover, with a record 3,054 men and women on death row in thirty-eight states, 1996 may see even higher totals.* (As of December 31, 1995, 2,998 men and 48 women were on state death rows, and 8 men were under federal death sentence. All had committed murder.) Richard Dieter, of the Death Penalty Information Center, a Washington research group whose focus is the inequities of capital sentencing, says that "the trend is fewer legal prohibitions and there's a sentiment towards speeding up the process."† Illinois nearly executed a woman, only the second since the country resumed capital punishment in 1976. Illinois last executed a woman more than fifty years ago. And in Utah, in 1996, John Albert Tayler, an inmate convicted of killing an eleven-year-old, elected to die by firing squad. Utah is the only state that permits such executions. When Jack Ford, of the Utah State Correctional Department, announced the execution, sharpshooters jammed his telephones volunteering for the job.

Such changes speak of a new, harsher attitude toward deviants—toward those who choose or who cannot escape life on the far edges. Lock them up and don't let them out—that's how we deal with crime these days. As James K. Kunen observes in "Teaching Prisoners a Lesson," prison officials have slashed programs of every sort, from drug counseling to medical care, "as get-tough-on-crime politicians shift the focus of corrections departments from rehabilitation to retribution and deterrence."‡ They

---

*Three hundred thirteen executions have taken place since January 1977, beginning with the execution of Gary Gilmore by firing squad, largely in the South and the West. No Court reinstated capital punishment in 1976. State governors commuted ten death sentences in 1991, which fell to one in 1994, and to zero in 1995.

†*New York Times*, December 30, 1995, sec. 1, p. 10. Dieter can make such a prediction in part because Congress passed the Effective Death Penalty Act in 1995, designed to increase the pace of executions.

‡James K. Kunen, "Teaching Prisoners a Lesson," *New Yorker*, July 18, 1995, p. 34.

have also begun to eliminate virtually every amenity for inmates, from large-screen TV sets, weights, and other recreational equipment, to coffee pots in cells, typewriters, access to the Internet, daily showers, and most dramatically, as part of the 1994 anticrime bill, all high school and college classes.* The governor of Alabama—followed by the governors of Florida and Arizona—has even resuscitated chain gangs for minimum security prisoners. At the Limestone Correctional Facility, near Huntsville, Governor Fob Jones, Jr., paraded prisoners (in the old striped uniforms) along a major highway in the summer of 1995 to combat the perception, he said, that prison offers a chance at easy living.

The most shocking move toward judicial meanness may not come from governors or wardens, but from Washington, with proposed legislation like the Stop Turning Out Prisoners Act (STOP). Introduced in the Senate by Phil Gramm and Kay Bailey Hutchison, Republican of Texas— who, in an amendment to the 1994 anticrime bill, also led the fight to deny Pell Grants for prisoners—STOP intends to void all federal court decrees aimed at redressing inhumane prison conditions.

These days, of course, it's getting hard to spot the convicts, as more and more young people, in an attempt, perhaps, to be taken seriously, affect a tough prison attitude, wearing the baggy denim clothing of inmates, sporting prison tattoos, spouting prison jargon, shaving their heads, and listening to rap groups like Public Enemy and Niggaz Wit' Attitude. Young gang-bangers "mad dog" each other—staring silently and coldly eye-to-eye—an animallike prelude to a showdown. Their dogs of choice are pit bulls, which they match in fights to the death, mixing gunpowder with their chow to make them meaner.

These young people mean business. In 1994, police arrested 2.7 million juveniles, more than a third of them under fifteen years of age. Juvenile offenders committed 14 percent of all violent crimes and a quarter of all

---

*The classes were cut even though recent studies show that one of the most effective deterrents to recidivism among released prisoners is education. Prisoners typically read and write very poorly. Twenty-five percent of New York's prison population, for example, read below the fifth-grade level.

property crimes. While males sixteen to twenty-four years old make up only 8 percent of the entire population, they account for more than a quarter of all homicide victims and nearly half of all murderers. The arrest rate for juveniles aged ten to seventeen for violent crimes rose 100 percent between 1982 and 1992. Between 1983 and 1993, the number of handgun homicides among juveniles increased fivefold, now constituting more than 80 percent of murders by young people. Finally, though FBI figures showed an 11 percent drop in 1996—the fifth annual decrease in a row—in the past ten years the homicide rate among young people aged ten to fourteen increased 165 percent.*

The goriest front-page murders have become a literary genre, devoured eagerly not only by those at the fringes of the spiked and studded punk movement, but by those at the far end of "Goth," who dress like characters out of gothic novels. True crime sells fantastically well these days— horrendous tales told with exacting detail that "touch the border where fantasy turns to fact, where the unimaginable becomes trite."† An awful lot of it, as with cheap handguns and expensive athletic shoes, has been designed expressly for the young consumer:

Another sub-genre of true crime links up with the punkish subculture of aestheticized violence—the friendly folks who have given us coffee-table books of autopsy photographs, exhibitions of paintings, by John Wayne Gacey, serial-killer trading cards, Amok Books in Los Angeles, certain novels of Brett Easton Ellis and Dennis Cooper, a Manson composition sung by Axl Rose, the pretentious gore of movies like "Seven," and so on. . . . One delightful release from St. Martin's Press explores the world of the Wisconsin Killer Ed Gein, who was the

---

*These figures were compiled by the National Center for Juvenile Justice, Pennsylvania. In May 1997, the Justice Department released its latest National Crime Victimization Survey, indicating the largest drop in a generation in practically all categories of violent and property crime. While the news might hearten some officials and relieve lots of parents, we should keep in mind the horrible statistics about young people in this country: 5.1 million Americans, including one-third of all young African-American males, are in prison, in jail, or otherwise involved in the criminal justice system. The independent National Criminal Justice Commission published a report in 1996 titled "The Real War on Crime." It found that one out of every four males in America has an arrest record and, more to the point, 50 percent of all inner-city children have at least one parent in jail or prison, on parole, or on the lam. Even more frightening, the Centers for Disease Control reported in 1997 that nearly three-quarters of all the murders of children in the industrialized world take place in the United States.

†Alex Ross, "The Shock of the True: Crime and Why We Can't Stop Reading about It," New Yorker, August 19, 1996, p. 70.

inspiration for "Psycho" and "The Silence of the Lambs." An address for the Ed Gein Fan Club's merchandising department is appended in the back [of the book], along with an annotated rock-and-roll discography. The author writes sunnily of one Gein-influenced band: "*Macabre* are so monomaniacally obsessed with death, so cartoonishly nihilistic, you must know they've got to be having fun."*

The mean streets promise to get even meaner for young people now that Congress has managed to pull off what it euphemistically calls "welfare reform." When massive cuts were first discussed at the beginning of the year in 1996, Marian Wright Edelman—head of the Children's Defense Fund and, in the words of the *New Yorker* "this country's most effective and passionate advocate for children"—saw "reform" for what it was:

I've never used the word "evil" in all my years in Washington, but what's going on down here is really quite evil. They're proposing to cut two hundred fifty billion dollars from programs for poor children, poor families, disabled children— and it's not even to balance the budget! It's to give a two-hundred-and-forty-five-billion dollar tax cut to the non-needy. The cuts they're talking about are six or seven times worse than the cuts we had in the Reagan years. The Republican radicals are trying to eradicate the role of the federal government as a protector of last resort for children and the poor, and for ordinary people during a recession. This is a major attack on government—what I call an ideological coup d'etat—without any consideration for its actual consequences. I have never seen less attention paid to facts or the truth.†

Want to be mean yourself, stylishly mean? "Bad Boy Entertainment" is the record label for you. Not mean enough? Try "No Fear" clothing. If you can't be right, or be heard, you might as well be tough. Lots of America's youth— a good number of impressionable young people, that is—see those folks behind bars as the toughest of the tough in this country. The meaner the better. Only machismo and swagger and a willingness to bust others in the chops can help you survive, say, in Pelican Bay Penitentiary. Inmates not only know how to take care of themselves—one cannot imagine a self-help manual, *How to Be the Model Prisoner*—but they absolutely *mean* what

---

*Ibid., p. 76.
†"Talk of the Town," *New Yorker*, January 15, 1996, p. 24.

they say. At a time when meaning is fast fading, no one knows conviction better than a con. Prosecuting attorneys struggle to provide jurors with the conviction that defendants are guilty of wrongdoing, so that every convicted person will carry the maximum sentence. Because of its connection with the criminal justice system, *conviction* has always suggested a steadfastness about ideas and issues. To have the "courage of one's convictions" requires summoning the nerve to act on one's beliefs.

Mark of the Michigan Militia demands of his followers nothing less. In small meetings and large rallies, he exhorts us to arm ourselves for the inevitable takeover of America by the New World Order, which, according to a bizarre document titled "Operation Vampire 2000," includes the Order of Illuminati, international bankers, the United Nations, the "Rothschild Dynasty," the Internal Revenue Service, CBS News, Communists, the Yale University secret society Skull and Bones, "humanist wackos," and quite possibly aliens from outer space. This millennial manifesto was written by Jack McLamb, a former Phoenix police sergeant. One of the bibles of the militia movement, it exhorts the police and the military to fight "against the ongoing, elitist covert operation which has been installed in the American system with great stealth and cunning. They, the globalists, have stated that the date of the termination of the American way of life is the year 2000."

Mark of the Michigan Militia carries forward the "2000" paranoia. He lectures about invasive government surveillance of our private lives and warns of the secret flights of unmarked United Nations helicopters. Just what the UN wants with America, Mark never says. But be prepared, have courage. The kind of courage one needs increases, in Mark's scheme, when you cradle an automatic weapon in your arms. (Want to know how to use it? Listen to G. Gordon Liddy's radio talk show, and he'll instruct you on the proper way to shoot government officials.)

The meanness goes on. Gangsta rap groups, like N.W.A. (Niggaz Wit' Attitude), scream in the foulest language imaginable about bitches, whores, and bloodthirsty cops. Rappers sport tattoos like "Thug Life" and "Outlaw" and write songs with titles like "Fuck the Police" and "To Kill a

Hooker." One can listen to the top of the line in gangsta music on a label with the chilling name Death Row Records. Its logo depicts a hooded convict sitting in an electric chair. The stars of this West Coast label include Snoop Doggy Dogg, who has faced a murder charge; Doctor Dre, who has served a five-month work-release sentence for violating probation on an earlier assault conviction; and Tupac Shakur, who received one and one-half to four years in prison for sexually assaulting a fan and who was shot and killed by an unknown assailant in Las Vegas. "Suge" Knight, the CEO of Death Row Records, evidently runs his business with the ruthlessness of a mafia boss. Suge was driving with Tupac down the main strip of Las Vegas when someone pulled alongside and shot the rapper four times in the chest. Six months later, perhaps to avenge Tupac's murder, someone gunned down the East Coast rapper Notorious B.I.G.

The crime-lord code has seeped into Suge Knight from movies like "Scarface" and "The Godfather." He has embraced the intoxicating toughness of that world—the maleness, the monied glamour, the us-against-them sense of power. His record company specializes in gangsta rap by artists like Dr. Dre and Snoop Doggy Dogg. Their lyrics can be violent and misogynistic, and they sell millions and millions of records. Suge—everybody calls him Suge—is the kingpin of this family, and his sensibility prevails. Some say that like the gangsters in the movies, he is to be feared, that he will mess you up if you cross him; others claim Suge is just a brilliant businessman who understands that the tough-guy persona works.*

In this light we can consider the fact that corporate executives now routinely use "hostile takeover" as a descriptive term. The title of a recent book by Bennett Harrison about corporate downsizing, *Lean and Mean*, says it all. As James Medoff, a Harvard economist, explains: "The name of the game is screw the loser to support the winners—a succinct if somewhat colloquial definition for winner-take-all markets."† The phrase "winner-take-all markets" comes from *The Winner-Take-All Society*, by Philip J.

---

*Lynn Hirschberg, "Does a Sugar Bear Bite? Suge Knight and His Posse," *New York Times Magazine*, January 14, 1996, p. 6.

†Medoff is quoted in an all-too-appropriately titled article by Steven Pearlstein, "No More Mr. Nice Guy," *Washington Post*, weekly edition, December 18–24, 1995, p. 11.

Cook and Robert H. Frank, which describes the new screw-you attitude of many large American corporations. Steven Perlstein blames a new corporate mentality for releasing a large dose of meanness into the mainstream of American life: "As the forces of the free market have been unleashed into every aspect of the economy, they have chipped away at the rules, the norms and the institutional mechanisms that used to smooth the rough edges of capitalism and share the distribution of economic rewards."*

Like "hostile takeover," the word "Borking" has also recently entered the language. As William Safire defines it in his *New Political Dictionary*, "to Bork" is "to attack viciously a candidate or appointee, especially by misrepresentation in the media."† Joseph Nocera, a fairly liberal journalist and no supporter of Robert Bork, makes the case that the viciousness with which the media attacked Robert Bork in 1987 "marked some kind of turning point in the disintegration of civil discourse in American politics."‡ No slouches themselves when it comes to viciousness, the National Rifle Association mailed out membership promotion letters in the summer of 1995 fingering the enemy as "jack-booted government thugs," language antagonistic enough to prompt the NRA's most prestigious spokesman, the former president of the United States George Bush, to resign his lifetime membership.

Washington politicians also spend their humanity in pursuit of meanness, as if they derive more authority and power by moving away from the center, preferring to yell and scream from the margins. One of those extreme politicians, the congressional freshman Republican Helen Chenoweth of Idaho (she insists on the male designation for herself), declares in no uncertain terms that "Westerners are at war with the Federal Government" and that "White Anglo-Saxon men are an endangered species." According to a *New York Times* article, she has become a "hero to

---

*Quoted in Philip J. Cook and Robert H. Frank, *The Winner-Take-All Society* (New York: Free Press, 1995), p. 10.

†William Safire, *Safire's New Political Dictionary: The Definitive Guide to the New Language of Politics* (New York: Random House, 1993), p. 19.

‡Joseph Nocera, "Getting Borked," *Gentleman's Quarterly*, September 1995, p. 18.

fringe groups around the nation who say no one else in Congress will speak for them."* The *Idaho Statesman*, the state's largest newspaper, had warned that fringe and hate groups would soon take up Chenoweth as their poster child. The *Statesman* had good reason to post such a graphic warning. E. R. Fields, a former Ku Klux Klan grand dragon in Marietta, Georgia, had praised Chenoweth's election to Congress as a victory for "race-based campaigns." Fields publishes *The Truth at Last*, a newspaper that carries headlines like "Racial Purity Is America's Security." The Militia of Montana sells videotapes of Chenoweth's speeches on the dangers of "world government" control of natural resources.

But one does not need to focus on Congressman Chenoweth to uncover a vein of meanness in Washington. Maureen Dowd, herself no stranger to biting sarcasm, describes the inner sanctum of the Senate itself as a no-holds-barred, bare-knuckle fight: "The world according to [Alfonse] D'Amato sounds more dangerous than inspiring. Things are always getting ugly. The time for turning the other cheek is always over. All hell is continually breaking loose. Punches are never being pulled, but nerves are always being hit."† Above the din, in an eerie echo of George Bush's "kinder and gentler nation," President Clinton pleads for a more gentle Congress in its 105th incarnation.

It doesn't look like Clinton will get his wish any time soon. Just moments after the conclusion of the Senate's hearings on the attempt to penetrate the Branch Davidian compound in Waco, Texas, by agents of the Bureau of Alcohol, Tobacco, and Firearms, thousands of irate citizens began sending faxes to members of Congress. A good many of those messages took aim at representative Charles E. Schumer, a Democrat from Brooklyn and the most vocal opponent of the hearings. One anonymous fanatic called the ten-day testimony a "wonderful piece of Yiddish theater," an obvious dig at Schumer's Jewish background. Another fax reproduced a

  *Timothy Egan, "Idaho Freshman Embodies GOP's Hope and Fear in 1996," *New York Times*, January 15, 1996, sec. A, p. 12.
  †Maureen Dowd, "Alfonse Unplugged," *New York Times*, July 27, 1995, sec. A, p. 15.

paragraph of anti-Semitic drivel from Hitler's *Mein Kampf*. And yet another carried a threateningly ironic couple of sentences: "I named my new rifle after you, Mr. Schumer. Please do not misunderstand me when I say, 'I'm going to shoot Chuck Schumer.' That just means I am going to the rifle range with your namesake, my trusty AR-15." After tracking virtually every piece of electronic hate mail following the Waco hearings, a *New York Times* reporter concluded that a good chunk of society seems to have moved to a frightening, almost psychotic edge: "The bottomless Congressional mailbag was as sulfurous on the closing Waco day as on the first, 94 witnesses ago. A perusal of some choicer offerings gave the feel of coursing through a series of mangled, woe-blotted Rorschachs toward the national psyche's ragged edge. ('Achtung African!' writes one constituent. 'Achtung Juden! Raus mit Sie!')."*

Pugnacity may make for great professional boxers like Mike Tyson, but in public life it subverts any possibility for reasoned and civil discourse. When fists begin to clench and tempers begin to rise, people stop listening and start shouting; they quickly retreat to opposite sides and dig in heels, defying anyone to cross the line into their territory. When civility disappears, thoughtful discussion, public discourse—the convivial pursuit of an issue or an idea—also vanishes. People become antagonistic; community falls apart. With the disappearance of public discourse, sophisticated, innovative solutions to social problems tend to fall by the way. Compromise becomes a scarce commodity. Those in authority find it easier to govern by dictating. More tragic than that, people—people on the streets, in institutions, on welfare, those with AIDS and disabilities—fade into an array of tables and statistics.

Who would want to enter politics these days? Certainly not the former governor of New Jersey, Thomas H. Kean, who lamented, after refusing to run for the vacated Senate seat of Bill Bradley, that Washington had become a "mean-spirited place. People are angry at one another, and use

---

*Frances X. Clines, "An End to Hearings, None to Hateful Faxes," *New York Times*, August 2, 1995, sec. A, p. 11.

language aimed at destroying one another. It's so mean-spirited down there that it makes it difficult to sit down and find compromise to get things done for the public, to bring people together."* Bradley himself says he retired in part for many of the same reasons. He expected to get kneed and elbowed in the NBA, but not in Washington. And besides, in basketball a referee can throw dirty players out of the game.

David Rosenbaum, political writer for the *New York Times*, sees the center aisle, where Democrats and Republicans have traditionally come together in compromise, becoming more and more narrow, and he attributes the increasing polarization in Congress to "the prevalence of negative ads in campaigns [which] make it harder for parties to kiss and make up after the election." Those ads may be a symptom or a cause. But whatever the case, as far as Senator William S. Cohen of Maine, a liberal Republican, is concerned, the current fashion among party leaders is toward a strident cry: "What we want is someone out there driving our flag into the ground, saying 'Here's where I stand! No compromise!'"†

Everywhere one looks: meanness. No wonder the Pew Charitable Trust funded a twenty-five member National Commission on Civic Renewal in 1997 to hold hearings in Washington on "the breakdown in civic trust." Headed by former secretary of education William Bennett and former senator Sam Nunn, the panel will explore, as it announced in refreshingly straightforward prose, why Americans have turned "so cynical, so distressed, so angry, so ticked off about so many things."

If I have at times blurred the distinction between meanness and violence, it is because their connection seems so obvious, in many ways inevitable. Meanness finds natural expression in acts of deliberate violence. Anger often gives birth to them both. The caricature of the angry person, muscles flexing and tense, bursting at the seams with suppressed rage, can stand as meanness personified. After all, *meanness* refers to a lack, a paucity

---

*Joseph F. Sullivan, "Kean Regrets 1996 Senate Bid in New Jersey," *New York Times*, August 31, 1995, sec. A, p. 13.

†David E. Rosenbaum, "In with the Ideologues, on with Deadlock," *New York Times*, January 21, 1996, sec. 4, p. 5.

of moral conviction and virtue. The word appears in this sense in the seventeenth century, a crucial time, as we will see, in the exploration of human interiority. To call someone "mean" is to describe a diminished moral space, a cramped interior architecture: "littleness of character or mind," the *Oxford English Dictionary* notes. An act we call "mean" falls short of moral excellence; it reveals a deficit. Mean acts make up such deficits with angry shouts, solid punches, and deadly guns. Those who are naturally expansive and generous, who can embrace, like Falstaff, the entire world, have less need to strike and destroy. They can risk standing in the middle and taking in both margins. But the mean ones need the edge (in all its senses), or so they think, in order to be heard, taken seriously.

In this book, I try to trace the reasons why so many discussions these days take place at the borders—"at the national psyche's ragged edge"—at the extremes where meanness overpowers meaning. Of necessity, then, this book begins with a discussion of borders as both geopolitical constructs and metaphorical conceits—ideas so deeply ingrained in popular imagination that they drive domestic and foreign policy not only in the United States, but virtually everywhere in the world. Here, in places like southern California and southern Texas, people demonstrate against open immigration policies along the borders themselves, as if the protests take on more power by virtue of their geographical immediacy.

Attitudes toward immigration laws themselves cut across traditional political boundaries. The ACLU opposes plans for registering illegal aliens, but so does the NRA and the conservative CATO Institute. On one side, Patrick Buchanan, president of the Christian Coalition, aligns himself with the Democratic senator Dianne Feinstein; on the other side, the conservative and former representative Robert K. Dornan sides with Barney Frank, the openly gay, Massachusetts Democrat.

In the summer of 1994, hundreds of people parked their cars along a stretch of the California border in nightly vigils, headlights on high beam and pointed toward Mexico, ready to corral anyone daring enough to attempt to cross into the United States. Later that same year, California passed Proposition 187, which denies medical and educational services to undocumented workers. Because of its inhuman stance, opponents of 187 called it the meanest political move in the history of the state. In 1996, along the border running east from Imperial Beach, California, authorities built a fourteen-mile steel fence, installing searchlights and motion detectors and placing hundreds of new agents in the field.

If the border can be made impenetrable, the thinking seems to go, the country can remain free not only of foreign people but of foreign ideas. Strangers bring with them new-fangled ways of thinking and acting. They talk funny and do things differently. They carry exotic illnesses. They work for less money and settle for less-skilled jobs. Their presence forces us to rethink our comfortable routines. Shutting down the border is easier than opening up the mind. Political and geographical borders thus easily become conflated with boundaries of acceptable behavior, with the abstract, moral edges that a culture continually draws and redraws for itself. No one describes this social dynamic with more precision and insight than the sociologist Kai Erikson. In *Wayward Puritans*, which chronicles the way that the seventeenth-century "community of saints" created its category of misfits and criminals, Erikson describes the dynamism of exclusion:

The deviant is a person whose activities have moved outside the margins of the group, and when the community calls him to account for that vagrancy it is making a statement about the nature and placement of its boundaries. . . . Members of a community inform one another about the placement of their boundaries by participating in the confrontations which occur when persons who venture out to the edges of the group are met by policing agents. . . . Whether these confrontations take the form of criminal trials, excommunication hearings, courts-martial, or even psychiatric case conferences, they demonstrate where the line is drawn. . . . Morality and immorality meet at the public scaffold, and it is during this meeting that the line between them is drawn. . . . Each time the community moves to censure some act of deviation, then, and convenes a formal ceremony to deal with the responsible offender, it . . . restates where the boundaries of the group are located.*

Most boundaries, of course, divide one state or country from another—the traveler has to cross a mountain range, or ford a stream, or

---

*Kai Erikson, *The Wayward Puritans: A Study in the Sociology of Deviance* (New York: Wiley and Sons, 1966), p. 106.

present the proper documentation at a checkpoint to gain entry. Government mandates may dismantle the Berlin Wall, but the border has already done its work: East Germany still remains distinct in outlook and style from West Germany. Battles in Bosnia and the Middle East take place nowadays in great part to reestablish fallen borders.* Take one step over a bridge into the town of Calexico at the southern edge of California, and you magically set foot in another country. The earth may look the same, the vegetation may smell the same. But the people on the other side eat different food, speak a different language. They walk with a slightly different gait, and sit with a bit more nonchalance. The poverty has a different cast to it.

Battles over GATT (General Agreement on Tariffs and Trade) and NAFTA (North American Free Trade Agreement) often devolve into border disputes. GATT in particular has enabled nations, with some exceptions, to move their products freely across international borders. The question, of course, hotly debated, is this: Does free trade result in more jobs and increased prosperity or fewer jobs and fierce competition?

Language has its own border crossings. A writer can push sentences only so far. At the edges of experience, where various feelings vie against one another, language begins to exhaust itself, unable to capture the significance and nuance of emotion. Frustrated and stymied, the writer has to stop short. Call the enterprise to a halt.† Or, in a brilliant metaphorical leap, one can abandon the logic of language, cross an invisible frontier, and enter a whole new world. Metaphor is the liberator of language, the avantgarde, the boldest explorer of critical thinking. Metaphor craves whatever seems strange and foreign. A border runner, metaphor rushes headlong into unmapped territory; and, because it carries meaning across contexts, every metaphor ultimately travels through space:

---

*Amos Elon, in *Jerusalem: City of Mirrors* (Boston: Little, Brown, 1989), sees peace in the Middle East only by removing "rigid boundaries of sovereignty in Jerusalem." See also Andrew Sinclair, *Jerusalem: The Endless Crusade* (New York: Crown Publishers, 1955), p. 278.

†For a critic like George Steiner, who continually returns in his writing to the poet Mallarmé for his discussions of language, words *never* mirror the world exactly. For Steiner, language always borders on ambiguity, on misdirection—on failure.

The word metaphor, used of words, is itself a metaphor. It means, literally, a "carrying over." In modern Greek it still carries its literal as well as figurative meaning. The adjective *metaphoroikos* refers to any means of physical transport. *Metaphoreas*, "a carrier," may refer to the national airline or to a railway porter.

In metaphor, words are "carried over" boundaries or "transferred," to reappear in new contexts. The "carrying" is done with varying degrees of conscious awareness.*

A language devoid of metaphor is inherently cautious and conservative and has to perform within a carefully delineated space. It cannot stray very far from home; it cannot visit strange lands easily. Without metaphor's poetic expression, speakers (and writers) must rely on other strategies to get at the heart of experience—on color, detail, and gesture.

Borders and boundaries are essential for keeping things and people in their proper places. Without boundaries, there can be no definitions. In fact, *definition* derives from the world of property rights—of deeds and maps—in which ownership demands precise measurements. Accurate property lines make for easy relationships between neighbors. Slippery, imprecise borders create confusion, in the management of politics as well as land, as Susan Trento makes clear in *The Power House*, her book about Hill and Knowlton, the public relations firm hired by the Pentagon to sell the Persian Gulf War to America. According to the Government Accounting Office, by the time Ronald Reagan left office, the Pentagon employed 3,000 public relations officers and maintained a total PR budget of $100 million. Such efforts undermine the integrity of government by blurring the borders and clouding the lines of responsibility. In Trento's words: "Something has changed in Washington. Boundaries no longer exist. The triangle—the media, the government, and the lobbying and PR firms—protect each other."†

My concern with borders and edges takes me directly to the connection between insides and outsides, for the metaphoric, interior space in which

---

*Nigel Lewis, *The Book of Babel: Words and the Way We See Things* (Iowa City: University of Iowa Press, 1994), p. 3.

†Susan Trento, *The Power House: Robert Keith Gray and the Selling of Access and Influence in Washington* (New York: St. Martin's Press, 1992), p. 59.

one entertains ideas, nurtures feelings, and concocts arguments affects the boundaries of one's behavior. The less deeply or fully one occupies that interior space, and the emptier and less powerful one feels, the more necessary it becomes to continually project oneself out at the borders, to "come across" —across some boundary of civility?—perhaps as excessive and strident, but certainly as a force heard and recognized. For those devoid of a large and rich inner life—those left only with a meanness—outlandish actions constitute a way of establishing a foothold in a world that feels overwhelmingly complicated. Such people have a difficult time "gaining some distance" or "getting some perspective" on life itself. Literacy changes all that, in the most fundamental way, by providing a brand new, emboldened outlook:

Notions of foreground and background, closeness and distance—the grid or perspective itself—exist first as a volumetric idea in the mind and then get projected back into the world. Youngsters deprived of language generally find those spatial relationships baffling. That is, they do not participate in the reciprocal relationship between what is out in front of them and what is inside them. They lack the *me* from which distance is judged. . . .

. . . A person must first hold the abstract notions of space and volume in mind before perspective can be described and analyzed, and certainly before it can be translated onto paper as vanishing-point perspective. That level of abstraction flourishes in literacy. Vanishing-point perspective requires more than mere seeing; it requires abstracting and shaping reality through conception and perception. Tuscan painters began rearranging reality through this new spatial grid in the thirteenth century. Before that time, artists depicted the world vanishing into a Euclidian space where parallel lines never converge. In the thirteenth century, a new conceptualized reality—a new relationship, that is, between viewer and experience—begins to appear on canvases. Painters found themselves in a more volumetric space, and they depict a world that has been conceptualized differently. Literacy develops a new space inside each individual—a mental space that gets projected out in the world. This is what Tuscan painters record, the discovery of seeing the world in a new, self-centered way: "The vanishing line, the vanishing-point and the meeting of parallel lines 'at infinity' were the determinants of a representation, at once intellectual and visual, which promoted the primacy of the gaze in a kind of 'logic of visualization.' This representation, which had been in the making for centuries, now became enshrined in architectural and urbanistic practice as the *code* of linear perspective."*

---

*Barry Sanders, *A Is for Ox: Violence, Electronic Media, and the Silencing of the Written Word* (New York: Pantheon Books, 1994), pp. 71–72.

Our inner lives thus fill out only under the conditions of literacy. One of the most astonishing things imaginable happens as one reads: The idea of the text is internalized, and day after day one inscribes on that text the events of one's life. As a creature of literacy I can return to that metaphoric text, to the permanent record inside the thing I call *me*, for consultation whenever I please. The record I carry around inside me creates a new kind of memory, something not found in oral cultures—a *conscience*. Permanently etched deep in my being, events continually dog me, causing me to feel remorse, sorrow, or regret about some of my actions. On that internalized text, the social contract gets written.

Literate people ingest reality—take it in, sort out what they need and discard the rest. Again, literacy makes the sorting, the critical thinking, possible. In speech, words disappear as soon as they are sounded. No listener can pin my meaning down. The recollection of my word must stand against the recollection of yours; the evidence continually flies away. Once letters remain fixed on the page, anyone can return to them, over and over again, a process that enables readers to arrive, in their individual ways, at that key concept, *meaning*. Historians of language, like Walter Ong and Eric Havelock, point out that abstract thinking—philosophy itself—begins at the same time the alphabet develops in Greece, sometime in the seventh century B.C.* Alphabetic literacy turns people into reflective, analytical beings.

To analyze and abstract, the mind must be able to return to a subject over and over, for review and reevaluation. The eye must see exactly what it saw the time before. Writing—in particular, alphabetic writing— enables this remarkable activity to take place. The reader can go over the same sentence time and again, puzzling out its sense, analyzing its structure, teasing from it every nuance of meaning. A sentence can be scoured and sifted for the last drop of its truth. Reading and writing provide the key

---

*See Walter Ong, *Orality and Literacy: The Technologizing of the Word* (London: Methuen, 1982), and Eric Havelock, *The Literate Revolution in Greece and Its Cultural Consequences* (Princeton: Princeton University Press, 1982).

exercise for the literate mind, allowing one, finally, to cast a critical eye on everyday experience and make sense of events. Most important of all, literacy allows one to carry on silent conversations with that other alphabetically constructed creature—the self—in an exploration of meaning at the deepest level.

I have tried to describe here, in the broadest terms, the way literacy sponsors and—I choose the word carefully—*authorizes* the process of reflective thinking; how it produces what we term, with deliberate attention to direction, *insight*: a looking inward to that cleared out, literate space.

While literacy itself may not behave in a democratic fashion, creating hierarchies of literates over illiterates—it still serves as the cornerstone of democracy. To be an informed citizen means more than to have someone tell you about an issue or problem. One must analyze and reflect for oneself. And that requires, above everything else, the ability to read. Illiteracy dismantles the enterprise of democracy. When people turn away from reading and writing, they lose their inner voices and thus the ability to carry out reasoned public discourse. They turn to easy alternatives—talk-show hosts, for example, usually conservatives like Rush Limbaugh and Michael Reagan—to instruct them on how to think about complicated political matters and crucial social issues. Twenty million "ditto heads" tune in to Rush, and the numbers keep growing.

As that metaphoric, literate, interior space—what we call private life—shrinks, the idea of borders assumes even more importance. More and more of life seems to take place at the extreme edge; limits on acceptable behavior fall away. Bluster passes for expansiveness, rant for power. Whatever details once constituted a private life, TV personalities have now turned into public advertisements. On shows like "Geraldo," "Oprah," "Sally Jessy," "Ricki Lake," "Montel Williams," "Jenny Jones," guest after guest unashamedly testifies to the most intimate details of his or her life to the overwhelming delight of millions of viewers. With each episode, the stories grow more bizarre, the events more lurid, as if the grossness of the details sounded the depths of an inner life*—as if every surreal and sodden detail bore witness to the existence of that life.

Sometimes the talk-show strategy backfires. A new term, "ambush television," came into use after an actual murder prompted by a television talk show. Jonathan Schmitz shot and killed an acquaintance, Scott Amedure, who had been invited to appear on the "Jenny Jones Show" in March of 1995 in order to reveal his homosexual attraction to the unsuspecting Schmitz. Schmitz justified the shooting, arguing that he had killed Amedure for humiliating him so publicly. As Milan Kundera brilliantly points out, "private and public are two essentially different worlds and the respect for that difference is the indispensable condition, the sine qua non, for a man to live free; that the curtain separating these two worlds is not be tampered with."†

It is human to be curious about others, and there seems to be no end to our desire for those interesting, hidden details that make up other people's lives. But those details—no longer simply exchanged in the gossip that spices conversation—are now trumped up, packaged, and marketed. Tabloids like the *Star* and the *National Enquirer* sell remarkably well in supermarket checkout lines, as does televised sleaze like "Hard Copy," "A Current Affair," and "Extra." As private life disappears, TV has scuttled serious documentaries; the uncovering of facts seems passé and bland in comparison to what people are prepared to tell about themselves. Another life, another reality—personalized, idiosyncratic—must surely lie behind the one we have traditionally been shown.

It is thus not surprising that trials have caught the public's hankering for that secret life: the owners of the McMartin Preschool, the Menendez brothers, Susan Smith, and the mother of all trials, of course, the O. J. Simpson double-murder extravaganza. In each of these trials, the details take on an air of unreality. Although we know that much of what counts in

---

*After all, *gross* initially referred to size, to depth.

†Milan Kundera, "You're Not in Your Own House Here, My Dear Fellow," *New York Review of Books*, September 21, 1995, p. 24.

life goes on privately, when private details are aired publicly on TV or radio, we dig for something deeper, something even more hidden and strange— something, that is, that might resemble what we used to recognize as deep interior life.

Then there's the spate of congressional hearings and senatorial investigations, starting in the fifties with the House Un-American Activities Hearings and the Kefauver Army Hearings, but picking up pace and publicity and, more important, seaminess, with Watergate, Iran Contra, Clarence Thomas, and more recently, Waco, Whitewater, and Ruby Ridge. How ironic that the lives we hear about on "Oprah" and "Geraldo" earn high ratings, but that the private lives of Lani Guinier and Dr. Henry W. Foster, do not play on Capitol Hill.

People sit, transfixed by the screen. Surely, here's where we'll learn the *real* truth about Jack Ruby or Ruby Ridge, or where we'll figure out why Vincent Foster, one of the president's closest advisors and an old friend from Little Rock, really took his life. If in fact he did. Even Hollywood cannot resist. Thus Oliver Stone's renewed, or continuing, interest in the Kennedy assassination (a Museum of Conspiracy, devoted entirely to JFK's death, has recently opened in Dallas). But of course no one is ever satisfied by any disclosure; everyone is disappointed. Not enough truth surfaced, not the right kind, certainly not in the right places.

Living has become porous, the outside flowing freely to the inside, as well as the other way around. Very few, if any, protections can prevent the exchange. Even condoms rip. And AIDS is not the only worry. Every illness these days seems to result from a breakdown of the immune system. As we grow more suspicious of the food we consume—with its fat, additives, sprays, bovine growth hormones, bone meal, and irradiated and spliced genes—we come to rely more heavily on vitamin and mineral supplements, on health-food remedies and ancient cure-alls like Kombucha mushroom tea or "blue algae."

The details of our lives have been downloaded into so many computer banks that any hacker, it seems, can reconstruct a pretty good picture of anyone else's existence. No wonder so many Americans—the richest and the poorest, the most conservative and the most liberal—believe in a hostile, nefarious government dead set on devising ways "to invade their lives." Timothy McVeigh, convicted for blowing up the Alfred P. Murrah Federal Building in Oklahoma City, on April 19, 1995, told his army buddies that, upon his discharge from active duty, military surgeons had implanted a computer chip in his buttock so the government could track his every move.

These days, a growing number of people seem to carry on a running argument with reality. Authority has to be shouted down or, in extreme circumstances, blown apart. When you possess little or no personal life, you become all too aware of the futility of positing a puny inner world against the vast stolidity of the world outside. Distinctions between interior life and external reality become jumbled and vague, and people need powerful aids to keep the two domains discrete.

Nowadays, internal human existence is largely constituted through legal action. Legislation like the Voting Rights Act, the Civil Rights Act, Freedom of Information laws, constitutional guarantees against illegal search and seizure, the shield of confidentiality, as well as other measures, help create the illusion of a thoroughly safeguarded, highly complex private life. Thus in December 1995, workers in Paris struck to keep their mandatory six-week vacations, free medical care, public transportation and education—all those entitlements by which the mass of workers define themselves as individuals in their public life. The first Amendment—"Congress shall make no law abridging the freedom of speech"—has assumed particular importance today when so many people have lost their voices. But freedom of speech means little without first enjoying freedom to think.

Where distinctions between inside and outside are falling away the most, security systems and alarm devices help to maintain the boundary. Few if any offices or factories have windows that open; workers spend their days breathing air that has been fully conditioned—filtered, cooled or heated, and carefully modulated. Who wants to breathe that polluted stuff outside, anyway? We lower our car windows only when we drive in for a burger, or drive by for a shooting. We put bars on windows, defining in concrete terms the outside of a house—a violent act of "breaking and entering" still required to breach it—and erect gates and walls around our communities to keep the outside out.

Nowhere does the distinction between inside and outside matter more than in prisons. At present, over five million people are either serving time or are otherwise involved— on probation or facing arraignment or sentencing or parole—with the criminal justice system. (Prisons represent one of the major growth industries in this country.) The world communicates its lesson over and over again: Seal yourself off, hermetically, from all external agents—biological, criminal, federal—before they do it to *you*. Seal away forever those foreign agents that threaten to contaminate *us*.

Public discourse—genuine conversation, motivated by openness and goodwill—demands a rich private life. Without that inner life, we can do little more than take up predetermined positions, which we then defend, like enraged warriors, in shrill tones and nasty language. In a country founded on the freedom of citizens to speak their minds in town halls and on village commons—an attempt, at least, at participatory democracy—we have descended into a perversion of reasoned public discussion. Reflection and critical analysis have all but disappeared, replaced by the stridency of those whose own voices have been so stifled that in order to be heard they have had to borrow the arguments of others.

Without an inner life, without the ability to reflect and analyze— the ability, in effect, to process daily experience—public discourse remains at best a remote possibility. In true discourse, people give and take ideas, they trust each other *and* themselves to move through complexities toward conclusion or compromise. They learn from each other. The coursing of ideas shows the same fluency, rides the same stream of consciousness, as talk. And like old-fashioned talk, public discourse can forge friendships and alliances. In town meetings, for instance, the chances are slim that only two sides—for or against—will emerge. Factions form and split apart, and come back together again in new alliances. Hierarchies collapse and take along with them divisions of class and color.

Moreover, a community knows that to choose up sides beforehand effectively puts an end to all discussion. Everybody must keep an open mind; everybody must listen. These days, public debate about political issues has taken just the opposite turn: Having neither the time nor the inclination, nor sometimes the ability, to arrive at their own conclusions, most people adopt positions that have already been established and ratified by some expert or agency—some news anchor or talk-show host. Like guests on "Oprah," too many of us latch onto positions that offer the easy satisfactions of certainty, that give us a sense of individual substance and strength. This translates into self-righteousness. We frame tough-sounding, hard-nosed proposals whose message to others—to the homeless, poor, disabled, the marginal—betrays the meanness of our understanding: Shift for yourselves. Find your own solutions or be damned.

Whatever the truth of where we find ourselves, it is less that the "center will not hold," as Yeats declared, than that there is no center, no middle or mean, as many of us reach inside ourselves and find nothing but a blank screen. Having displaced the text, the computer screen serves as our internalized, controlling metaphor: We can boot up our internal machines with a program in family values if we listen to Dan Quayle; with a program in morality if we listen to Newt Gingrich; or with a program in virtues if we listen to William Bennett. And no matter where we are in this country, we can tune in Rush Limbaugh and turn on to vitriol and rage. Quayle and Gingrich, Bennett and Limbaugh all know that public debate is bankrupt and have rushed in to speak for the vast majority of those without public voices.*

Because public discussions have little substance these days, they

---

*Surveyed at polling places in November 1994, more than half the voters said they turned to political talk shows for direction at least some of the time; the most frequent listeners voted Republican by a three-to-one ratio. Radio talk-show hosts "brag of their new status as political power brokers" ("Triumph Has Talk Radio Pondering Next Targets," New York Times, January 1, 1995, sec. A, p. 11).

The brokering is tough and the power is nasty. As Timothy Egan reports, some talk shows encourage "open racism and hatred." Evidently, a staple of some talk-show hosts, "following the lead of Rush Limbaugh a few years ago, is to make fun of the way some black people talk." Limbaugh, by the way, claims 20 million listeners on shows syndicated on more than 650 radio stations across the country. The New York Times credits him with creating a trend that saw the news-talk format move from 360 stations in 1990 to 1,168 stations in 1994. Personalities like Limbaugh not only speak to America, they speak for Americans. Ventriloquists of power, they have turned millions of listeners into their dummies. See Timothy Egan, "Talk Radio or Hate Radio?" New York Times, sec. A, p. 11.

quickly become strident, entrenched, extreme, and mean-spirited—witness Gingrich's orphanage solution for mothers on AFDC—and automatically bestow on professional toughs like Oliver North and Norman Schwarzkopf a two-fisted eloquence. Colin Powell, able to engineer a stunning victory in the Middle East, commands extraordinary respect and attention. (His autobiography, *My American Journey*, still stands as the fastest-selling book in the history of publishing in this country.) How odd, how utterly sad, that meanness, rather than meaningfulness, should chart the course of public debate today. But meanness hits opponents with power, force, and above all, with authority. We even say, in common speech, that meanness "carries an edge": It doesn't give a damn about politeness and manners and so makes itself heard no matter what, no matter where. It's a substitute for substance. With the death of private life, public discourse has become confused with public power, or worse yet, is tangled up with public bullying. In a sense, then, meanness takes the spirit of the Persian Gulf War—the chilling authority of Colin Powell—and transfers it to the domain of politics.

Indeed, I see the Gulf War as a watershed event. It gave America the opportunity to make an invigorated, tough-minded stand on the international stage. The roots of this war reach far back in time. Politically, we began preparing for the war just after the last American helicopter lifted the last GI out of Saigon in 1975. Emotionally, perhaps we began preparing for it even earlier—in the thirties and forties.

2

Bloom and Bush—Literary Criticism as Foreign Policy

How are we to explain America's fit of awful aggression against Iraq, just as the country entered the last decade of the twentieth century, an attack where the ordnance we dropped far outstripped the aim we articulated: the liberation of Kuwait?* And how are we to explain America's jubilation over such savagery? High school youngsters, college students, long-hairs and yuppies, foreigners and natives, joyous rednecks and uneasy liberals—a solid cross-section of the country—behaved like spectators at a small-town parade, their tiny flags waving in patriotic tribute to the White House claim of staggering victory. As if the outcome had ever been in doubt. As if America had just barely managed to come out on top, victory the result of breathtaking military strategy and battlefield finesse. In some very primitive way, the killing of more than 100,000 Iraqis, and the maiming of probably 100,000 more, raised the hopes and heartbeats of an enormous number of Americans. Suddenly, it seemed, everywhere one looked, men, women, and even children felt alive and red-blooded once again.

---

*According to a report released by the Government Accounting Office in July 1996, the United States deployed nearly one thousand combat aircraft in the Persian Gulf War. Those planes dropped nearly as many tons of bombs *each day* as were dropped on all of Germany and Japan daily during World War II.

   Despite the GAO report that American "smart bombs" did not perform nearly as accurately as the Pentagon claimed, the cost of new smart bombs planned by the Pentagon totals around $58 billion, more than three times what the government spent in 1996 on the FBI, the war on drugs, immigration control, customs, federal courts, and prison construction combined. The GAO report concludes: "The cost of guided munitions and the limitations of their effectiveness demonstrated in Desert Storm need to be addressed by the Department of Defense." The Bush administration sold a story about those smart weapons to what they must have considered an extremely gullible public. See "Implementation of Lessons

Like a patient recovering from a prolonged illness, America had rebounded with extraordinary strength, its vital signs proclaiming a renewed, hallelujah health. Politicians might have been promising it for quite a while, but the recovery began in earnest when Allan Bloom, a literary critic of all things, diagnosed the illness in his *Closing of the American Mind*, published in 1987. The nation had turned sickly, he declared, having contracted a strain of crippling jungle fever, picked up in the thick undergrowth of Vietnam. The malaise weakened the collective will and the collective willingness. How feeble: The United States of America, the most powerful, the most technologically advanced, and the wealthiest nation in the world, could not manage to beat up a pack of raggedy peasants on bicycles armed with nothing but resolute nerve and sharpened bamboo sticks.

Bloom fingered the enemy: Student power movements—particularly insidious, the free speech advocates, Students for a Democratic Society, Congress of Racial Equality, and Student Non-Violent Coordinating Committee—feminists, and black power activists had conspired in "the collapse of the entire American educational structure." Such openness in the universities of America, Bloom went on, likening the New Left to the Hitler Youth, had led to a damned near fascist closing down of education. Those political upstarts had single-handedly destroyed "the West's universal or intellectually imperialistic claims, leaving it [as] just another culture." America knew Bloom had the right diagnosis and kept his book on the *New York Times* best-seller list for close to eight months. It sold more than 800,000 copies, the second best-selling hardback book of 1987.*

It came as no surprise to many people—at least not to all those who believed as Bloom did—that America could not beat out a solid victory in Vietnam. We fought as a nation seriously divided. As the war slogged on month after month in Southeast Asia, it began to overflow into the streets of Chicago, Los Angeles, San Francisco, Miami, and Washington,

Learned from the Persian Gulf Conflict: Joint Hearing before the Subcommittee on Coalition Defense and Reinforcing Forces and the Subcommittee on Military Readiness and Defense Infrastructure of the Committee on Armed Services," United States Senate, 103d Congress, 2d session, April 18, 1994.

*Allan Bloom, *The Closing of the American Mind* (New York: Simon and Schuster, 1987), pp. 27, 33.

D.C. Worse yet, it infected the imaginations of young college students across the country. They demanded change and turned the enemy into their hero. The National Liberation Front infiltrated America so thoroughly, its philosophy even penetrated the dense pages of college catalogs.

New groups and new voices found a place in the college curriculum—black studies, women's studies, ethnic studies. Liberation ran rampant, and no one knew where it would stop—or if it ever would. Disenfranchised, marginal, cross-cultural, formerly colonized, gender—these were the catchwords of the New Left curriculum. The new curriculum, Lawrence Levine points out, demolished, for many guardians of ivied gates, distinctions between inside and outside. The academy was suddenly porous: "the outside world [crept] within the walls of the university and . . . radically altered the curriculum according to the critics. 'Superman is as worthy of study as Shakespeare,' Gertrude Himmelfarb has charged. 'Comic books are as properly a part of the curriculum as *Hamlet* or *Macbeth.*'"*

Young professors awoke to a startling truth: The enemy's way of life—the Southeast Asian, Third World way of life—could stand up to anything the First World had to offer. Bloom fumed. He laid the blame for such misguided—indeed, traitorous—thinking at the house of anthropology, and in particular at the doorstep of the cultural anthropologists.

Relativists—that's what those anthro profs had turned into, the result of all that wandering about outside the borders of the United States, doing their so-called fieldwork. Back home, they weighed Third World values alongside Western values and announced that the pans had reached a happy balance. Not content to keep the word to themselves, they brought the contagion home to a whole generation of students. Bloom cried foul and demanded a return to reason and order. As a consequence of such borderline madness, Bloom maintained, American college students had managed to close their minds against and loosen their grips on absolute truth.

---

*Lawrence W. Levine, *The Opening of the American Mind: Canons, Culture, and History* (Boston: Beacon Press, 1996), p. 12.

They had been brainwashed into believing that their own culture was all right, but no more all right, no more advanced or sophisticated, say, than that of a Pintabi somewhere in the outback of Australia, or a North Vietnamese peasant, or even an Iraqi in some godforsaken desert or other. Even more shocking, some of those Third Worlders seemed happier, more content, than we—or at least they did before we mucked up their lives.

George Bush, the commander-in-chief, the president as pharmacist, could fill Bloom's prescription. He—the president of the United States—knew how to make the nation feel good again. Bush could pull the country out of its doldrums. The opening of the American mind simply required clenching the American fist. An adrenalin rush of unquestionable victory—that would certainly cure America's listlessness. American intelligence assessed Iraqi military capability only too well: Bush knew we would wipe out the enemy in one or two or even three dozen sorties. Even the name for that war, "Desert Storm"—the PR firm of Hill and Knowlton hard at work to give killing just the right cache—suggested something cosmic, something larger than anything any human could create, or control.

In actuality, however, Bush had no real desire to wage war. He had something more insidious, much more politically exquisite up his sleeve. He would decimate the entire population of Iraq if necessary—wholesale and fully sanctioned serial killing—to pull us back to robust health, to get every citizen to believe in this country once again. And the president pulled it off. Millions of Americans watched CNN as if the screen registered their collective heartbeat, blood pressure, circulation. For those who couldn't see the connection, Peter Jennings and Wolf Blitzer made it clear: Our vital signs looked good indeed.

It takes some kind of guy, a man with guts, to call the bluff of a monstrous, Middle Eastern Hitler. Standing tall, Colin Powell by his side—the military as supreme equal-opportunity employer, affirmative action put to its highest aim: Why, we entrusted the security of the nation to a black man—George Bush drew a line in the sand and dared Saddam Hussein to cross it. America had established a brand-new frontier, out there in some dry, desolate place called the Middle East.

45

BLOOM
AND
BUSH—
LITERARY
CRITICISM
AS
FOREIGN
POLICY

While historical accident had brought Bloom and Bush together
—one an educator, the other the "education president," one who says what
he means, the other who means what he says—the roots of literary criticism and foreign policy share a long and cozy history. They aim for the
same goal: to discipline the most unruly organs of the literate body, the
eyes. The eyes need to be prevented from wandering off to the edges—to
the frontiers and the fringes—because that's where change and upheaval
begin. That's where the activity goes on, the place where villains like Saddam Hussein think they can pull off their dirty work and go unnoticed.

Troubles begin at the borders. That's what we mean by the fringe element,
the irrelevant, unruly, and unfinished strands of society. They stand out
from the rest: those long-haired, bearded ones, or the ones with no hair at
all, the skinheads—marginal types of all descriptions, who hang out at the
edges of society peering in, or more accurately, lately, leering in. They operate beyond the reach of rules and regulations, beyond the confining grid of
civilization. In a sense, they operate far out there because, more than most
citizens, they recognize the rules all too well.

To control its citizens, the authorities must determine what people
can and cannot see. Governments walk the finest of lines here, staying a
course between free expression and censorship—between virtually unlimited viewing on cable TV versus the V-chip, for instance, or unlimited
surfing on the Internet versus legislation against indecent images and language. At the borders of behavior, something strange happens to the eye:
restraints on behavior loosen and at times fall away altogether. Social critics
like Andrea Dworkin and Catherine McKinnon, for example, argue that
pornographic images lead to shockingly aggressive behavior, degrading and
even physically harmful to women. At the fringes of society, images, even
words, constitute action.

The borders spell trouble for literature, too. Early medieval scribes
understood that the eye characteristically moves to the edges. They took
advantage of such wanderings, placing illustrations in the margins of manuscripts—*marginalia*—designed to illuminate, shine light on, the text itself.

Those illustrations guided readers back to the heart of the text, to focus on their own core—the soul. Turning inward, the eye could stay as close to home as possible.

The process, however, began at the margins. There, medieval readers discovered what they should take to heart, what they ought to commit to memory. For alongside the text, in the margins, monks would draw an index finger pointing dramatically to a critical passage, like an arrow indicating an exit in a theater—except this finger said, "Enter here!" "Know this!"—an artistic practice that culminated, in the ninth century, in that incredibly useful scholarly apparatus, the index.

Later medieval monks—after the late twelfth century, say—given free rein to work at the margins, took their role as border runners to heart and painted figures designed to subvert or upset the text: "Lascivious apes, autophagic dragons, pot-bellied heads, harp-playing asses, arse-kissing priests and somersaulting jongleurs."* A dwarf winks back at the reader; the devil aims his anus off the edge of the page, ready to let fly a thunderstroke of a fart. The theologian as artist turned trickster: operating at the outskirts of the page has its dangers. But these illustrations, which argue and play with the text, only made the margins a more sophisticated partner of the center. The center plays off the margin, and vice versa, in a never-ending carnival dance of meaning.

47

BLOOM
AND
BUSH—
LITERARY
CRITICISM
AS
FOREIGN
POLICY

Whether for instruction or entertainment, the eye instinctively wanders to the farthest reaches to see what's going on. William Carlos Williams captures the act of seeing this way: "Everything is a picture to the employing eye that feeds restlessly to find peace."† That's the essence of reading, and it lies buried in the word's Latin root, *legere*, which initially meant "to gather" (including the related activity "to choose"), underscoring the eye's desire to wander tirelessly, picking up one letter here, another there, a group of words way out there, until there was a bundle of meaning

---

*Michael Camille, *Image on the Edge: The Margins of Medieval Art* (Cambridge: Harvard University Press, 1992), p. 9.

†William Carlos Williams, *Selected Essays* (New York: New Directions Press, 1954), p. 282.

to carry away. For that reason, medievals referred to collections (even that word comes from the same reading root, *legere*) of prayers as *florilegiae*, "bouquets of flowers." Every object stands before the eye like a bloom, ready for picking.

The eye devours everything. It's the real adventurer, the true colonizer. The eye needs to wander if the mind hopes to broaden its understanding. Some natural historians even argue that one trait in particular led to expanded consciousness in the large primates—binocular vision. An animal that can stand erect and cast its eyes on a large wedge of nature, makes little distinction between roots and raccoons for its food. It devours it all, as omnivorous in perception as in appetite. It sees more space than the animals that roam on all fours, and it sees differently. Indeed, every last scrap the eye sees it hands over to the brain, gives over to the mind's eye. Reading is to hunting and gathering as writing is to agriculture.* The writer plants the seeds; the reader harvests the plants.

The printing press eliminated the metaphor of reading as gathering. By policing the borders and cleaning them up—by making them rigidly uniform—the press trained the eye to move in a mechanical way, back and forth in precisely measured spaces, like today's laser printers, across each and every line of each and every page. Justifying the right-hand margin created more than rock-solid columns of print; it also exerted a political force. For when you put limits on the eye, you alter perception—especially peripheral vision. Uniformity suddenly presented itself as a standard.† The press made writing by hand look unfinished and unprofessional; unjustified margins suddenly seemed raggedy and fringey.

In 1927, the poet Paul Valéry published selections from Poe's *Marginalia*. Fifty years later, the literary critic Lawrence Lipking added his own gloss to Valéry's, discovering that the margins offered a wonderful place—a playground of white space—in which to have fun. Poe observed that in the

---

*The ancient Greeks called their writing *boustrophedon*, so named for the way it gets inscribed back and forth across a page, as if an ox-drawn plow had made furrows of words.

†The word *cliché*, a "click," is the repetitive sound made by a press during the printing process.

margins "we talk only to ourselves; we therefore talk freshly—boldly—originally—with *abandonnement*—without conceit." So after the printing press made the page a much more serious, engraven artifact, the margins offered an opportunity for a little mischief. Poe turned medieval monk. And he admits to the bad boy impulse: "Just as the goodness of your true pun is in the direct ration of its intolerability, so is nonsense the essential sense of the Marginal Note." Lipking found his own truth in the margins, not so much about play as about the infinity of space located there:

Only the limitations of space prevent Valéry's margins from going on forever. The mind—Valéry's mind, at any rate—cannot bear the idea of finishing. To finish, as to know thyself, would involve a kind of immortality, or a kind of death. Thus the apparatus of the margin, with its constant suggestion that revisions are possible, explanations are needed, delivers a vivifying truth: however much the text pretends to finality, it is always open to change. And even the gloss requires in turn a gloss.*

49

BLOOM
AND
BUSH—
LITERARY
CRITICISM
AS
FOREIGN
POLICY

Allan Bloom, in contrast, represents the full flowering of a school of literary criticism known as New Criticism, which took radical measures, beginning in the 1930s, to sweep the margins clean once again and to further domesticate the eye. The New Critics knew the importance of the margins and based their methods on a printed page bounded by well-protected borders. The cultural strategy of the New Critics required that works of literature appear on the page stripped of all details of historical context or biographical fact, even place of origin—anything in short that might situate them. The poem or story assumed a new centrality by denying all secondary sources as support. In fact, the true critic, too, felt obliged to shun such help: Criticism as xenophobia. A New Critical reading subjected all poetry —no matter its country of origin or date of composition—to standards of universality, treating each poem as if it were "one of ours." In this way, a select group of literary experts both promulgated and reified the canon. Poems stood or fell against a few models of excellence—primarily Milton, Eliot, Pound, the metaphysical poets of the seventeenth century, and one

---

*Lawrence Lipking, "The Marginal Gloss," *Critical Inquiry* 3, no. 4 (summer 1977): 611.

or two others. The two major proponents of New Criticism, Cleanth Brooks and Robert Penn Warren, threw a half-nelson around literature, holding it fast in two textbooks, *Understanding Fiction* and *Understanding Poetry*. Virtually every student who took up the study of literature in the mid to late forties entered it through those two gates.*

What immediately strikes one about these anthologies—besides the confidence conveyed by the titles, as if something as complicated as understanding were a textbook possibility—is the table of contents. *Understanding Fiction* (1943) contains a very narrow, safe selection of foreign writers: Balzac, Chekhov, Alphonse Dudet. Brooks and Warren include these authors, they say in a preface aptly titled "Letter to the Teacher," because the stories endorse an "ironical ambivalence" as powerful as that of any English-speaking writer.

These foreigners illustrate a point, then, quickly and safely, without much fuss: They read just like American fiction. To maintain this illusion, the reader will find no surreal stories here. In fact, only one twentieth-century, non–Western European writer makes the cut—Franz Kafka. What a different volume it would have been with artists like Hermann Broch, Karl Krauss, or Robert Musil, or even Dostoyevsky. But the point of the anthology is not to show difference, but to uncover similarity. The editors include just enough foreign literature to be ingested easily; by taking it in, readers could strengthen their critical and aesthetic immune systems, a safeguard against odder and more quirky writers. An anthology of European literature that resembles American literature only serves to cast the experimental beyond the pale. Imagine students fed on Brooks and Warren. Once they had read their stories, Broch and Krauss would seem too bizarre, too outre, too marginal even to categorize.

A reader could deem an individual story or poem as good or bad—as having succeeded or failed—insofar as it looked or felt ("smelled") like a shot from the canon. So long as the object on the page sounded like

---

*Cleanth Brooks and Robert Penn Warren, eds., *Understanding Poetry* (New York: Holt, Rhinehart, and Winston, 1959); *Understanding Fiction* (Englewood Cliffs, N.J.: Prentice-Hall, 1959).

us, like one of the authorized models, everything was all right. New Criticism thus had woven into its very method a powerful strain of exclusivity. Anything written by Russians, Africans, Indians, would not be picked up. Unsurprisingly, New Critics like Cleanth Brooks, Robert Penn Warren, Kenneth Burke, and John Crowe Ransom had nothing to say on the subject of ethnicity and cultural diversity. Those subjects lay beside the essential point; they drifted in a no-man's-land, well outside the borders of the poem.

Discussions by design were narrow, roaming no further than the ends of lines; the marginal, in every respect imaginable, remained off limits. Students politely raised their hands and framed reasonable questions, using terms like irony, paradox, complexity, or devices with strange-sounding names like "vehicle" and "tenor"; poems distinguished themselves from the rest of the pack as "well-wrought urns" or "verbal icons." Students could play literary critic by uncovering seven levels of ambiguity, or four kinds of pastoral, in a poem or story. No matter what, the answers lay on the page, secondary sources were disqualified from playing in this game. Each poem existed as an isolated, hermetically secure, aesthetically intact object, just waiting to surrender its layers of meaning. One just had to ask the right questions.

51

BLOOM
AND
BUSH—
LITERARY
CRITICISM
AS
FOREIGN
POLICY

In the hands of the New Critics, the margins of the page acted like the borders of a country: No one—nothing—gained entry without the proper credentials. What authors claimed to be the meaning of their own poems made absolutely no difference; writers only deluded themselves into thinking they could interpret their own works of art. R. P. Blackmur, one of the most eminent of the New Critics, called this error "intentional fallacy," and it became a central tenet of the new system. As if they had learned a lesson from the Second World War, the New Critics warned readers not to grant authors the power to dictate meaning. The New Criticism silenced authors by stuffing gags into their mouths. They did not need to speak.*

---

*Authors took their first step here on the way to their final execution at the hands of contemporary literary theorists.

In a profession that provides little if any training in the art of teaching, the New Critics offered teachers a way to shine in the classroom, a pedagogical strategy as practical as a blueprint for building a house. They provided professors of literature the tools and terminology for dealing with even the most difficult poem without having to venture into the ambiguous and confusing details of literary history or biography. Recall, the goal of a close reading is always *understanding*. Nothing stands in the way of reaching that understanding: Reason and intellect drive the reader into the heart of meaning. "Practical criticism," I. A. Richards called it, for the reader needed nothing but a sharp pair of eyes, carefully focused on the sequence of words on the page.

I have not forgotten my original problem—the Persian Gulf debacle—I am closing in on it. But I am still trying to understand the way the New Critics treated readers as if they needed to be protected against contamination, or invasion, by anything too foreign, too strange. To make readers stronger, the New Critics subjected them to small, mild doses of foreign material. In the past, we called that inoculation. Jonas Salk built a reputation on it in the early fifties, in the fight against polio.* Notice that we are still talking about the eye, for buried in the word *inoculation* is the word *ocular*: The eye somehow moves underground, becomes internalized. This, too, will be important for our analysis of literary criticism, for inoculation has, oddly enough, a political beginning. Those in charge must recognize the eye as both all-seeing and very private before they consider implanting it within the human body. Those in authority must first entertain the idea that the eye can eavesdrop, quietly observe without giving itself away with a wink. That sounds awfully like spying. The act of spying for a foreign

---

*Inoculation has reached new technological levels in the late twentieth century. Consider a program proposed in Baltimore, whereby high school girls would have voluntarily received implants of Norplant, a long-term contraceptive. Citizens groups successfully defeated the program through demonstrations and protests, despite the fact that people quite routinely submit to nicotine implants. See Willard Gaylin and Bruce Jennings, *The Perversion of Autonomy: The Proper Use of Coercion and Contraints in a Liberal Society* (New York: Free Press, 1996).

government—what the sixteenth century called, in a quasi-medical phrase, a "penetrating agent"—was first performed with great skill and some daring by Giordano Bruno, who worked underground for Italy in England from 1583 to 1585, to frustrate a Catholic conspiracy bent on overthrowing Queen Elizabeth. An eye implanted in the body politic, Bruno carried on his work in court.*

By 1665, spying had become so routine and gentlemanly that the phrases "foreign office" and "foreign affairs" had entered the English language. Other countries had grown so alien that leaders saw the need to handle them diplomatically, militarily, and, moreover, craftily—through "private eyes." Like doctors, spies diagnose the situation and prescribe remedies. Doctors in turn work like spies, undercover, probing parts of the body they cannot see, diagnosing illnesses they will not readily reveal, operating in rooms few can enter, writing prescriptions in language that almost no one can understand. Clandestine activity marks their profession. Espionage appeals to them.

Thus, medicine took quite naturally to spying. Why not insert an eye in the body to warn the system against invasion by foreign bodies? By 1714, doctors were doing just that—giving inoculations to patients to strengthen their immune systems against smallpox.

During Bruno's time as a spy—beginning in 1601 to be exact—the idea of the canon as a standard of taste, as a safeguard against foreign invasion, first enters the language. Borrowed from the Church, as in canonical texts, the word is cognate with military ordnance, a *cannon*. Both words derive from the Italian *cannone*, a hollow "reed," and ultimately from Greek *kanon*. (One can fire projectiles through a hollow reed or, in a more sophisticated way, through an iron cannon.) The *canon* can be utilized as a switch, a stick for hitting those who step out of line—or, in the domain of literature, those who read the received and authorized texts in a heretical or

53

BLOOM

AND

BUSH—

LITERARY

CRITICISM

AS

FOREIGN

POLICY

---

*The British call spies "moles," creatures that burrow relentlessly underground and, with exceedingly small but not blind eyes, see everything.

misguided way, or worse yet, the wrong texts altogether. The canon symbolizes power, then, both centralized and focused.

Inoculation can provide some protection, but it is no match for armament. The canon keeps the borders of literature militarily secure, an idea that takes on renewed significance during the period when the New Critics thrived. Brooks and Warren tried inoculation, using small bits of foreign literature to build up an immunity in students against a wholesale onslaught of wild European and Third World poetry and prose. But New Criticism worked best because of the canon behind it. Inoculation becomes ineffective over time unless the potency of the dosage is regularly increased. Viruses mutate, evolve, increase their strength. Influenza viruses change rapidly enough that new vaccines have to be prepared almost yearly. Tuberculosis has recently returned in several new, drug-resistant strains. Scientists work to stay ahead, and in a frightening way, push diseases on ahead of them.

By the mid 1960s, the New Critics had to admit it: The precious texts they had tried so hard to guard had now fallen to invaders. The inoculation had failed. In newspaper jargon, "the war had come home." The National Liberation Front, the enemy from that far-off place in Southeast Asia, had penetrated our borders. Could it be, could it actually be, that America, too, was just another colonized nation in need of liberation, and only now, only against the backdrop of Vietnam, could we finally recognize that shocking reality?

The New Critics, who had attempted to sanitize the text and to insulate professors from any classroom discussions of politics or culture, gradually lost their authority in the turbulent years of the late fifties and early sixties. Their demise, hidden behind a history of larger issues, reflects the political stakes of much of that period. Their fall has already begun by the time Mario Savio climbs on top of a police car at the University of California Berkeley campus in 1964 to address a crowd, not in the language of tenor and vehicle, but in a deeply spontaneous and heartfelt eruption. The New Critics said, Let the text speak for itself. The free speech movement countered: We are the text! We will speak out!

The first official transformative literary event took place at Johns

Hopkins University, at a historic conference in 1966, when the now-famous theorist Jacques Derrida described a new wave of literary theory—something he termed poststructuralism. Few knew then exactly what he meant, but everyone in attendance recognized that the world of literary articulation had been forever changed. We are all now "post-" something. Then, in May 1968, against the background of student riots in Paris, Derrida rallied the new cadre of literary professors in a paper carrying one of his typically ambiguous titles, "The Ends of Man," which suggested society's goals—its ideals—would be its undoing. Indeed, the good-natured academic humanism of the previous several decades, he declared, had to be seen now as the enemy of reason.

Events moved faster and faster. On May 10, 1968, at Columbia University, students themselves crossed some crucial borders. While black students occupied Hamilton Hall, members of the white radical Students for a Democratic Society entered the inner sanctum of President Grayson Kirk's office in Low Library and refused to leave. The Students lasted there an entire week, periodically releasing their demands, before the police finally broke in, beating some of the students and dragging all of them off to jail. On August 8, Nixon and Agnew received the Republican nomination amid riots at the convention in Miami; and on August 28th, Humphrey and Muskie received the Democratic nomination amid even wilder riots in Chicago.

E. P. Blackmur and Company gasped its last breath at the end of that year, quite appropriately, at the 1968 meeting of the Modern Language Association, in New York City:

At the Americana Hotel, which served as the convention's headquarters, three activists—a professor and two graduate students—were arrested after a scuffle with hotel guards. The guards had tried to tear down a poster on which the words of William Blake appeared as a call to action: "The tigers of wrath are wiser than the horses of instruction." The incident sparked a mini-rebellion at the MLA Convention, and it had a lasting symbolic significance. The war in Vietnam was radicalizing the profession. And what in literary studies was more radical than critical theory?

In the ensuing decade, the American lit-crit profession slowly but steadily shed its tweedy English image in favor of foppish French fashions. The result in time

55

BLOOM
AND
BUSH—
LITERARY
CRITICISM
AS
FOREIGN
POLICY

was a transformation of the very nature of literary studies. Thenceforth the study of literature could be primarily theoretical in outlook. Theory would reign where practical criticism once held sway.*

How fitting to choose Blake, probably the most radical poet of the early modern period—the vanguard of the Romantic poets—and a frightful enemy of the New Critics. And the line! To choose the unbridled power of wrath over the tempered reason of instruction—tigers over horses. The horses of instruction had been let out to pasture. And tigers, as everyone knows, will never submit to domestication.

Theory ranges outside the borders of any poem, beyond the borders of any country, for that matter. The most exciting ideas in the mid sixties came from France, from Germany, and from Italy; the stars of the new theories had names like Benjamin, Adorno, Horkheimer, de Man. America's inoculation against the foreign invader had lost its efficacy. That was becoming as clear on the page as it was in Vietnam. Indeed, so powerful a model of liberation did the North Vietnamese present that many students embraced the National Liberation Front for the very same reasons the U.S. government viewed it as the enemy—for its singular power and determination, its efficiency in translating its ideals to the people of Vietnam, its staunch refusal to submit to outside authority. The key word was *liberation*—freedom. In a country founded on freedom, young Americans wanted that word to mean something. They wanted to turn abstraction into action.

The National Liberation Front would thus inspire revolutionaries in this country—ranging from Students for a Democratic Society and the Student Non-Violent Coordinating Committee to the Black Panthers, the Weather Underground, and the wildly unpredictable and violent Symbionese Liberation Army. All these groups had the same rallying cry—liberation. America, that bully among nations, could no longer dish it out, would not be permitted to lord it over smaller countries. Vietnam provided the

---

*David Lehman, *Signs of the Times: Deconstruction and the Fall of Paul de Man* (New York: Poseidon Press, 1991), p. 48.

key lesson. The American military had lost its firepower. So had that other piece of armament, that other canon. New Criticism had given way to New Historicism, Deconstruction, Lacanian Psychoanalysis, Poststructuralism, Feminist Theory, Queer Theory, along with a dozen other theoretical approaches to the study of literature and culture. Allan Bloom likened the black power movements of the sixties to the populist movements of Nazi Germany. As Lawrence Levine reports, Bloom "compared the New Left to Nazi Youth, the Woodstock concert to the Nuremberg Rally, and the professors who 'collaborated' with the American student movements to such supporters of Hitler as Martin Heidegger, the Nazi Rector of Freiburg University."*

The new theorists roamed everywhere, borrowing from anthropology, sociology, the history of ideas, even chemistry and physics. They held nothing sacred, exempted no discipline or idea or assumption from political scrutiny. No definition—not even "man" or "woman"—could stand up against such total revision. Out at the fringes, the margins and the borders, young people plotted and schemed. Who could have seen that sitting in a classroom and explicating a poem or story could register as an exercise in foreign policy? But it did, and the shared perception of foreign policy and literary criticism—a construction all of a piece—came tumbling down.

Michel Foucault makes the following point in the introduction to *The Order of Things*. Locking objects into categories of their own, he observes, "localizes their powers of contagion." Foucault goes on to place the notion of contagion within an expanse of space. He ponders the question, an appropriate question for this study, of what happens when something shatters "all the familiar landmarks of my thought—*our* thought, the thought that bears the stamp of our age and our geography—breaking up all the ordered surfaces and all the planes with which we are accustomed to tame the wild profusion of existing things, and continuing long afterwards to disturb and threaten with collapse our age-old distinctions between the

57

BLOOM
AND
BUSH—
LITERARY
CRITICISM
AS
FOREIGN
POLICY

*Levine, *American Mind*, p. 6

Same and the Other."* This question goes to the heart of the meaning of *mean* in our contemporary world; Foucault is asking *where* meaning lies, and of even more interest, *how* meaning lies.

In the next chapter, I will argue that something much more fundamental than definitions have shifted. Something at the core of our convivial humanness—deep down where we contact the self and where we project that self back out into the world—has altered to such a radical degree that our inability to rely on traditional definitions, one of the key ways we negotiate the complexities of our surroundings, has made many people frightened for their very lives. We don't know who to trust, or what to believe. In the face of liberation movements, the collapse of the self means something particularly devastating, for liberation absolutely depends on a sense of self.

Without the canon to guide them, and without definitions to protect them from intellectual contagion, Allan Bloom argued, young people laid themselves wide open, not only to literature from every colonized and formerly colonized nation, but also to unreliable theories about that literature—a sure sign of moral degradation. New Criticism, as I have pointed out, had handed teachers a neat pedagogical tool. Everything they needed to carry out their analyses appeared on the page. No teacher had to spend hours and hours in preparation. But with the introduction of theory, everything changed. Teachers lost their hold on meaning. Their power receded, and to the forefront came books of critical theory to ponder, new approaches to understand. Literature required a different kind of rigorous study, with arguments couched in a carefully reasoned, sometimes highly abstract prose that sounded much of the time like philosophy. The new theories came with a new set of technical terms—sign, text, reader-response, *sous rature*—some of which conflated literature and politics—hegemony, valorization, resistance. Such unconventional and permissive thinking made young people more vulnerable, much more susceptible, the Christian

---

*Michel Foucault, *The Order of Things: An Archaeology of the Human Sciences* (New York: Random House, 1970), p. xv.

Coalition screamed, to a dreadful disease that appeared in the late seventies, AIDS, or in Pat Buchanan's ruthless phrase, "gay cancer."

AIDS has generated images of monstrous proportions, along with stories of deep paranoia and hatred. Every issue that used to describe America's fall from greatness in the sixties has now attached to AIDS, bringing together as it does fear of the Other, of vulnerable borders and fuzzy definitions, of the alien and the invader, of depravity that places no value on life—*our* life—and, finally, of immune systems so wasted that those afflicted become utterly defenseless.* To stay healthy, young people must learn to distrust their partners, questioning where they have been, who they have been with, and what they have done. A blood test precedes intimacy, spontaneity a potentially dangerous kind of behavior. Patients must be quarantined, kept at bay, beyond the usual distance of an arm's length. It is much safer to talk behind a grid or a mask or anonymously on the Internet, in that sanitized way MTV encourages young people to practice safe sex.

Homosexuals, the first to fall to the disease, themselves blur boundaries and definitions, threatening complacent thought with their refusal to stay within even the most basic categories of male and female, threatening, as Foucault implies, to infect deep-seated, traditional meaning with their linguistic—let alone physical—contagion. Now AIDS has snapped Americans to moral attention, prompting a good many of us to narrow our ideas of boundaries and tolerance of definition *and* geography: How much safe space to give those whose sexual past we fear is suspect. What about a sneeze? A handshake? Can we trust restaurants? If medical science could promise an entirely antiseptic country, with the aim of keeping

59

BLOOM
AND
BUSH—
LITERARY
CRITICISM
AS
FOREIGN
POLICY

---

*The Centers for Disease Control has considered the frightening possibility of new viruses arising from the transplantation of animal organs and tissues into humans. Both the CDC and the FDA intend to publish safety guidelines for such operations, a move prompted by the 1995 bone marrow transplant from a baboon to Jeff Getty, an AIDS patient. A virus can change, and "AIDS is the best example of how an unknown virus can cause an epidemic. Two immuno-deficiency viruses found in African monkeys, HIV-1 and HIV-2, infected more than 12,000 people through blood transfusions before the disease was recognized and the virus discovered. Today, an estimated 17 to 18 million people are infected with HIV. Clearly, our record for catching and containing a virus with a long incubation period is not good" (Jonathan S. Allan, "Fear of Viruses," *New York Times*, January 21, 1996, Sec. A, p. 15).

us all virus-free, we would probably vote for it. Fear, hate, anger, and anxiety all find a justification in AIDS.

Plague, as Susan Sontag says, "is the principal metaphor by which the AIDS epidemic is understood."* One thing about plagues, from their earliest descriptions in the Middle Ages through Daniel Defoe and on into the modern world—smallpox, bubonic plague, influenza, yellow fever, Ebola, AIDS—the general population believes, needs to believe, that those diseases all come from somewhere else: "AIDS is thought to have started in the 'dark continent,' then spread to Haiti, then to the United States and to Europe. . . . It is understood as a tropical disease: another infestation from the so-called Third World, which is after all where most people in the world live, as well as a scourge of the *tristes tropiques.*"†

In an unconscious way, perhaps, but nonetheless in a most pervasive way, AIDS has become for us the vessel into which our fear of the interloper—foreign and domestic—can be poured. That kind of displacement occurs with all plagues, but with AIDS, a sexually transmitted disease, those images are overlaid with notions of depravity, of dissipation and excess. Not surprisingly, Pat Buchanan equates "AIDS and moral bankruptcy," while Jerry Falwell argues that "AIDS is God's judgment on a society that does not live by His rules." The Religious Right lays the blame for the sexual plague on the sixties, and that period's fraudulent "free love." Why not call AIDS a divine punishment for all those traitors who fought against our resolve in Vietnam: "Although . . . specialists in ugly feelings insist that AIDS is a punishment for deviant sex, what moves them is not just, or even principally, homophobia. Even more important is the utility of AIDS in pursuing one of the main activities of the so-called neoconservatives, the *Kulturkampf* against all that is called, for short (and inaccurately), the 1960s. A whole politics of 'the will'—of intolerance, of fear of political weakness—has fastened on this disease."‡

*   *   *

---

*Susan Sontag, "AIDS as Metaphor," *New York Review of Books*, October 27, 1988, p. 89.
†Ibid., p. 90.
‡Ibid., p. 93.

It is impossible to conceive of Colin Powell or Norman Schwarzkopf infected with HIV—generals, who, like guard dogs, secure our borders. In the boldest way, they represent the opposite of AIDS: the American immune system at its toughest. Indeed, the entire military denies the ambiguities and weaknesses that AIDS has come to represent. It is an organization that operates best with discrete categories. Orders and commands keep its lines as crisp and sharp as starched uniforms. Obeying orders stabilizes definitions and keeps them inert. In many ways, the Persian Gulf War was a general's war. But it can also be seen as the surgeon general's war, a fight against a distant enemy in a dark country—don't those people have swarthy complexions?—who threatened the health of the body politic.

Vietnam changed attitudes about war, or more precisely, about enemies. Just after the national embarrassment of Vietnam, America had to confront yet another indefatigable killer—AIDS. Some people even argued that GIs had brought the deadly virus back from Southeast Asia. Every international skirmish and battle, every bomb dropped and missile fired by our country after Vietnam has been an effort to keep America, not only militarily safer, but hygienically secure.

61

BLOOM
AND
BUSH—
LITERARY
CRITICISM
AS
FOREIGN
POLICY

The treatment of disease has employed military metaphors for more than one hundred years, as Susan Sontag points out. In the 1880s, bacteria were said to "invade" or "infiltrate" the human body. Cancer in particular has lent itself to such descriptions. Sontag notes that cancer cells

do not simply multiply; they are "invasive." Cancer cells "colonize" from the original tumor to far sites in the body, first setting up tiny outposts whose presence is assumed, though they cannot be detected. Rarely are the body's "defenses" vigorous enough to obliterate a tumor that has established its own blood supply. . . .

Treatment also has a military flavor. Radiotherapy uses the metaphors of aerial warfare; patients are "bombarded" with toxic rays. And chemotherapy is chemical warfare, using poisons. Treatment aims to "kill" cancer cells. . . . There is everything but the body count.*

---

*Susan Sontag, *Illness as Metaphor* (New York: Farrar Straus and Giroux, 1978), p. 66.

Comparisons of the way cancer has been battled and the Vietnam War in particular surfaced in the mid seventies: "Reporters covering 'the war on cancer' frequently caution the public to distinguish between official fictions and harsh facts; a few years ago, one science writer found American Cancer Society proclamations that cancer is curable and progress has been made 'reminiscent of Vietnam optimism prior to the deluge.'"*

AIDS, too, has the tenacity and subversive power of the National Liberation Front: Medical science, which has won virtually every battle with every mysterious virus, has fallen helpless in the face of what Susan Sontag calls that "quintessential invader." If AIDS results from a profound moral failure, as Bloom and others would have us believe, visited on us from some "dark continent," then bombing Iraq was the *ne plus ultra* of moral acts as articulated by Bush and his legions of PR consultants. We may have failed in Vietnam, but at least we could try to outsmart *these* moral incorrigibles with our smart bombs. Out of the eerily dark night of that beleagured country, we could finally fashion a smashing victory.

An extreme act, that fierce bombing of Iraq. But our wars must become more and more fierce. That's the nature of American production. Fueled by industrial and technological know-how and progress—a progress that continually pushes against the foreseeable limits—demand increases, business expands, budgets mushroom, profits rise. War is just another one of America's powerful industries, defined by the drive for a better product, to reach the top-of-the line status:

One of the messages of the society we live in is: Consume. Grow. Do what you want. Amuse yourselves. The very working of this economic system, which has bestowed such unprecedented liberties, most cherished in the form of mobility and material prosperity, depends on encouraging people to defy limits. Appetite is *supposed* to be immoderate. The ideology of capitalism makes us all into connoisseurs of liberty—of the indefinite expansion of possibility. Virtually every kind of advocacy claims to offer first of all or also some increment of freedom. Not every freedom, to be sure. In rich countries, freedom has come to be

*Ibid.

identified more and more with "personal fulfillment"—a freedom enjoyed or practiced by oneself for oneself, whatever involvement with others one may have.*

Consume. Grow. Do what you want. Amuse yourselves. Defy limits. We grow up in America with that idea constantly drummed into us—grow and consume, consume and grow, expand your *self*. We took up that instruction with immense seriousness in the early years of the sixties. That was a transitional time, the high point of the self before the global economy and the cyberworld, before the fall of the Soviet empire and the Wall in Germany— before the demise of the nation-state when we began to designate countries as "former." Now, more than any other time, as boundaries tumble all around us, the self must stand fast, must mean with strength and clarity, as we navigate experience.

Therein lies the problem.

63

BLOOM
AND
BUSH—
LITERARY
CRITICISM
AS
FOREIGN
POLICY

*Sontag, "AIDS as Metaphor," p. 90.

3

The idea of the self is a particularly American obsession. While the self takes form in the crucible of Reformed Christianity in seventeenth-century America, it announces its arrival in literature with Cotton Mather, the first American to use the term *biography*, in his *Nehemias Americanus*, the life of John Winthrop, the first governor of New England.* Many literary historians point to autobiography as a purely American invention, associated first with Benjamin Franklin's unfolding of his inventive self in prose. The celebration of the literary self culminates in that first-person masterpiece of supposed self-revelation and discovery, *The Adventures of Huckleberry Finn*, narrated by the semiliterate Huck into a magical tape recorder that manages somehow to transcribe vernacular speech onto paper. The novel's true author, Samuel Clemens, takes on a new self—Mark Twain—a stage self, if you will, for retailing purposes.

The self gets shaped by the strong habit of Puritan theology for good reason.† In a Lutheran appendage to Reformed Christianity, a seventeenth-century concept called *sola fides* shifted authority dramatically from ecclesiastical institutions to a place deep inside the individual—

---

*Nehemia led the Israelites back from Babylon to the Promised Land. Mather uses that story as a template to impress the outlines of Winthrop's life on the reader's imagination. I do not intend to imply that Mather invented biography: scholars locate the beginnings of biography in the sixteenth century, with the humanists—Thomas More, Richard Roper, George Cavendish—and with the Reformed biographies of the next century: Francis Bacon's *Life of Henry VII*, or Izaak Walton's portraits of contemporaries, or John Dryden's *Life of Plutarch*.

†In America, the self is urged into existence first by religion, and immediately after, as we will see, by political philosophy. On the Continent, both religion and politics played less of a role in its formation. Instead, seventeenth-century analytical philosophers like Descartes tried to capture the meaning of human nature through understanding self and self-consciousness.

the elect soul. Abetted by that radical notion, the self nagged away inside every Puritan, impatient to make itself heard—and felt. But, one could not simply give free rein to that urging. Used unwisely, the idea of the *sola fides* could generate "dis-grace," luring the too arrogant Puritan headlong into too worldly concerns. One had to have enough of a self to exercise free will and thus carry out a program of practical work—good deeds—but not so much of a self that you risked turning your back defiantly on God.*
This simultaneous celebration and exorcism of the Puritan self character-ized a culture in transition, but one that would eventually yield, by the end of the eighteenth century, the thoroughly modern idea of the liberated per-sonality, which slightly later developed into that American archetype the Rugged Individual. The idea of personal liberation initially, however, was fraught with danger, for following close on the heels of political freedom, it could only come about by pushing the definition of the self past the mean and out to the extreme, which meant running the risk of casting oneself as a renegade and a rebel.

Once America began expanding west from the Atlantic seaboard, it needed, even cultivated, renegades, depicted in literature as a new Ameri-can type, rugged and fiercely independent, the "frontiersman." A water-color from the Missouri Historical Society painted by C. B. J. Févret de Saint-Mémin in 1807 shows Meriwether Lewis in modified Indian dress: buckskin and fringe, and a string of white weasel tails draped around his neck, the present, perhaps, that Sacajawea gave Clark in 1806. His clothing speaks to the fringe position he occupies, running the border between what his boss, Thomas Jefferson, might describe as the white, civilized world and the rougher world of the Indians that Lewis explored with Clark. These two icons of the frontier opened up, for President Jefferson, the far edges of America—the Northwest Territory.†

---

*Sacvan Bercovitch, in *The Puritan Origins of the American Self* (New Haven: Yale University Press, 1975), situates the conflict of self as "the basis of Puritan psychology," which "lies in this contest between per-sonal responsibility and individualism" (p. 17).

†The *frontier*, meaning the extreme edge of a country's settled area, is an American coinage, attrib-uted first to Ralph Waldo Emerson in 1870, in an interesting observation on the civilized life: "'Tis wonderful how soon a piano gets into a log-hut on the frontier" ("Civilization," *Society and Solitude*, 3:8).

The majority of Puritans tried to stay the path, to hold the quotidian, hoping all the time that those reassuring signs of election would gather around them. But others, those who stood outside the center anyway, found a kind of freedom from their own vantage point—out at the edges. One need only look at Anne Hutchinson, an early rebel, who took the idea of *sola fides* so seriously she declared herself above all authority—or more accurately, perhaps, declared herself *as* an authority. As a woman, an outsider, she had little to lose. She served as a model for others who lived and worked outside the tight circles of power, attracting around her what turned out to be the most individualized of Puritans—the early Quakers.

By broadening the *sola fides* and locating the divine center—the Mean of Power—inside each person, man or woman, elect or not, Anne Hutchinson defined a new kind of *self-reliance* for all Enthusiasts, that is, a new, emboldened category of staunch independents in New England, the social and religious deviants. She envisioned a life that Emerson would later argue for, and that Wordsworth, Byron, Carlyle, and Nietzsche would later write about. Her goal—self-reliance—should have been congenial to the Puritans, for a strong dose of selfhood had enabled those adventurous New World radicals to entertain ideas and perform deeds that broke with the most stringent rules. Who knew broken conformity better than they? Even the highest, most valued of Christian virtues—good deeds—as Emerson later declared in his bracing essay "Self-Reliance," should push against the norm: "Your goodness must have an edge to it,—else it is none." What would goodness with an edge look like? It might arrive with a bold announcement, but most certainly it would make itself felt with unforgettable assuredness and rock-hard determination. Goodness, for Emerson, should be unsettling, a thin line separating right and righteousness.

Self-reliance often grows quietly but doggedly into defiance—at least that's why those in authority often tend to fear it. Governor Winthrop found Anne Hutchinson so dangerous to the Puritan project that he banished her first from the City on the Hill, and when that failed to straiten her behavior, he cast her out of New England altogether. In her actions and attitudes, she had proven herself unredeemable. At Anne Hutchinson's trial, the chief prosecutor accused her of disregarding definitions—of breaking boundaries—by acting like a husband rather than a wife, by preferring to give instruction rather than accepting teaching. Such crimes of the self the "community of saints" simply could not abide.

Imagine now the American self, cut out of religious cloth, encouraged by the Church to restraint, but propelled in the opposite direction by the ethic of work, and particularly by the engine of capitalism, toward total assertion, in unrelenting pursuit of success. Situate this self in a young country with seemingly endless borders, boundless ingenuity, and a limitless appetite for whatever smacks of the new: Progress! In America, the self is not only continually tantalized but downright encouraged to fill itself out to its capacity—and beyond.

Once the self had been set in motion, no amount of success could satisfy its need, or quell its drive. On the contrary, while we have lived by the myth that financial success—and only financial success—can provide satisfaction, each incremental taste of financial gain has only served to fuel the self in its resolve for more. The captains of industry in this country, the masters of money—Carnegies, Rockefellers, Fords, Vanderbilts—all proved they had reached election by amassing vast amounts of money. Most of them never slowed down, never paused. J. Paul Getty once revealed in an interview that he woke up each morning panicked that he did not have enough money. The theological logic, as Max Weber pointed out, runs very simply: A just God would only grant such largesse to those whom He deemed righteous and virtuous. Emulate them, gain recognition and amass great fortune, and you, too, just might prove that the Lord had showered you with grace. The meeting of the Puritan self and the capitalist spirit sired the American enterprise as we know it.

In the sprawling context of the capitalist free-for-all, the adjective "self-made" has a very particular ring. It suggests that while one can take actions and register accomplishments, something called the self, distinct from the physical person, really directs the show, impelling a player on to ever greater amounts of success. The self holds fast the rudder, keeping the otherwise hapless body on a precise course. The phrase speaks of inner drive, a public recognition garnered, not merely by being born into the right family, or through some lucky break, or by accident of timing, but through sheer resolve, grit, determination. Anyone can pull off magic American-style: To be self-made is to be remade, a figure of dynamism and fortitude. Well, almost anyone—in actuality, only a few are chosen—overwhelmingly male, white, and Protestant.

In my description of the sovereignty of the self, interiority is power. The self serves as the locus of judgment, reflection, and perhaps above everything else, responsibility—a self-centered responsibility that develops through one's encounters with other beings. If the self is to avoid the dangers of a consuming egomania, it has to bow in the face of another Other. In just the way a poem always addresses an imagined audience—a reader or readers, a disembodied ear—the self assumed its civic responsibility in continually positing a "You." That's all that tempers the self; it must recognize the needs of the Other and say, "After you." In that spirit, it automatically turns philanthropic—another sign of possible or even probable election. The great age of American philanthropy built municipal buildings (legislative institutions for ministering to the communitarian You) and, most conspicuously, libraries (humanistic institutions for strengthening the individual You).*

For some philosophers, like Martin Buber, the I and You (Thou) requires reciprocity: Because I acknowledge you, you must therefore acknowledge me. Out of this obligation develops a sense of community. For the French philosopher Immanuel Levinas, the I demands no such reciprocity, a situation resembling at times that of the unrequited lover. I acknowledge you and, more important, respect you simply because it is my moral

---

*Between 1886 and 1919, Andrew Carnegie's various endowments financed a total of 1,679 libraries in 1,412 cities and towns across the country at a cost of $41 million (more than $1 billion today). Carnegie's other diverse programs helped launch many more during those years in out-of-the-way, rural villages.

Not coincidentally did Carnegie turn his attention and influence to books: The good Protestant knows that through the written word one reaches the Truth. If you cannot read, you run the risk of having some priest interpret for you. Literacy is as indispensable for the Protestant, for reaching salvation, as it is for the literary critic, in reaching meaning.

duty to do so, because my natural inclination (leaning) is to forge a coalition of selves. In Levinas's words: "When I acknowledge you, a society begins to form, a community of people who are addressed, although only some of them may choose to respond. A society is the gathering together of those who speak and listen." Notice that for Levinas, community arises out of social discourse, out of the experience of speaking that reaches deep down into literacy for the shape of its argument. I point here to an articulation that finds its home within the self. In Levinas's seminal work, *Totality and Infinity*, he asserts that the encounter of self with self ends in an affirmation of engaged and responsible civic life, for the "essence of discourse is ethical."*

The self, even a vastly expansive self, is thus tempered in the presence of a vibrantly alive Other. This tempering is not possible, however, when the self meets another it perceives as enslaved or diminished. Feeling powerfully alive and expansive, the self must always posit the sanctity of You—equally vibrant—to keep from turning tyrannical or abrasive. In the seventeenth century in Europe, the Church still sponsored a series of *xenodochia*, houses of hospitality for receiving Catholic strangers. America saw itself as a kind of *xenodochium*, welcoming to its bosom the immigrant stranger from every distant land.† The country, like a person, constituted and extended itself in that democratic, all-inclusive, sometimes coercive "*We* the People." Independence is of course a quintessentially American ideal, and I can think of no better place to see its grand reciprocity than with the "good grey poet," Walt Whitman.

On an auspicious day, July 4, 1855, Walt Whitman delivered to America his paean to liberty (liberation). *Leaves of Grass* speaks of an assertive, highly confident, and curious self that peers into every nook and cranny, scoops up every neglected and outcast soul until the poet has embraced the whole of

---

*Immanuel Levinas, *Totality and Infinity*, trans. Alphonso Lingis (Pittsburgh: Duquesne University Press, 1969), pp. 130, 134.

†I am aware of our periodic immigration quotas, especially with the Chinese in the nineteenth century.

America. One has the experience of flying at an eagle's height over the heart and soul of the United States. I include here a large chunk from the Preface to the 1855 edition, because what amounts to Whitman's homage to America sounds so foreign, so terribly alien, to anything one gets to hear today:

The Americans of all nations at any time upon the earth have probably the fullest poetical nature. The United States themselves are essentially the greatest poem. In the history of the earth hitherto the largest and most stirring appear tame and orderly to their ampler largeness and stir. Here at last is something in the doings of man that corresponds with the broadcast doings of the day and night. Here is not merely a nation but a teeming nation of nations. Here is action untied from strings necessarily blind to particulars and details magnificently moving in vast masses. Here is the hospitality which forever indicates heroes. . . . Here are roughs and beards and space and ruggedness and nonchalance that the soul loves. Here the performance disdaining the trivial unapproached in the tremendous audacity of its crowds and groupings and the push of its perspective spreads with crampless and flowing breadth and showers its prolific and splendid extravagance. One sees it must indeed own the riches of the summer and winter, and need never be bankrupt while corn grows from the ground or the orchards drop apples or the bays contain fish or men beget children upon women.

Other states indicate themselves in their deputies . . . but the genius of the United States is not best or most in its executives or legislatures, nor in its ambassadors or authors or colleges or churches or parlors, nor even in its newspapers or inventors . . . but always most in the common people. Their manners speech dress friendships—the freshness and candor of their physiognomy—the picturesque looseness of the carriage . . . their deathless attachment to freedom—their aversion to anything indecorous or soft or mean—the practical acknowledgement of the citizens of one state by the citizens of all other states—the fierceness of their roused resentment—their curiosity; and welcome of novelty—their self-esteem and wonderful sympathy—their susceptibility to a slight—the air they have of persons who never know how it felt to stand in the presence of superiors—the fluency of their speech—their delight in music, the sure symptom of manly tenderness and native elegance of soul—their good temper and openhandedness—the terrible significance of their elections—the President's taking his hat off to them not they to him—these too are unrhymed poetry. It awaits the gigantic and generous treatment worthy of it.*

What a falling off of the idea of self and of nation there has been in little more than a hundred years. Not quite thirty years after Whitman set

---

*Walt Whitman, *Leaves of Grass*, ed. Malcolm Cowley (New York: Viking Press, 1959), pp. 5–6.

forth his vision of America—1884, to be exact—Huck Finn slipped into the Mississippi River as if he would penetrate the very heart of the country. In a land where the frontier seemed endless, the imagination, too, could roam forever. By 1884 the real frontier had been reached, so that Huck's desire, at the end of the novel, "to light out for the Territory, ahead of the rest," must be read with a certain amount of irony. Still, we know what he means. He speaks *American*. He needs the horizon ahead. Immensity forms his imagination.*

The two—self and nation—can only move in concert, the latter depending on the former for its life: Only an expansive spirit can bear witness to—can, in some very real sense, produce—a broad-shouldered nation. Here, I think we get a hint of what Emerson meant by goodness with an edge: unequivocal statements, bold claims, outspoken love, not a sharp and cutting goodness, but one of persuasive friendliness.

No wonder Walt Whitman gave the New Critics fits. In effect, he observed their tenets—no author's name on the title page, no geographical details, no location except all of America—but in the most flamboyant and transgressive way. He crosses all the borders. He has no need to light out for the territory: He *is* the territory. The New Critics gave up on him because no page, no margins, could contain him. Too much the bad-boy self, too much the bardic deviant, this Walt Whitman character could never adhere to rules. He offends sensibilities through his choice of subjects and the sheer force of his self. His biography—his *bios*, his "fleshy life," as the Greeks call it—stalks virtually every line like a wild beast. He refuses domestication. Whitman possesses the uncanny ability to bow before the Other without lowering himself.

In his outspoken love of both men and women, his embrace of every race and class and color of people, his compassion for the poor, the

---

*I can mark in my own lifetime a significant change in attitude toward open space. In the late fifties and early sixties, Ford manufactured a station wagon called the Town and Country—a genteel utility vehicle for tooling around town loaded with packages and groceries, or loaded with camping equipment, for excursions into the country. Four-wheel-drive vehicles have replaced station wagons in the nineties, rugged minitrucks for off-road trips across deserts or in mountains. In the fifties families stayed at campgrounds. In the nineties, families stay in their "four-runners" and make their own space.

derelict, and the outcast, Whitman embodies the liberal/progressive ideal of the self-content and fully liberated American. But even the most ardent liberals often have a tough time with his bold assuredness.

This prompts a fundamental question, a question that can only be framed in the most awkward manner. For it is a question that attempts to peer into the deep, interior space that the Puritans had begun with such skill to excavate: the metaphysical space occupied by the self. The question is hard to frame, first, because it seems on its face to be so tangential and so elusive and, second, because in the rare moments we explore that secretive space, we usually do so only with intimates, or professional intimates—with doctors, therapists, priests, and rabbis. No one explains it to us; we receive no training in how to utilize its particular strengths.

When we describe Whitman as a poet with an expansive spirit, we must ask, what fills out that space? What do we believe that interiority contains—if anything? Where do we locate it? Conversely, what has caused that expansive self, in recent times, to collapse to the point where its meanness is charted daily in acts of the most violent, anticommunitarian behavior? To follow the argument out, the country, too, must have shrunk without our ever noticing it. Perhaps the diminution of the vast world into a global cybervillage may carry more serious implications than we like to admit. In addition, of course, the infinity of cyberspace exists nowhere but in the mind's eye; it is a figment, a mote really—more ethereal than any subatomic particle. It is, in the end, a flat-out disappointment and a frustration.

We believe without question in PC megabytes, IQ potentials, Nielsen ratings, horsepower ratings, Richter scale readings, Dow-Jones averages, GDP outputs, SAT scores, box-office dollars, cholesterol counts, T-cell numbers; but the soul registers on no quantifiable set of scales. Indeed, everything we say tells of its absence—our words point to moral decline, loss of civic virtue, disintegration of community. We buy William Bennett's *Book of Virtues* by the hundreds of thousands as a possible fix, as a manual for negotiating a world stripped of all virtue. Look up a confounding, morally demanding situation under the right chapter heading, find the corre-

sponding parable, and meet the problem head-on. With Bennett's guidance, you can avoid every ambiguity. He makes it all seem so tidy and neat;
there is no need for introspection. But Bennett misses the point. The communitarian collapse—of morals, of virtue, of compassion—begins on the
inside first, with that personal interiority I have been exploring. Bennett
only exacerbates things by framing the problem and the solution so pro-
grammatically. To fix what is broken in the outside world, we must first
begin with its analysis in our own inside worlds, in dialogue with the self.
The self does not exist in isolation; we continually project it back into society, weaving it into experience, casting its net over social and emotional
configurations. When our interior lives begin to fray, the cultural fabric
unravels as well.

Perhaps the world of art offers an even better way to describe the
dynamics of this interior space: Vanishing-point perspective requires more
than mere seeing; it requires abstracting and shaping reality through conception and perception. You must have the ability to entertain space and
volume as abstract concepts, as I have pointed out, before you can translate
them onto a canvas to capture reality. Tuscan artists began processing the
world through this new spatial grid in the thirteenth century. Earlier artists
had depicted reality receding into a Euclidian space where parallel lines
never converged. In the thirteenth century, a new conceptualized reality—
a new relationship, that is, between the viewer and the viewed—began to
take shape on the canvas. Painters found themselves in a more volumetric,
more fully rounded space and struggled to depict the new world they were
conceptualizing. They began to paint this reformulated reality, not out of
some new aesthetic theory, but because they had been reading and writing.

Literacy forges a new space inside each individual, a mental space
that is then projected out into the world. This new space is produced
through a reciprocal relationship negotiated between a literate mind and
the concrete world that the mind encounters. Tuscan painters recorded a
radical vision, the world perceived in a new, self-centered way: "The vanishing line, the vanishing-point and the meeting of parallel lines 'at infinity' were the determinants of a representation, at once intellectual and

visual, which promoted the primacy of the gaze in a kind of 'logic of visualization.' This representation, which had been in the making for centuries, now became enshrined in architectural and urbanistic practice as the *code* of linear perspective."*

Youngsters deprived of language generally find spatial relationships, like foreground and background, closeness and distance, baffling. They live in a world of undifferentiated space. They do not yet participate in that major reciprocal relationship, between what lies inside them and what lies out in front of them. They lack the Me from which they judge distance. We have several historical examples of children who have grown up without language, and who describe their world as if it had been flattened by some gargantuan mallet.†

One of those feral children, Kaspar Hauser, suddenly appeared in the city of Nuremberg on May 26, 1828; he spoke not one syllable and uttered only grunts and groans. A criminologist, Anselm von Feuerbach, who met the young boy on July 11, set his age at around seventeen. Von Feuerbach assembled the most detailed account of Hauser's life. He gave an interesting sketch of an afternoon walk with his young charge, the two of them strolling through two distinct realities, one volumetric and the other flat: "He had not yet learned by experience, that objects of sight appear smaller in the distance than they really are. He wondered that the trees of an alley in which we were walking became smaller and lower, and the walk narrower at a distance; so that it appeared as if at length it would be impossible to pass [through] them."‡

On another occasion, von Feuerbach asked Hauser to look out an open window, "pointing to the wide and extensive prospect of a beautiful landscape, that presented itself to us in all the glory of summer. . . . He

---

*Henri Lefebvre, *The Production of Space*, trans. Donald Nicholson-Smith (London: Basil Blackwell, 1991), p. 41.

†Some fifty accounts of "wolf children" have been written since the fourteenth century. For an interesting summary, see Douglas Keith Condland, *Feral Children and Clever Animals: Reflections on Human Nature* (New York: Oxford University Press, 1993).

‡Anselm von Feuerbach, *Kaspar Hauser: An Account of an Individual Life in a Dungeon Separated from All Communication with the World, from Early Childhood to about the Age of Seventeen* (London: Simpkin and Marshall, 1833), p. 354.

instantly drew back, with visible horror, exclaiming, 'Ugly! ugly!'" Later, when he had learned sufficient German, Kaspar explained his reaction: "When I looked at the window it always appeared to me as if a window-shutter had been placed close before my eyes, upon which a wall-painter had splattered the contents of his different brushes, filled with white, blue, green, yellow, and red paint, all mingled together. Single things, as I now see things, I could not at that time recognize and distinguish from each other."*

The question of an interior, feeling life is connected, not just to the idea of space, but to the production of meaning itself. To ask how one feels inquires after a person's state of health. But to ask how one feels about some event or idea asks about a set of beliefs—an attitude or inclination—as well about what we call an emotional outlook. The two—belief and feeling—have to be related, for the question "What do you mean?" probes that indeterminate, internalized space where thinking brings emotions to life. The word *feel* betrays that same inside/outside duality as the word *mean*. To feel refers to a *tactile* act, but it may also point to something hidden, deep, and interior. And what goes on in reflection in part determines how something feels to the touch. One can use *tact*; one can simply employ *tactics*—both require feelings. We move through the world by sending out *feelers* from our inner beings.

The threads of these connections come together in the account of another feral child. In the story of Genie we can see just how essential feelings are to the way we fathom the world.† In 1970, a young girl strolled into the Department of Social Services in Temple City, California, with her mother. Genie, as she was called by the psychologists who took her case, had lived since birth with virtually no one speaking to her. Her existence had been confined to a darkened room, where she lay strapped to a bed or to a potty seat. Her contact with others did not extend beyond being fed a bowl of gruel twice a day. The clinical psychologists who worked with

---

*Ibid, p. vii.
†Russ Rymer, *Genie: An Abused Child's Flight from Silence* (New York: Harper Collins, 1993).

Genie reported that she had great difficulty negotiating space, and that to avoid banging into things, she walked with her hands in front of her face. When given objects to hold, she would touch them to her face to determine how hard they were, how sharp, even how large. Bereft of language, Genie's perception *was* her sense of touch: She had to feel her way through her world quite literally.

Genie feels, but only on the surface of her skin. What she feels, everyone can see. Once one has an interior life, however, it is possible to hide one's emotions. You may ask me how I feel, but I can always decline to tell you the truth. That's why the Middle Ages considered wrath and envy sins. One can keep them hidden from view for long stretches of time. Other emotions, like guilt, embarrassment, and even shame, which did not gain attention until late in the fourteenth century, also carry the taint of sin. Dissembling hangs over social interaction as a constant threat to civilized life. One has to stay alert, act cautiously, and listen carefully around a literate creature. We plumb each other for honest responses, learning to pay attention to certain clues and details of language, gesture, and behavior. That's what it means to be social in a literate world. Considered, civil life requires analysis and reflection, judgment and perception. Such informed interactions rest on the assumption that one has not just the ability but the obligation to read complicated situations, which come to us as often as not through discourse. In life, we get where we're going, in great part, by uttering a series of sentences, at times to others, but most often to ourselves. While Adam and Eve are obviously not literate, their story is presented to us by the People of the Book. They, and the rest of the characters in the Bible—including Christ—sound like literate people. Though we never hear of Jesus reading, he speaks in sentences that no unread person would utter. Irony and paradox inform his parables: He loves riddles and conundrums. His utterances are rarely straightforward, grammatically unambiguous. Christ thus acts as a moral tour guide, taking those around him on the zigzagging road to truth.

With an internalized text, regret, remorse, sorrow, and shame become a permanent record of one's life. In a literate world, you can direct your attention inward, scan that metaphoric text, reflect on past events, and relive them in the present moment. You can then talk about the details of those events—confess your actions—to a friend, a priest, a therapist, or in more considered moments, silently to yourself. Memory is always present, a constant companion. The possibility of talk, of conjuring another self to talk to, always exists.

But sometimes confession is not possible, or even appropriate. Talk just will not help, in which case the events burn themselves more deeply onto that internalized page. One returns to them time and again, ponders their meaning, and measures them against acceptable standards of behavior. In a literate society, one's acts will continually be judged against those standards—judged by friends and family, by those in positions of secular or religious authority, and most often and perhaps most critically, by oneself. One may come to feel good about one's accomplishments, or one may feel a strong sense of guilt, sorrow, or regret over what one has done.

Until very recently, people had both public and private lives. Except in the most intimate situations, the private life remained private; it tempered and made possible a socially reasonable, public presentation. Oprah and Geraldo have exploited what may come to be seen as one of the most profound changes—if not the most profound change—in human development in the twentieth century: The collapse of a self-sustaining interior life. I maintain that interiority began to disappear as reading and writing began to drop out of people's lives, replaced by hours and hours of staring at screens. The interior life began to collapse, that is, when the screen drove out the text as the internalized metaphor for organizing private life. Again, until very recently, one's private life was not material for this TV program or that radio talk show. It did not affect ratings.

Whatever the case, what enables the emotions to work, what holds the emotions together, is that most crucial of literate constructions, the self—the self with whom we carry on our silent conversations, ranging from the most trivial of subjects to the grandest. We talk to ourselves about our state of being, and in those discussions try to discover—or uncover—how we feel, and to refine those feelings. Out of those conversations, we articulate something called a conscience:

The idea of a self that continues to glimmer in thought or memory, occasionally retrieved and examined in the light of day, cannot exist without the text. Where there is no alphabet, there can neither be a memory conceived as a storehouse nor the "I" as its appointed watchman. With the alphabet both text and self became possible, but only slowly, and they became the social construct on which we found all our perceptions as literate people.*

When we say that someone is expansive or narrow, we use those terms to refer to an in-dwelling metaphorical volume—a book, a dimension, a loudness—that we continually write and rewrite inside ourselves. This space is, of course, unlocatable. Not the surgeon, not even the coroner can excavate this region. Only the therapist, the archaeologist of metaphor, knows where to dig. And thus, we can only talk about interiority in the most immediate of ways—in spatial metaphors that try to capture the motion of emotion, the meaning of being moved. "I have arrived at this conclusion," we say, even when we have not given an inch. Or we remark, in the most casual way, "I have come to believe this or that," when we have not gone anywhere. Even in terms of feelings, people get moved without themselves ever really moving.†

The self has been nourished in large part as a by-product of the Protestant Reformation, which succeeded first as a bookish, literate revolution. The Protestant Church devoted itself to the cultivation of an interior life, as each Puritan reached salvation, theoretically, through an individual reading of the Bible. Literacy offered the means; the Bible presented the ends. No priest had to intercede or interpret. Puritan theology recognized the need for a reflective, interior life, for God bestowed election not on a

---

*Ivan Illich and Barry Sanders, *ABC: The Alphabetization of the Popular Mind* (San Francisco: North Point Press, 1988), p. 72.

†For Aristotle, *motion* and *emotion* stick to each other as twin terms. Even in modern English, they have not quite separated.

body, but on a consciously willed, reflective self. The upstanding Puritan fashioned a presentation to the world. Posture, bearing, dress, language— all made up the public face. The righteous Puritan represented an upstanding self to the community. Illiterates—those who could not read the Bible, and concomitantly those who had no internalized place to inscribe the lessons of scripture—had little if any chance of attaining election. The Book remained closed to them.

I have tried to describe the interior architecture of the human being, the many-storied space we can know but never see. I return now to questions I raised earlier in this chapter: What has happened to the American expansiveness that Whitman unfurled so magisterially in *Leaves of Grass*? How has the *vox populi* become so strained and nasty, so narrow? Why has the self collapsed so thoroughly? For the answers to these questions we must search in two very different places: One, ironically, the seventeenth century just as the self comes into focus, and the other, the world of computer technology in the last decades of the twentieth century.

The scientific revolution of the seventeenth century touched people's lives in strange ways. At its inception, with Kepler, Copernicus, and Galileo, the talk centered on pure science, on theory and formulation. The average person could not relate to, care about, let alone understand, something as arcane as the retrograde motion of the planets. But by 1615, the sciences had taken many practical turns and informed daily life. For the first time, for example, physicians had an accurate means of determining a patient's condition, a new measuring instrument, the thermometer, capable of gauging internal fluctuations of what even Hippocrates had recognized as the key to health—body temperature. Although Galileo had developed a similar device a bit earlier, in 1597, it could register only gross changes in the ambient air and served solely as a laboratory instrument. In 1615, however, Robert Hooke filled a thin glass tube with alcohol that rose and fell in small increments, tracking precise variations of heat and cold. On the tube he also marked a fixed zero point—originally the freezing point of water—for ease of calculation.* The medical community gradually settled on 98.6 degrees Fahrenheit as the baseline for normal body temperature—as the proper number, that is, for good health.† Before the introduction of the thermometer, doctors thumped their patients' backs to hear if they were *sound* of health or not. Patients had to rely on the doctor's judgment, on his ear and intelligence, on his ability to attune himself to their conditions, for a decision about their physical state. Doctors had limited diagnoses: Patients fell into melancholia or turned sanguine, choleric, or phlegmatic. These were called "dis-orders," the unbalanced eccentricities of people out of their humors. (In the nineteenth century, Dickens would fill his novels with eccentric, "humorous" characters.)

To be ill before 1610 meant one had what the modern period would call a certain type of personality. The melancholic person, filled with an excess of black bile, thus spends a good deal of the day brooding in private, sullenly reviewing all the depravities of society; and the phlegmatic, beset with an excess of phlegm, feels cold and clammy and cannot be roused from indolence and apathy. After 1610, people came down with a "dis-ease" or fell ill. To be sick meant quite specifically to vomit up the contents of one's stomach, inside turning outside, in one of the most disgusting breaches of border management.

Before the scientific revolution of the seventeenth century, the four humors—blood, phlegm, black bile, and yellow bile—coursed through the body in undetermined proportions, cold balancing hot, moist balancing dry. Cold and hot, in association with dry and moist, described the "complexioun" of all things in the universe—the elements, the seasons, the planets, herbs and drugs, stones and rocks, and most important, people—their skin color, hair color, nostril size, beard shape, and so on.

---

*Mercury thermometers did not appear until much later, around 1720.

†Before the late sixteenth century, *health* described one's general condition. You might fall ill, but that illness merely constituted one part of an ongoing condition, your *health*. During the late sixteenth century, and all through the seventeenth century, *health*, for the first time, had to be modified and qualified: one enjoyed *good* health, or one suffered from *bad* health. Ill health, tolerable, crazed health, sickly health—all described states of internal being. Its linguistic inevitability appeared in the late sixteenth century in the adjectival form *healthy* (from Anglo-Saxon *haelig*, meaning "holy"), "possessing or enjoying good health."

For the medievals, cold and hot had little if anything to do with what we call temperature; they stood for states of being, or more accurately, states of mind. For instance, medieval texts described the earth as dry and cold, but those terms correctly captured the essence of mud as well as of dry desert sand.* Likewise, water was moist and cold, air moist and hot, and fire dry and hot. Melancholia and choler, autumn and Saturn were dry and cold; phlegmatics, winter, Venus, and the moon were moist and cold.

This medieval tempering of the humors—an organically regulated mean—resulted in a balanced, well-proportioned, healthy person. Such a tempering gave you your "temperature," or "animal temperament." An improper balance of the four humors, an excess of one of them, brought on a "distemper," fits that first affected the body and then moved to the mind, so that the word in Chaucer's day referred to insanity or madness.

After the introduction of the thermometer, one *had* a temper but could also, for the first time, by getting too hot, lose one's temper.† Exposed to too low a temperature, one could also come down with a cold, chills accompanied by catarrh, hoarseness, and a cough. The thermometer, able to register precise changes in heat, focused on movements off the mean. That is, its calibrations caught the slightest deviations from the mean, which before would have either gone undetected or would have over time evened out. The thermometer, like the camera, captures brief moments of time—no more time than it takes to take one's temperature—but physicians typically use the information as an atemporal description of a patient's condition. By the seventeenth century, Aristotle's Mean no longer served as a metaphoric, abstract description. Medical people could suddenly measure movement away from the mean, and could thus record deviations and categorize deviants.

In the Aristotelean scheme, harmony, proportion, balance, and

---

*We still use figurative—or alchemical—temperatures in our language. When someone describes a celebrity as "cool" today, the term does not refer to that person's ambient temperature. Likewise, when a young person today calls a particular car "hot," we know that vehicle is either terrific or stolen.

†One tempers metal by heating it red-hot and then quickly plunging it into ice-cold water. Such tempering permits flexibility without breaking.

order—the hydraulic complementarity between liquids—regulated the interior life of a person. When the doctor thumped, he listened to the humors resonate; he distinguished the sound of phlegm from that of black bile. But the keen physician had eyes as well as ears. He could tell the state of a person's health through an informed reading of physiognomic details—skin color, hair length, lumps and pimples, and so on. A complete separation of inside from outside simply was not possible.

True, in our modern world, a fever, let's say, does flush the face, but many illnesses do not show up except in sophisticated tests.* The thermometer represents an important moment in the creation of interior space. A new, scientific measuring device led the way in replacing a system of interior health detectable mainly through the senses. In that older, Aristotelean system, a whole range of feelings found a welcome home in which to wash around and flow. The medievals believed so strongly in those fluids that they attributed most of their aches and pains to a tidal action operating in their bodies, pulled by one planet or another passing through the zodiac. Thus, both men and women experienced periodicity. In a certain sense, then, after the middle of the seventeenth century, feelings began to dry up. That is, the medium in which they had circulated slowly drained from popular imagination. What replaced it was a state measurable (temperature), describable (diagnosis), and controllable (prognosis) solely by physicians. Medicine displaced healing; prescriptions displaced proscriptions.

The self thus took shape in this country, not in the old internal system of proportion and harmony—the four humors—but in the new regime of science. The thermometer merely clinched a radical, conceptual change in the world. In that new regime, the emotions—which above all

---

*People have always had fevers; the word dates back to Anglo-Saxon and probably even earlier times. But people did not "have a temperature" except insofar as they were normal, balanced, healthy, and flexible. Temperature served as a normative term.

The thermometer appeared at virtually the same time as did the mechanical means for making ice. The two, cold and heat, are twins. When liquids vaporize, they absorb heat from surrounding areas, thus cooling them down. Perspiration cools a body off in just that way. Cooling chambers of refrigerators operate on the same principle. Thus, both heat and cold were reconstructed as scientific, measurable concepts in the seventeenth century.

mark us as human—made their appearance but, at the same time, took second place to a negotiated set of rights, that over the years would come to constitute the self. Just as states' rights would come together to form the United States, so the self would coalesce as an agglomeration of entitlements granted to it through documents carefully drafted by local and federal authorities. The Declaration of Independence enunciated the "*self-evident*" truths about people's knowable privileges and rights: "Natural laws" exist prior to, and outside of, any written laws and can be discerned by any rational person, utilizing the power of deduction and the gift of common sense. Individual selves, in turn, form a union, a community, which John Locke calls "a compact," what later goes by the name "social contract."

John Locke, in his *Two Treatises of Government*, followed the same year (1690) by *Essay Concerning Human Understanding*, provided the philosophical foundations for natural law and natural rights, both of which concepts, of course, would inform the writing of the Declaration of Independence and the Constitution, as well as that quintessential American creature called the *individual*. In 1690, just seventy-five years after Robert Hooke introduced the thermometer, thus helping to create interior space, John Locke began to navigate that interiority in an attempt to describe it.*

The *Inquiry* introduces a new philosophic notion called "personal identity," Locke being the first philosopher to discuss the problem of what constitutes a person's identity in any modern sense. Locke defines a person as a "thinking intelligent Being, that has reason and reflection, and can consider it self as it self, the same thinking thing in different times and places" (2.27.9). Rationality and consciousness, including *self*-consciousness, define personhood. Locke says nothing, however, about the emotional life. The closest he gets to the emotions is to point out that a person's private commitment and obligation to public, civic life can be determined by sub-

---

*Robert Hooke had worked as a laboratory assistant for the famous physicist/chemist Robert Boyle. Coincidentally, a short time later John Locke held the same position. Only three years separate the older Locke from the younger Hooke. Locke came to study medicine later in his education and never took a degree. But he always approached situations with the precision of a medical mind and in his own way can be said to have taken the temperature of human beings.

mitting the question to rational thought and to a concept that some philosophers believe Locke created—common sense.

In the pre-Newtonian, seventeenth-century world, ideas still existed as Platonic Forms, in God's mind. The Form of the Good persisted, uncorruptible, in some undefined, externalized location outside human beings. But in the West, with John Locke's insistence, ideas began to take up residence within the person, paving the way for modern notions of originality. The *Oxford English Dictionary* cites the *Essay Concerning Human Understanding* as the first use of *idea* in this modern way: "[Idea is] that term, which, I think, serves best to stand for whatsoever is the object of understanding when a man thinks (1.1). . . . Whatsoever the mind perceives in itself, or is the immediate object of perception, thought, or understanding, that I call idea" (2.8). A secular version of the *sola fides*, really, the idea of an idea generated by an individual person shifts attention away from institutions, away from religion, even away from the body, and concentrates attention on the mind. That shift ought to grant great autonomy, but as I want to show, in actuality it bestows very little power. Perhaps even worse, it creates an awful illusion of power.

Under Locke's scheme, the Form of the Good no longer calls a disparate collection of people together under some abstract, standardized code of behavior. Instead, a very personalized version of the good drives the ethical life of each and every one of us. When Emerson suggested that even good deeds should have an edge, he may have had some sense of this self-generated idea of the good. Confronted with such competing definitions of the good, however, community splinters and falls apart. Natural rights offer a way to pull it all together again. Under a regime of natural rights common to all, regardless of social rank, physical ability, class, race, or gender, diverse individuals can draw together knowing they enjoy equal protection under a higher authority—in this case, the law. Rights provide the bedrock for adjudicating conflict; they grant power and limit power at the same time. In theory, a well-reasoned, well-implemented system of natural rights eradicates all superficial differences and re-creates us as equals.

Since Locke's day, institutions have increasingly come to define people, not as a conglomeration of selves with a range of emotional responses that require expression, but as citizens with an innate set of inalienable rights that need protection. In practice, continued attention to equal protection—education, say, for blacks—serves to underscore the unequal treatment that society deals out to the have-nots. In the name of equality, politicians debate these injustices year after year, define and promulgate rights as a way of correcting imbalances, and then legislate them back into the lives of each and every citizen. Every conceivable facet of a person's life, every idiosyncratic move—imagine something called "reproductive rights"—ultimately finds protection within that system of rights. In a Lockean democracy, even criminals enjoy extensive rights; and beyond that, those who cannot claim rights for themselves still can be seen to benefit from such a legal system.*

Buried within Locke's comprehensive program of rights there also lies the promise of a privilege we now take for granted—the right to good health. In the revolution of the seventeenth century, scientists reduced all problems to their mechanical essences. Locke, a scientific man himself, likens illness, for instance, to the phenomenon of color, a secondary quality of objects, made visible to the perceiving eye only under the right conditions. Alter the conditions, eliminate the light, and the color ceases to exist. Secondary qualities, Locke points out, "are no more really in [bodies] than Sickness or Pain is. . . . Take away the Sensation of them and [they] are reduced to their Causes" (2.8.17). Locke describes "causes" as powers or dispositions bodies possess that produce sensations of, let's say, color. So for Locke, illness is no more than a disposition that needs changing or, since secondary qualities have no permanence and can be perceived only at certain times and only under certain conditions, why not strive for the ideal and eliminate illness altogether? Early modern medicine set itself that very goal—the eradication of all disease—as something new, something more

---

*In 1976, the New Jersey Supreme Court voted 7–0 in the case of Karen Ann Quinlan that the constitutional right of privacy encompassed a person's decision to forego life-sustaining medical treatment in certain circumstances. It also ruled that, in this particular case at least, the patient's father could make the decision on her behalf. In a very real sense, the court ruled on her right to die.

satisfying than merely returning patients to health. These days, we can more accurately read "health delivery system" as a "prolongation of life" system. Twenty short years after the publication of Locke's *Essay*, doctors routinely began to inoculate their patients against dreaded smallpox—a secondary quality of the human body—to make them whole again. Today AIDS not only stumps scientists, it blasts a hole in the philosophy underlying medical treatment. Medical victory means absolute extermination of every bacterium, every virus, every microbe. Today, as a logical result of Locke's argument, we equate broad medical coverage with excellent health and long life—a version of the great trinity: life, liberty, and the pursuit of happiness. Moreover, we take health care as a natural right, and we hold politicians responsible—the president, more than anyone else—for delivering adequate and reasonably priced health-care coverage.

Emotions have a difficult time surviving under such restrictive, tightly defined conditions. Or rather, the emotions slowly get *legislated* out of existence. Every time I am wronged—the legal equivalent of having "my feelings hurt"—the law intercedes and takes care of me by arguing on my behalf. I do not need to say a word. In fact, those in power—those who judge from the bench—can hear me more clearly if I keep quiet. A "mouthpiece" can plead my case in court with more finesse than I could ever muster. The court does not condone discourse. To argue convincingly, all parties must set their feelings aside. I lose all title to my feelings. More than that, even, I am encouraged not to feel a thing. Justice long ago lost her sight: She cannot read, has no perspective, holds no emotions. She needs to feel only one thing—her scales in perfect balance.

These days, the legislative or judicial system legitimates and directs my emotional responses. I have no *right* to feel envious about any other person's higher status, unless a court of law can show that my rival's wealth has been derived illegitimately—through insider trades, say, or junk-bond deals, payoffs, kickbacks, shady lobbying. Only then can I find officially sanctioned vindication. A woman has a *right* to feel jealous about her husband's affair because she has entered into a *contract* of marriage; a man has a *right* to feel angry if a thief steals his car because his property rights have been violated. In both examples, the pans of justice reach equilibrium once again, not through retaliation or retribution, but through socially established, institutionalized forms of equity—meted out in rewards and punishments—within a reasonably ordered criminal justice system. Jealousy and anger are never fruitful. If I take matters into my own hands, I violate the rights of others. Society stops me short, and I am left, ironically enough, empty-handed, with only my feelings of jealousy or, more likely, anger.

In a legally constituted society—where the law views every person as a layer cake of rights, and virtually every move finds sanction in some legislative act—the emotion that seems to allow people to feel most alive is anger.* The emotions, those second-by-second reactions to experience, do more than make us human. They also plague us, taunt us, and test our humanity. We learn to suspect the emotions for good reason. Shame and guilt come tinged with sin from the Middle Ages, but the corrective influence those two emotions once exerted on overly aggressive behavior now seems to have vanished: In a society where the top 20 percent of Americans account for 94 percent of the total financial wealth of the country, shame has not obviously tempered behavior very well, and guilt just seems silly.† The other emotions fare no better. Who wants to admit publicly to envy or jealousy? Likewise, embarrassment is not an emotion in which one can take pride. What's left? Pride itself, perhaps, if that indeed counts as an emotion. Love, of course, but the specter of death hangs over the most innocent of relationships: nowadays, a blood test precedes a kiss. And then anyone serious about love must confront those staggering divorce statistics, must account for a society strewn with crippled and broken families. Except in the movies, courage and caution—for a few, foolhardiness—characterize

---

*I use the term *emotion* here, but I am not entirely convinced that anger constitutes an emotion. Perhaps only some kinds of angry responses fall into the category of emotion.

†The Twentieth Century Fund, in a report dated 1995, gives the following figures for 1989: "In 1989, the top one percent of families as ranked by financial wealth owned forty-eight percent of the total wealth in the nation." According to the Fund, "the sharp increase in disparity [between the rich and the poor] since the late 1970s has made the distribution of wealth in the country more unequal than in what used to be perceived as the class-ridden societies of Northwest Europe. Today, the United States is the most unequal of any industrialized country in terms of income and, more importantly, wealth."

contemporary attitudes toward love. And so, finally, we fall back on the one emotion that, like love, can overcome us without warning—anger. Both love and anger, the somatic emotions, course, in an adrenaline rush, throughout the entire body.

For a democratic society, anger is an acutely troubling, even devastating emotion. You cannot have people walking around hitting each other whenever they choose. Our country has passed an enormous amount of legislation—perhaps the bulk of its legislation—against the expression of this emotion.* Ironically, since anger is by nature already a thwarted, frustrated emotion, such legislation only serves to intensify people's feelings. Anger breeds at the intersection where one feels the overwhelming urge to strike out at another and at the very same time feels constrained from doing so because of fear of reprisal or punishment. As a consequence, people shake and tremble in the tenseness of anger, working one muscle group against an opposing group to hold themselves in dynamic check.† The least expansive of the emotions, anger has its root in the Latin *ang-*, meaning "strait" and "narrow," as well as "trouble."

By holding two contradictory feelings—to strike and not to strike—in a rigidifying standoff, anger countermands the binary logic of a computer program. In electronic programming, circuits switch on, circuits switch off, but an electronic impulse cannot turn both on and off at the same time. The computer cannot record a bit of information as 0 and 1 at the same time. Digital information can tolerate no such ambiguity. As the computer comes not just to dominate life but to alter behavior and shape

---

*Beginning in the late nineteenth century in this country, professionals urged parents to take a firm hand against their children's angry outbursts. At the same time, child-rearing experts pointed out that anger, properly channeled—in sports, business, schoolwork—could produce a nation of youngsters with "spunk": "Children incapable of anger lacked individuality and independence and were truly 'pathetic.' The notion that anger reflected a kind of admirable spunk, at least in males, had not been totally foreign to the earlier period, but now it became a central strain of the emotionology rather than an insignificant aside" (Carol Zisowitz Stearns and Peter N. Stearns, *Anger: The Struggle for Emotional Control in America's History* [Chicago: University of Chicago Press, 1986], p. 75).

†In the late fifties, dynamic tension (sometimes called isometrics) as a bodybuilding technique enjoyed great popularity. One can only wonder today about "hard bodies": Are they supposed to look like a permanent state—a petrified state—of rage, signaling to others that they had better keep their distance? (Compare this usage to descriptions of the tough private eyes of detective novels in the thirties as "hard-boiled." How tough can such eggs really be?)

perception, anger has established itself as the most vigorous nontechnological, antimachine emotion. It braces us as only an invigorating emotion can. It enlivens and thrills, and carries with it, always, a taste of danger. That anger acts in a manner so dramatically antithetical to computer logic may just be a happy coincidence, but the way anger narrows and straitens certainly reduces the interior space in which we function. And in a time when narrowness characterizes the interior lives of so many, anger suits us well. We feel comfortable—at home, if you will—with anger.

Anger has made a most remarkable journey, from a predominately private emotion, confined to the home and "ventilated" most effectively in a therapeutic situation behind closed doors—a model popularized by Sigmund Freud—to a public declaration, on TV talk shows, in movies, concerts, and on city streets. Even in the home, anger now explodes in at least a perception of increased violence. One can only wonder if the breakup of the family in recent years has permitted anger to escape its traditional confines, free to terrorize not just domestic life but public life as well.*

Fire, a holdover from the older, Aristotlean world of humors and elements, dominates the imagery of anger. We get hot under the collar; we become incensed; we explode with rage; we blow our tops. We seethe, stew, simmer, sizzle, boil, fume, steam, flare up, and burn—hotheads all. As our temperatures rise, we lose our tempers. Short fuses make us blow particularly fast. What else is there to say at those moments but cool off, chill out, or simmer down.

Still connected with the idea of fire, we make *caustic* comments, a word derived from Greek *kaustikos*, from *kalein*, "to burn," akin to *kausos*, "a burning fever." In a strange journey, Greek *enkaustos*, "burnt," yields the English *ink*. This relation between fire and writing may be due to the Greek *enkaustic*, "to burn in," reinforced by the deep purple ink used by Greek monarchs, and later by Roman emperors, for their royal signatures. In con-

---

*One can find discussions about anger in the late nineteenth century in two significant areas: one, as I have already pointed out, in child-rearing texts, and the other, in advice books about marriage. Juvenile and domestic violence still occupy much of our own concern.

trast to the fiery hue of those ancient, aristocratic signatures, black ink looks sooty—the aftermath of fire.

Fire insists on its meaning. The Greeks and Romans wrote with it. And in the late twentieth century, in our attempts to make meaning, we use it to speak—we yell and belt and scream epithets and sentences. We arm ourselves with firearms. It all demands attention, from the shoutings to the shootings.* All of us have a deep-felt need not just to be heard, but to be understood and appreciated. But, first we have to grab the attention of other people. Brandishing a gun generally gets someone's attention, and in a hurry.

For anger our vocabulary seems endless, the nuances and gradations running on longer than for any other emotion, including love. Like the Eskimo, who have dozens of words for *snow* and who therefore, according to some linguists, can distinguish many more delicate shadings of the frozen stuff than non-Eskimos, Americans seem obsessed with articulating every small degree and minute change of anger. From all appearances, we take great pride in living in a culture defined by rage. Tough-minded, heir to Puritan defiance and frontier ruggedness, self-possessed and self-made, Americans ask no quarter and give no quarter. Given the slightest provocation, this country can make anyone else in the world, damned near, cry "Uncle" and submit.

Besides anger, wrath, ire, rage, madness, fury, and outrage, we Americans feel irked, cross, offended, miffed, peeved, exasperated, piqued, annoyed, indignant, resentful, irritated, infuriated, provoked, aggravated, nettled, galled, riled up, worked up, fed up, pissed off, roiled, vexed, frustrated, and just plain sore. Even acrid and vitriolic comments partake of heat or serious burning. That extensive vocabulary of anger gets pumped directly into mainstream culture. Consider the slams of dancing, and the fiery language of street talk.

Nowhere, however, does anger get played out so dramatically and so graphically, nowhere does it get dangled with so much dazzle, before so

---

*The image of a "firearm" is menacing indeed. Think of a handgun as an extension of the index finger, spraying fire and causing death, or an entire arm converted into an instrument of destruction.

many eyes, than in movies. Stallone, Schwarzenegger, Willis, and Company have screamed, kicked, shot, and tortured their way to box-office millions. Perhaps we have left Aristotle far enough behind that watching such movies may provide a release of our own frustration and anger: catharsis through crime. If this is so, Americans have replaced the pity and terror of tragedy with the thrill of wholesale revenge. No matter the case, anger sells big in Hollywood.

And anger persists. One can remain angry for an exceedingly long time, even a lifetime. A rigorous case of anger can outlast many love affairs. In the Middle Ages, enough anger over a protracted period could drive a person crazy, hence the conflation of anger and madness in modern English. Indeed, it is sometimes hard to distinguish between a mad person and an angry person: Angry people do irrational, weird things. They act crazy. But anger can find expression only in such excessive moments, in what we call acts of hostility, or hatred, or outright meanness. Angry people strike out. Three of those strikes and the authorities can indeed call them out—out of the entire game itself.

Imagine, then, a society in which a great many people walk around angry and frustrated, and a great many others vent their anger in acts of aggression. As robberies and batterings, rapes and killings increase, politicians push through more and more legislation designed to protect the rights of the victims (to the delight of the conservatives), although on the other side, the rights of criminals must also find safeguards (much to the horror of the conservatives). As of mid-1997, America had more than 5 million people in prisons and jails, on probation, or awaiting sentencing, with an incarceration rate for black males that exceeds South Africa's during the time of apartheid. No wonder penal institutions operate at 165 to 185 percent of their capacity in this country.*

---

*Children get angry, just like adults, and act on it, too. The Centers for Disease Control and Prevention reported in 1996 that nearly three-quarters of all the murders of children in the industrialized world occur in the United States. The United States also has a higher rate of childhood homicide, suicide, and death by firearms than any of the world's twenty-six richest nations. The suicide rate for children under fourteen is double that of the rest of the industrialized world, the CDC reports.

On the sidelines, Americans grow angrier and more frustrated as the government tries to define our lives by making deeper and deeper intrusions. American society seems caught in a state of dynamic tension, ready at any moment to erupt in one wild incident or another. Angry outbursts provide an effective way of establishing one's space: a clenched fist has always said, "Stand back!" or "Come closer and you'll get clobbered!" Oral cultures, not generally marked by great privacy, tend toward ritualized kinds of verbal aggression, partly because of the intensity of personal interactions, but also, perhaps, as a way of establishing boundaries, of creating personal spaces.

Some Americans, tired of it all, hole up in places like Waco or Ruby Ridge or Jordan, Montana, or in a remote cabin in Lincoln, Nebraska, defying all local and federal authority. They declare their right to bear arms, and at times they claim the further right to pull the trigger. These days, to be a free man, a lot of Americans believe, requires being a Freeman.

The computer has made the situation all the worse. As we have abandoned the book, the screen—TV, movie, video, video game, and of course, computer—has gotten under the skin of our culture, as I have said, and replaced the text as the artifact for organizing internal space. The text and the screen cannot share the same metaphoric space at the same time. The electronic media are too powerful, too present, and too persistent. They overpower the book, so that the screen eventually drives out the text. Moreover, the screen behaves in a radically different way from the text. Sentences move freely about on the screen; ideas leave one location and trade places, like dance partners, with other ideas. Images made of light shine and then disappear. The screen simply cannot begin to match the permanence of the text.

Once letters get written with light, the self, too—that interlocutor of the inner life—shimmers ghostlike in its fleshy home. If nothing holds fast—whole paragraphs, entire pages, deleted with the stroke of a single key—then one has a much more difficult time experiencing more permanent, socially situated emotions like guilt, remorse, and shame. Once the screen replaces the text, experience comes and goes, without catching in the heart. Nothing gets permanently etched on the interior screen anymore. Sven Birkerts, who writes intelligently about computers, says this about screen-composing:

The words on the screen, although very possibly the same as the words on the page, are not felt to dead-end in their transmitting element. Rather, they keep us actively aware of the quasi-public transparency out of which they emerge. These words are not *found* in the way that one can thumb forward in a printed text and locate the words one will be reading. No, they emerge; they are arriving, and from a place, moreover, that carries complex collective associations. To read from a screen—even if one *is* simply scrolling *Walden*—is to occupy a cognitive environment that is very different from that which you occupy when reading a book. On a small scale this does not amount to much. But when the majority of reading acts take place at the screen, then we might argue that a blow of some sort has been dealt to solitary subjectivity. Especially as the book has always been more than a carrier of information or entertainment—it has traditionally represented a redoubt against the pressures of public life, a retreat wherein one can regroup the scattered elements of the self.*

One experiences guilt as a result of a particular kind of transgression, not just a breaking of society's rules, but of one's own internalized set of rules as well. Literacy reinforces this reciprocity between interior life and external reality. When that nexus breaks, one can kill without feeling bad, without feeling much of anything. Without letters that hold fast, interiority collapses. An indelible inner record—what I have been calling the interiorized text—cannot take hold in words punched into an electronic text composer: pixels of light ultimately disappear from view.†

The consequences of unanchoring the self can best be seen in young people on the street, particularly those in gangs, most of whom cannot read or write above a fourth-grade level. For many of them, literacy presents just another form of control and authority, a set of rules and constraints imposed from outside. After all, only those in positions of power have access to reading and writing. Street youth know literacy largely

---

*Sven Birkerts, "The Fate of the Book," *Antioch Review* 54, no. 3 (summer 1996): 266.

†Printing out a text after composing it on a word processor does not eliminate the problem. A person must write, from the beginning of a text to its end, with tools that make an indelible impression. One must come to understand the doggedness of written sentences and paragraphs.

in *sentences* and *paroles*, or when some judge throws the *book* at them. Beyond that, young people find themselves, as they say, "jumped" into gangs, and complain that they have no way out, no choice. They get carried along by the on-rushing stream of daily craziness—the current sweeps them up; events wash over them. They have an impossible time standing back from the scene and reflecting on their lives. No self to talk to, no interior life to draw on, no reflection or analytical power left to them, young gangsters try to survive through expressions of anger, rage, and violence. They make themselves heard and felt in the few, dead-end ways left open to them. They sound a strange note, for a good part of their innards has dropped out of their lives.

Read interviews with young people who have been charged with or convicted of murder: They almost never express regret over what they have done. They betray no feelings of remorse or guilt. They admit to no shame. They do not even use the word "murder." They "blow away," "dust," "whack," "ice," or "drop" their victims. This erasure of the most fundamental feelings—the constituent elements, I would argue, of the social contract—has begun to make itself felt in the general population. People pull off the nastiest acts, shout the most foul, obscene epithets, without *feeling* bad about their actions—without even seeming to notice. If I have no sense of self, how can I recognize some other self? A flat interior life blinds us and silences us to the complexities and concerns of others. Drive-by shootings, aimed at random passersby, distinguish modern-day murder. The self seems to glow nowadays only when heated by anger.

Thus, the most alarming change of all lies at the deepest levels of interiority. From a shimmering screen of light we can expect only the most evanescent, the most insubstantial sense of the self. And with the self gone, or even with the self greatly reduced, down comes everything. The Lockean compact, the social contract, the Declaration of Independence are all null and void. To be bereft of emotions is to be tired in a house without furniture: no comfortable place to sit or lie down and certainly no place to relax. One merely paces, grows weary, and eventually collapses in exhaustion.

Lately, reading the morning paper brings us face to face with the harshness of the times. The numbers numb. Consider the following accounting from the April 19, 1995, bombing in Oklahoma City: at first 8 dead, then 17, 35, and on it climbed to 130, 140, 160; 4,000 to 5,000 pounds of explosives; 9 floors ripped away; 300 buildings damaged; 1,000 FBI agents; 244 militia groups with perhaps up to 100,000 members throughout the United States. Seventeen days after the explosion, the search ended: 166 killed, 2 victims entombed in the rubble. Most astonishing of all, perhaps, federal agents fed over 2 million tips into a mainframe computer operated by NASA.* The fury of the Unabomber too, is tabulated, in 16 incidents, over 17 years, resulting in 23 people injured and 3 dead, 27,000 to 35,000 words in his manifesto. He sounds like someone in his late forties, the newspapers conjecture; no, in his early fifties, we read later. Each bombing takes place twice. A building may blow up, but that same bomb, loaded with statistics, goes off in the newspaper, reducing the victims to ciphers.

One struggles to fend off the statistics in order to imagine the people. TV provides only images of life, fleeting ones at that—no help at all. Only words and the imagination offer a way through the mazy stretch of numbers to reach real human beings. Only language can retrieve all those bodies from the bombed-out buildings. How fortunate the timing, then, that a "Summit of the Word" took place the week of April 24, 1995, in Atlanta, Georgia, just five short days after the Oklahoma City bombing. FBI agents could still smell Oklahoma City in the Georgia night air, making security especially tight around the Carter Presidential Center, where eight Nobel laureates had been invited to speak on language and society. The eight men and women of letters spoke with one voice. It was time for America to confront its most disturbing paradox: the freedom of the First Amendment in a society "grown inarticulate, and unused to expressing itself in language."

---

*According to a report released in early 1997 by Klanwatch, directed by the Southern Conference on Law and Poverty, membership in hate groups has increased about 6 percent since the Oklahoma City bombing. The report lists eighty-three armed militia groups active in this country.

At least that's how the summit's moderator, Ted Koppel, described the state of the union. Koppel went further, shockingly further, by linking the Oklahoma City bombing to a country so tongue-tied that some of its citizens had come to equate explosives with a powerful voice. Seated beneath the protective gaze of Jimmy Carter, each speaker in turn expressed the writer's obligation to defend the sanctity of the word: Toni Morrison, Kenzaburo Oe, Joseph Brodsky. Wole Soyinka put it in terms the audience could not easily miss: "I want to preserve a special level of communication, a level different from Oprah Winfrey."

While the laureates were helping to kindle the Olympic flame in Atlanta, they could not help referring to those who had already lighted their own fuse in Oklahoma City. Regardless of whether Timothy McVeigh acted alone, it cannot be denied that scores of militia groups, from California to Nebraska, from Michigan and Montana to Idaho, with their rhetoric of violence and hate, had set the stage for the bombing of the Alfred P. Murrah Federal Building on April 19. That act constituted a strike against what every militia group perceives as excessive government control of citizens' lives. The computer, in their view, has made government surveillance all the more insidious and pervasive, the "clipper chip" the hallmark of government stealth.

On April 24, 1995, just as the Nobel laureates were uttering their elegant, impassioned sentences about the dangers of computerized communication—"pseudocommunication," Oe called it—a little-known lobbyist for the forest-products trade, Gilbert P. Murray, opened a small package, detonating the bomb wrapped neatly inside. Murray died immediately. Two thousand miles from Atlanta, federal agents could see the smoke of Oklahoma City hanging over yet another capital city—Sacramento, California. This time, the explosion came with an explanation, a fairly lengthy, fairly literate manifesto, plunked out on a typewriter and sent by the Unabomber to the *Washington Post*: "Through our bombings we hope to promote social instability in industrial society, propagate anti-industrial ideas and give encouragement to those who hate the industrial system. . . . Oppo-

sition to the industrial-technological system is widespread and growing."*
The Unabomber (Theodore Kaczynski?) made revisions by crossing out
words with a series of Xs, the form of his manifesto a further stand against
technological advance. Mail carriers—letter bombs do not work on
e-mail—unwittingly delivered the Unabomber's deadly work into the
hands of the scientists and engineers who produce the new electronic
technology.

The manifesto, itself a bomb, threatened more terrorism unless a
major, widely read periodical agreed to publish the Unabomber's manuscript. It's as if the writer were saying, O. K., now that I have your attention,
I want you to read me—to listen to me and to each of my 37,000 critical
words. The Unabomber's words carried a very real charge. They could only
be dismissed as empty and hollow at great peril to human life. Only the
most literate FBI agents—the laureates of the bureau—were permitted to
analyze the Unabomber's prose for telltale signs. He had made critics of
them all, every word a clue to his identity. In a perverted way, the Unabomber was trying to restore to language its authenticity and authority—
no illiterate he. He knew what language can do, what power it holds, or
used to hold. And he wanted to bust into print. The Unabomber's trail led
the FBI back to Berkeley, and to the student activity of the sixties. Had he
participated in the free speech movement? Is that why he cared so much
about language? Or did he come a bit later, during the time of the antiwar
movement, hence his concern with the military-industrial and technological complex? Did Unabomber represent, finally, the sixties gone wrong,
drifting into violence and coming full circle?

Can it be that the word somehow lies at the root of such violence, or more
specifically, that the degradation of the word, and along with it the human

---

*I find it interesting that the Unabomber used the politically charged "we," when all signs seem to
suggest he operated alone. The Unabomber's manifesto appeared in the *Washington Post*, September 19,
1995. Donald E. Graham, publisher of the *Washington Post*, and Arthur Sulzberger, Jr., publisher of the *New
York Times*, made a joint decision to publish the manifesto on the recommendation of Attorney General Janet
Reno and Director of the FBI Louis J. Freeh.

capability for making intimate, meaningful contact, has provided the fuse for the bombs? Early interviews with members of the Aum Shinrikyo, the secret Japanese cult that allegedly released the deadly Sarin gas in Tokyo in the summer of 1995, revealed that they, too, philosophically opposed the computer technology they saw as having ravaged their country. A letter from the Unabomber to another of his victims, David Gelernter, a professor of computer science at Yale University, who like Murray received a booby-trapped package on April 24, 1995, called him a "techno-nerd" and blamed computers for serious invasions of privacy. Gelernter's idea for computer-generated "mirror worlds" aims at absolute electronic control of reality. That scheme in particular fired the Unabomber's rage—or outrage.

While a horrific tear in the social fabric may be opening through terrorist acts, they may be only a symptom of something much more basic, much more significant: not just our failure, but our inability to converse with one another, an inability to create the kind of discourse that made the social contract possible in the first place.

Terrorists like Timothy McVeigh and the Unabomber engage in a kind of remote violence—driving a truck up to a building or sending a package through the mail. Each drive-by or mail-by is shrouded in anonymity, an anonymity encouraged by the virtual worlds of TV programs; by passwords, encoded addresses, and made-up names that zip along the information superhighway; by ghostly phone calls that pass between radio talk-show hosts and their listeners.

A profound change is taking place in this country. A 1995 Gallup survey interviewed over one thousand Americans, 39 percent of whom said they believed the federal government has become so powerful that it poses an immediate threat to the rights and freedoms of ordinary citizens. These numbers do not point to a nation of lunatics and bombers. Rather, these people may simply have been saying that they themselves do not feel powerful enough. The degradation of the word has begun to affect even those most capable of resisting it—the literate—whose once rich inner life is also showing holes. *Everyone* wants to be heard. If I am right and there are such metaphorical hollow spaces inside a good many people these days, then more than a few of us have passed beyond shouting, beyond nastiness and even guns. There is fire in the hole. Our very beings are armed, just ready to go off. Push the wrong button, and watch out!

The bombings of recent years demand serious discussion, not just by the world's literary elite, the Nobel laureates, but by every concerned person in this country. We must finally ask the big, tough questions about the technological revolution: How is it altering, perhaps altering forever, the way human beings interact with each other? Can we maintain our humanity, shaped as it has been by literacy, in the face of a technology that threatens to transform, even to erase, identity and individuality? Is the numbing impersonality of the computer forcing people into warped and violent reactions, in ways that we can only barely understand? Have pipe bombs replaced pipe dreams?

Paradoxically, McVeigh and the Unabomber, too, have become the technology they profess to hate. Militia groups carry on a determined life over the Internet, even exchanging recipes for explosives by e-mail. The Oklahoma City bombing is the largest terrorist event in American history, a technological achievement of sorts. The Unabomber boasted, like the CEO of some electronics conglomerate, of producing ever smaller but ever more powerful bombs. I have said that the screen is no substitute for the book; it is also no substitute for human rights. Modern media have the power to eliminate all sense of humanness.

Ted Koppel is no social critic, but perhaps these days the keenest insights into electronic culture have to come from those who know media—electronic media—from the inside. Perhaps more than the laureates, Koppel understands the horrible consequences of the degradation of the word into mere communication. The Unabomber area of Time Warner's Pathfinder site on the Internet makes an eerie kind of sense, then, with its game called "Find the Unabomber." Pathfinder invites visitors to join a forum that asks, "Is there a little of the Unabomber in all of us?"

I began this chapter by mentioning *The Adventures of Huckleberry Finn*. I would like to end with it. Twain breaks out the irony in the first sentence of this deeply ironic book. He gives us a story narrated in the first person: the highest, boldest order of self. In a running narrative of forty-three chapters, Huckleberry Finn reveals, however, that he possesses no self. He runs on cunning. He gets by with clever lines and wisecracks. He is selfish; he goes for the moment. He can, for that reason, tell us something about our contemporary troubles.

Huckleberry Finn thrives only in open space. Even the new clothes the Widow Douglas provides make him feel "all cramped up." Once out of her care, and having escaped imprisonment in his father's cabin, he feels the world open up before him. He moves through great chunks of space, describing each leaf and wave, in paragraphs of precise detail, as he floats down the Mississippi (even the name of that mighty river takes up an inordinate amount of space): "The great Mississippi," as Twain says, "the majestic, the magnificent Mississippi rolling its mile-wide tide along." Huck needs space, he thinks, to thrill with freedom. Ironically, though, he experiences freedom most intensely on his tiny floating home, the wooden raft, in face-to-face conversations with the slave Jim.

At the end of his journey, however, when Aunt Sally threatens to "sivilize" him once more inside the narrow confines of grammar and spelling, Huck vows to get his freedom back. Huck cannot go beyond equating freedom with space.* In the end, as he feels the world close in on him, his desire for space intensifies: Huck declares that he will not only "light out for the Territory," but he will have to do it "ahead of the rest."

No matter that the frontier had already shut down by the time the novel was published, in 1884—an essential part of Twain's irony—Huck still talks *territory*. That's the one way the reader knows Huck has not really grown out of adolescence: Huck can only measure freedom in hectares, in miles, in fathoms, in the always meandering bank of the mighty river. Even his creator has a name that measures space—"mark twain"—telling the depth of water at various places on the Mississippi.

100

THE
PRIVATE
DEATH
OF
PUBLIC
DISCOURSE

---

*The cover of Bill Gates's book, *The Road Ahead*, shows him standing on a long stretch of open highway in some desolate place. Gates, like Huck, craves space.

Huck lays the blame on everyone else; he always manages to get off scot free. He feels superior.* In that way, *The Adventures of Huckleberry Finn* lays bare the American grain: To find Huck these days we would have to track him down in some remote outpost in Idaho or Montana. The ending of the novel connects less with free men than with the Freemen. One can only wonder how Huck would vote in the late twentieth century. The title of the novel means to imprint Huck's character indelibly in our minds—he is all adventure. It's mostly fun—a helluva ride on the water. But what about Jim? He's left behind, and he can't light out.

From the beginning of the novel to its very end, Huck remains quintessentially American: He wants room to roam. That may be why Hemingway, with all his own safari adventures and European treks—in war and out—found Huck's story so compelling, his judgment so commonplace it now appears as a blurb on most editions: "All modern American literature comes from one book by Mark Twain called *Huckleberry Finn*." Huck is frontiersman, cowboy, gambler, rover, railroad worker, and oil rigger. No wonder he and Tom Sawyer love Sir Walter Scott's romances and medieval knights. America, with all its vast democratic vistas, had space to spare.

America even measured the emancipation of its slaves in the possibilities of space—forty acres of it to plough and work. Through federal legislation, space spelled freedom. This solution to a deep-seated racial crisis only meant that most Americans did not really have to treat Negroes as liberated men and women; they were handed forty acres of freedom, and not an acre more. That should or would suffice. Those forty acres might as well have been cyberspace—virtual room—for the space on the ground did not reflect an equivalent inner space on the part of those who granted it. Without every white American creating space inside themselves for blacks, racial hatred would burn on and on.

In a very real sense, Huck embodies failure—America's failure, as Twain pictures it. Huck can see Jim as free only when he knows Miss Wat-

---

*The *Dictionary of American Regional English* defines a huckleberry person as a "desired or suitable" one. It cites 1892 as the first use. I can only assume Twain knew the connotation.

son has written a letter granting his freedom.* Otherwise, Jim's freedom extends no further than the edge of his skin. Without that slip of paper, he remains a slave to every white person who sees him. Huck simply cannot entertain freedom as an abstract idea that might occupy the immensity of one's imagination. He lives in the concrete and the now. Jim is free only so long as Huck finds him interesting in conversation. Like the lightning storms on the river, however, those conversations illuminate only briefly. Jim appears to have taught his friend nothing lasting.

Nothing sticks inside Huck. How can it? He has no interiority. For that, ironically, he needs someone like Aunt Sally. With her insistence on reading and writing, only she can get him that precious indwelling space. Without it, he can only know Jim as a specimen of articulated legal rights, a man freed by a proclamation, a man who is not a whole man. Twain makes Jim the obverse of Huck—a person constructed and defined only through documents, through literacy. Without the written word to free him, Jim does not even exist.

102

THE
PRIVATE
DEATH
OF
PUBLIC
DISCOURSE

Without an indwelling space, Huck has no ground from which to create those invisible connections to the larger world. Nothing supports him. Twain never mentions Huck's mother, and his no-name father, Pap, appears only briefly at the beginning of the novel, stumbling into the narrative dead-drunk and falling out again, drunk and dead. Practically everyone Huck touches has some kind of title or appellation, some tag that makes relationships instrumental—*Aunt* Sally, *Nigger* Jim, *Judge* Thatcher, *Widow* Douglas, *Uncle* Silas, *Aunt* Polly, *Miss* Watson. Those titles create hierarchies and take the guesswork out of social encounters, a perfect system for Huck, who has no interior architecture and who thus has a hard time "re-lating" to strangers.

The last thing that Jim tells Huck in the novel would appear to be of colossal significance: He breaks the news to the boy, finally, that Pap has

---

*I find it hard to believe Huck's melodramatic crisis when he scribbles a note turning in Jim to his legal owner, and then, after a momentary deliberation, after ripping up the note, announces, "all right, then, I'll go to hell." Huck does not believe in hell. Sin frightens him not at all. This boy suffers very little.

died some time back, on the river. Huck now has no parents; he has become a free agent in a most bewildering way. Jim announces, quite flatly: "Doan' you 'member de house dat was float'n down de river, en dey wuz a man in dah, kivered up, en I went in en unkivered him and didn' let you come in? Well, den, you k'n git yo' money when you wants it; kase dat wuz him." But Huck has absolutely no reaction to the news. Like a gang kid from a broken home, he shows no emotion—not so much as a glimmer of sadness or even relief. Everything is dead for that young character. Twain uses the floating house here, with Huck's dead father inside, as a metaphor, really, for Huck's unhoused, fatherless, floating life.

In fact, after all he has experienced, Huck confesses, "if I'd a knowed what a trouble it was to make a book I wouldn't a tackled it and ain't agoing to no more." It's as if he has had a thrill ride down the Mississippi, a momentary pleasure. To postpone gratification, to do some hard work . . . well, "there ain't nothing more to write about."

As proof that he has no real, lasting connection to anyone, not even to Jim, Huck leaves without uttering so much as a goodbye. Begrudgingly, he at least recognizes the one who has been with him the longest, the one who has gone through every adventure with him, the loyal and lonely reader, but only with the most perfunctory, the most formal farewell, the way one might end a letter to a stranger: "The End. Yours Truly, Huck Finn."

People spend most of the day in utter silence. We think, listen, read, ponder, watch, observe, eat, and sleep without mouthing so much as a single syllable. The thinker, the reader, the drifting daydreamer—nearly everyone who moves to silence retreats into some internalized, metaphoric space. Only in such metaphorically constructed space can we entertain thoughts, conceive ideas, pursue desires, or cultivate emotion. Moreover, by becoming periodic loners, we lay the groundwork for community. We come alive—and contact our aliveness—in what Adam Philips, a psychotherapist, calls a "nourishing solitude."* Civilized life moves back and forth between the private and the public, sometimes exchanging places, so that private in one culture belongs to the public in another: "Each language draws taboo lines in quite different places. Things which in one language are the bedroom's final wild privilege are in another language almost public, and vice versa."†

We human beings prepare the deep business of life, the civilizing strategy of our interactions, in the most charming, most intimate and private location imaginable: "It is in our idleness, in our dreams, that the submerged truth sometimes comes to the top," as Virginia Woolf instructs in her profound exploration of solitude.‡ In idleness, ideas and desires remain safely

---

*Adam Philips, *On Kissing, Tickling, and Being Bored: Psychoanlaytic Essays on the Unexamined Life* (Cambridge: Harvard University Press, 1993), p. 121.

†George Steiner, *No Passion Spent* (Chicago: University of Chicago Press, 1996), p. 84.

‡Virginia Woolf, *A Room of One's Own* (New York: Harcourt, Brace, 1929), p. 141.

insulated from the corruption of time and the corrosion of day-to-day activities. We only know what we think, or think how we feel, by working underground. Whatever stories finally get articulated, whatever conversations eventually get transacted, take place first in rehearsal, in a silent, guarded, phantom voice deep inside us. And then, at least for the great majority of us, that voice becomes audible through those stories and conversations. The ultimate sorrow, the great cosmic pain that fills the gut, occurs when we stifle that voice, when we choke it off and try to keep it, not just silent, but secret—Adam and Eve's tragedy.

If writers have a difficult time describing that voice—the sound of the self—they have an even more devilish time describing the space in which we carry on our inner conversations.* Adam and Eve bit off a furtive space for themselves as they ate the forbidden fruit.† Myriad other invisible spaces, the antimatter of existence, characterize a great deal of our conscious and unconscious lives. Where do we go, for example, when we fall in love, or fall asleep, or when we enter into a relationship? Do all those excursions drop us, like Alice, down an ink-black hole, or entice us, like Hansel and Gretel, into deep woods? A woman staring out the window, lost in lazy contemplation and just disappearing behind her eyeballs—we may call her "zoned" or "spaced," but where has she gone? We can go all the way back to one of the first great poets of the Middle Ages for an answer. When Virgil takes Dante's hand and leads the poet across the threshold down into the first level of Hell, Dante begins the primal descent into the black night of the soul, into the netherworld of the self.

This descent, however, need not always be dark or portentous.

---

*Most of us learn early in our lives not to talk out loud to ourselves, that it is a sign of craziness. We learn to shut up, just as we learn to read silently, as a sign of maturity. Indeed, we may learn these two lessons of silence at the same time.

†When God commanded Adam and Eve not to eat, they must have struggled, in vain, against imagining the opposite—eating—much as a child's challenge to a playmate, "Try not to think of elephants," immediately calls up the image of hordes of the beasts. Likewise, the apple's absolute convexity calls into being the possibility of its opposite, its concavity.

Adam and Eve presumably took only a single bite, leaving a startling vacancy on the fruit itself, startling for the concave space of sin that it symbolizes. What if they had eaten the entire fruit, devouring both convexity and concavity? Would they have committed a much larger sin, entered a space that only God has the capacity to occupy? To eat the entire fruit with impunity, one might imagine, would be to become God.

Someone reading a novel, for instance, enters a rich but carefully circum-scribed world in the imagination, each book generating its own colorful microcosm. Furthermore, a reader returning to a familiar passage may find there an entirely different world from the previous encounter. But that iden-tical someone sitting in front of a computer—Windows 95, a view of what landscape?—rides off along the superhighway, to nowhere each time, a place thoroughly drained of all detail in the desert waste of cyberspace.

In a review of Mary Gordon's 1996 *The Shadow Man*, Michiko Kakutani describes the intricate act of writing such a memoir: "As Ms. Gor-don began looking into her father's past, she began to realize that the man she revered was partly an invented persona, and partly an invention of her youthful imagination. There was a public person behind the doting father, she realized, a public person, accessible to her through the paper trail he left behind as a writer."* Where has Mary Gordon gone, to what unex-plored territory has she traveled, in recovering her father? Of course, we immediately respond: Back in history, back in time. But more important, she has also tunneled her way to a newfound truth, a truth she has exca-vated from the space in which her father once lived. And she has had to clear out enough debris—the old truths—from that space to make room for a new father. In the process, she has reshaped space. In the process, that is, she has designed new memories that will slowly rearrange themselves, like so many atoms, into the image of that new father. From now on, when-ever she thinks about him, she will have to "re-member" him differently.

All feeling, all emotion certainly, must begin as a private act, a per-sonal retreat into the cavelike interiority of being—a flight, as Hannah Arendt says, from the world into the self. Emotions demand that kind of enclosure. Privacy, or the withdrawal from public view, likewise involves a retreat into some sheltered space. Actual physical privacy, of course, demands a physical space, but the two private worlds of emotion and motion cannot be separated from each other. Every time we walk inside a

106

THE
PRIVATE
DEATH
OF
PUBLIC
DISCOURSE

---

*Michiko Kakutani, review of *The Shadow Man*, by Mary Gordon, *New York Times*, May 3, 1996, sec. B, p. 14.

building or a room or an antechamber, we also walk, however unconsciously, into the idea of interiority. In varying degrees, with greater or
lesser intensity, actual space and metaphoric space converge.

Entering a theater, either to watch a play or to view a film, brings
one face to face with the two kinds of space conjoined. Audiences sit in a
darkened auditorium—a tantalizing imitation of the mind?—in the interiority of their own imaginations. The auditorium is a public building
designed for the private experience of entertainment. When the lights dim,
the mind's eye opens wide. Imagination rules the world. Under cover of the
dark, fantasy spirits away all the rules, both natural and artificial.

Productions staged under the glare of the sun break the magical
spell that only the dark can deliver. In daytime productions, the world
shifts so far off center that the dislocation prompts George Steiner to ask,
"Why is it that a daylight visit to a movie theater is peculiarly and deeply
unsettling?" Quite simply, leaving a darkened theater to emerge into the
broad daylight breaks the hallucinatory spell of cinema. Daylight seeps into
the dark crannies of the imagination and calls our fantasies to a halt. Illumination—"I see the light"—operates on both a literal and a figurative level,
in both the public and the private domains.*

While the performing arts (drama, dance, cinema) succeed in part
by playing with varying degrees of light, from full glare all the way down to
dimness, drawing and painting, even sculpture—what we call the visual
arts—require focused light. They demand carefully controlled, directed
light, which transforms objects on public display into private, individual
experiences. Such directed light narrows and concentrates perception,
shines as something called illumination, framing mere observation as a singular act of perception.

As in auditoriums, the interplay between public and private is
exploited quite deliberately in museums, public institutions housing art

---

*Broadway shows move closer and closer to pure spectacle, apparent in plays like *Cats*, *Les Misera-
bles*, and *Phantom of the Opera*, making up, it would appear, for audiences unused to conjuring images since a
variety of screens—TV, computer, video, movie—produce the images for them. Plays also move closer, of
course, to film and special effects, to more easily satisfy the expectations of audiences trained as filmgoers.

that has been purchased with predominately private funds for the community's benefit.* Even the word *museum* reveals that interplay between public and private. Museums serve as storehouses of memory, so named after Mnemosyne, who reigned not only as the mother of the Muses, but more important, as the goddess of recollection. Ancient Greek poets (*rhetors*) would invoke Mnemosyne's name for inspiration and rhythmic guidance—a private act anticipating their public declamations. In classical myth, Mnemosyne dwells in that old hydraulic world as the waters of a babbling brook, to whose banks every *rhetor* must travel to drink deep from her magic potion. The poet's subject resides there, beneath the self-reflecting skin of the brook, for the dead can reach the netherworld only after passing through Mnemosyne's waters, washing off the shadow of individual experience. Thus, each person's experiences mingle with everyone else's. When poets drink from Mnemosyne, they ingest those mingled lives, singing them out loud as one grand, public event—the poem. The poet's skill enables the group to see (remember) the dead once more. The *rhetor* erases the border between living and dead.

108

THE
PRIVATE
DEATH
OF
PUBLIC
DISCOURSE

Illumination is all. The impulse of art is an impulse toward the light. The Romantic artist moves easel and watercolors (the liquidity of painting no less important than the liquidity of poetry) out into nature; or earlier, the Renaissance master limns the portrait of some noble, in a clean, fully illuminated sitting room. Still earlier, medieval scribes use gold to capture light on the margins of the manuscript. Light drives the artist. And it guides the viewer, as well. Critics judge museums and galleries by how well curators train light on their pictures, how airy and bright the gallery space seems. Light inflects the gallery toward the public.

Without light, the eye stops working. That's the point of art, after all, to set the eye sailing, and to bring it back home—to put what it has seen

---

*The paintings in, let's say, the Metropolitan Museum of Art are legally owned by the museum's foundation or corporate board, but the Metropolitan Museum is one of the municipal facilities of the City of New York. Do all the residents of New York City hold those paintings, then, in common? Certainly no rational New York tax payer would list his or her share in those paintings as assets on a loan application.

on view. The artist transcribes and translates. Whatever can be seen is food for the insatiable appetite of the imagination. But the artist produces in the light—under sun, candle, kerosene lamp, or electric bulb. No one paints in the dark. Braille can put into relief the contours of each letter and thus convey the meanings of words to the blind, but the fingertips lose all tact in trying to retrieve, say, the color blue, the nuances of a cerulean or Prussian hue. One can write, albeit in sloppy fashion, in the dark; one might even compose music. But painting demands light—and more light. No one would deliberately walk into a darkened room to create a canvas.

That's what makes all the more remarkable the cave drawings at Lascaux, Altamira, Trois Freres, and the recently discovered gallery of Cro-Magnon animal drawings in the great cave of Niaux, deep in a gorge of the French Pyrenees. Carbon tests date some of the images at more than 30,000 years old. These prehistoric peoples, in seeming disregard of common sense—turning their backs on the light—had to walk more than a mile inside the earth to get to the walls of those caves. Jean Clottes, president of the International Committee on Monuments and Sites, comments, "Imagine those people coming this far inside the earth. This place is wet and dank. It's dangerous. They walked more than a mile. They had to have a very strong reason for coming here."

Even today, wearing the most advanced hiking gear and a miner's lamp, Clottes has a difficult time negotiating the precarious descent into those dank drawing rooms: For two hours he picks "his way through an underground warren of caves, zigzagging across the spongy and slippery floors. He clambers over high piles of rocks and sometimes squeezes between them."* He needs his miner's lamp. That far beneath the earth, very little light penetrates the cave, and the oxygen dissipates fast. Anyone who studies the caves has to account for the light: How did those primitive peoples see? From 30,000 years in the past, the Cro-Magnon make us moderns aware of that one thing—the curious problem of the light. If prehis-

---

*Marlise Simons, "Why Ancient Images Haunt Modern Minds," *New York Times*, January 30, 1996, sec. B, p. 30.

toric peoples burned grease lamps for illumination, as many scholars believe, the light would have been dim and the oil would have been consumed fairly quickly. Even tallow-soaked wicks after a time start smoking. Pine torches would have probably blazed for no more than a few moments. The Cro-Magnon could draw with their charcoal and red earth only in brief snatches, in moments of fleeting insight.

Given all the troubles and obstacles, why would anyone venture into the dark and forbidding recesses of a cave to leave impressions of animals rather than tracing them on the flat rocks outside those caves? Perhaps the drawings needed protection from the weather. Or perhaps the drawing rituals demanded absolute secrecy, total privacy. No one, of course, can know for certain. One is thus free to wonder at the far edges of the imagination: What metaphoric possibilities, even for the most ancient of peoples, were liberated as they entered those remote, dark, and treacherous galleries?

110

THE
PRIVATE
DEATH
OF
PUBLIC
DISCOURSE

Most scholarly debate about cave drawings centers, not on the light, but on their elusive aesthetic nature—hundreds of bears, horses, aurochs and lions, rhinoceroses, woolly mammoths, deer and reindeer, almost all of them in motion, some of them with spears sticking in their sides. Drawn with elongated lines, each creature borders on caricature. Why are they so strangely distorted? Were those primitive people artists? Did only the most creative (whatever that term could mean 30,000 or more years ago) of them—the ur-artists—volunteer for the cave project, the Sistine Chapel work of the Ice Age? To call it art seems logical: Who could look at those fantastic, weirdly contemplative beasts and not call them modern, or contemporary, or see them as almost but not quite, lifelike?

I prefer, however, to rescue them from art, not because I do not like them, or do not appreciate them, but because I think they occupy a different category, absolutely distinct from the domain of creative art. Historians call them art, I suggest, mainly because of their presentation—lines that stylize objects on a surface—or out of sheer habit; or they cast them as ritual merely because they allow the so-called primitive world such a narrow range of definition and categories. Here, for instance, Mario Ruspoli, who has produced an elaborate, well-documented volume on Stone Age art, describes the gallery at Lascaux in the way a critic might review a New York opening:

The hundreds of images inscribed on the walls of Lascaux, both paintings and engravings, all display the same stylistic conventions and a great homogeneity in execution. The artists would have been the same people, belonging to the same tribe, or else their children or descendants, the inheritors of an impressive culture and skill together with a mastery of complex technique. The stratigraphic study confirms that in a very short time—perhaps within two or three genera-tions—the sanctuary was decorated, frequented and then abandoned. The art at Lascaux suggests the existence of a real "school" with its representatives con-tinuing to give instruction over several generations.*

But I would argue that those drawings at Lascaux, and at other cave sites as well, are not "art" at all. Rather, they stand as the earliest tracks of language. I do not mean that those cave scratchings constitute a written language. But I do believe they record early thought, not in pictures—a word I reserve for more consciously rendered and organized attempts—but in images.

The most primitive beginnings of language must surely start with *gesture* (the Latin word *geste* means "story"). Someone points to an object—an animal, say—and grunts. Language is born in the teeming crush of experience. But thought begins in removal, away from the group, in reflection *outside* of experience, and *inside* the person. To think, one must metaphorically or physically leave the group. The human impulse always lurches toward expression—a fleeting bit of truth uttered either to self or society, in silent conversation or in noisy discourse, in graffiti slo-gans sprayed onto warehouse walls, or in animal images tattooed onto cave walls.

Who knows what thought looked like inside the head of a Cro-Magnon man or woman? No trace of it has been left behind, quite obvi-ously, in words. Ideas existed in that early time, not in reflective, analytical thought, but in the word's earliest etymological sense, *ideal*: forms and

---

*Mario Ruspoli, *The Cave of Lascaux: The Final Photographs* (New York: Harry N. Abrams, 1987), p. 78.

images. A record of those forms can be examined, I believe, on the walls of caves from the Magdalenian Period, beginning some 17,000 years ago, and extending even further back in time. Arrangements and placements of animals in the caves just might represent meaning. Bears, for example, almost always appear in the back of caves, in the narrowest of passageways. The caves provide a model of meaning through pointing, definition through location.

We can thus view those cave images as metaphor, something linguists usually consider an advanced, sophisticated trick of language and writing. In flashes of insight (a curious kind of light that fills the entire body), metaphor illuminates by making the burden of reality a bit lighter. I am suggesting that the exaggerations and elongations of those images result not from a need for style in art but from a desire for expression in language. To walk into any of those caves, then, is tantamount to walking inside the head, to a particularly startling and revealing event: the moment at which a certain kind of rudimentary consciousness dawns and begins to break away from the stream of experience.

In a wistful moment, perhaps, the master scholar of cave images, Andre Leroi-Gourhan, said of the Cro-Magnon: "Oh, I should like to think that his first invention, the first condition of his survival, was a sense of humor. If he did not have one, it is all too easy to imagine what a miserable creature he would have been."* Having said that, Leroi-Gourhan nevertheless excludes cave images from the category of play. Instead, claiming those images as examples of high seriousness, Leroi-Gourhan titles his books *Paleolithic Cave Painting*, *The Dawn of European Art*, and the *Art of Prehistoric Man*. If one can entertain the idea of a prehistoric sense of humor, already a considerable stretch, many would argue, by laying modern sensibilities onto the primitive world, then why not glimpse a bit of that playfulness in momentary outbursts of metaphoric abandon in the dark interiors of caves? In this context, distortion through elongation suggests movement,

112

THE
PRIVATE
DEATH
OF
PUBLIC
DISCOURSE

---

*Andre Leroi-Gourhan, *An Introduction to Paleolithic Cave Drawing* (New York: Cambridge University Press, 1982), p. 142.

motion—images (fleeting e-motion) racing across the mind—one creature in the process of turning into something else and, under the spell of metamorphosis, loosening its defining lines. There go the edges of bear, the certain shape of rhino.* What is an antonym—or anodyne—for *nightmare*, for the images that capture our soul's fissuring in the dead of night? Maybe *daydream* will suffice, or Shakespeare's more immediate "thick-coming fancy," or perhaps, an odd-looking lion will do even better.

The caves may just represent a very early and unconscious step, then, toward a break between the full gaze of public activity and the more removed, more opaque world of privacy.† This separation, necessary for human thought and thus for social intercourse—even at a most rudimentary level—presents itself as a possibility the moment the Cro-Magnon first sees an image of an animal with the mind's eye. Without naming it, of course, that Cro-Magnon imitates the experience by walking inside a cave. It is just easier to prime the imagination when we somehow feel that we are stepping *inside* the imagination—inside, to use Hermann Hesse's term, the Magical Theater. Mimetic action, a most powerful impulse for learning, must start somewhere.

Whoever walks inside an enclosure, walks inside twice at the same time: once into the structure itself, and second into the *idea* of interiority—into the metaphysical idea of "indwelling." Architecture, of whatever sort, natural or constructed, cave or castle, reverberates with "responsibility." Every enclosure encourages reciprocity, an answerability from anyone who enters. Whether audible or physical, or both, a person "responds" to an interior space, an exchange between place and person.

Jean Clottes, in speaking about his favorite caves, unconsciously points to this architectural doubling I describe. Standing one mile under-

---

*Whatever one feels deeply *inside*, even at the subterranean depths where secrets hide out, one usually has a desire to express *outside*—the private becomes public. Indeed that's what *e-motion* means. The prefix *e-* means "out of," and *motion* means "bodily movement": thus "to draw out of someone." I do not find *emotion* used in the modern sense before the seventeenth century, and not until John Locke describes the way bodily agitation produces an emotional response (1690).

†The earliest definition of *private*, in the fifteenth century, refers to architecture, to space. The word points to a place—a retreat—and situates tranquility.

ground in front of the Cro-Magnon drawings, Clottes makes the following, revealing remark: "This art speaks to all of us. It touches something very deep." Deep under the earth, yes; deep in meaning, certainly; but also something deeply invasive in our psyches. I want to pursue this meaning for a moment more, as to what we walk into when we enter any sheltered space—houses, huts, dwellings, and caves. But the most studied, certainly one of the most sophisticated entrances anyone can make, takes place when the reader opens the covers of a book and enters the narrative flow. I can find no better place to *enter* such a discussion—the subject itself (any subject, really) generates its own space, one you can peer into—than through Virginia Woolf's brilliant little book about private space, *A Room of One's Own*.

Woolf makes clear from the outset the thesis of her book: "A woman must have money and a room of her own if she is to write fiction." She follows this statement with a rather disarming disclosure, that she will allow her readers to figuratively enter her mind by unfolding, in some detail, her reasoning as she goes along. That is, she refuses to give her readers revised, finished prose. Instead, she intends to think "out loud" as she writes, letting readers bear witness to every false start and quick judgment, every wrong move and silly turn: "I am going to develop in your presence as fully and freely as I can the train of thought which led me to think this. Perhaps if I lay bare the ideas, the prejudices, that lie behind the statement you will find that they have some bearing upon women and some upon fiction."* Why lay herself bare? Because after all, a woman cannot write, Woolf believes, without making herself vulnerable.

The book ends with a dictum: Only with money comes intellectual freedom; and only with a locked room that one can enter at will can come independence of thought. In the end, then, and here the book unpacks both its metaphoric and architectural vigor, to enter one's own room is to enjoy the freedom to do nothing but contemplate. A woman can-

114

THE
PRIVATE
DEATH
OF
PUBLIC
DISCOURSE

---

*Woolf, *A Room of One's Own*, p. 129.

not entertain the same abstract, disconnected, meandering thoughts in the rooms where her family silently consigns her to carry out the necessary tasks of the house—the kitchen or the sewing room. She needs her own retreat. Woolf dwells on this point: Entering such a room works a metaphoric as well as a social magic; one enters absolute privacy and, at the same time, walks into some fuzzy sense—the only sense we can have—of the mind. Entering is essential; crossing the threshold is important; and closing the door behind one is utterly crucial. One enters to entertain the most scintillating of guests—ideas, thoughts, visions, and idle speculations.

Every good writer practices a form of literary architecture, and so Woolf has a few more rooms she wants to show us. Her book itself is also one great room, and when we enter—open its covers—we have the privilege of watching her mind work. As she says, "a book is not made of sentences laid end to end, but of sentences built, if an image helps, into arcades or domes."*

Woolf's mind is a room; the book is a room. One room remains. And that of course is the mind of the reader. As we read the book, the form of which follows Virginia Woolf's thought processes—an architectural shape she has already conceded—we take in her story and overlay it with our own thoughts. That is, we take in, quite literally, the story as in-formation, the story as in-dwelling shape and form and layout—as architecture.

Virginia Woolf makes clear that reading is just as important, just as spatially challenging, as writing. Both require rooms, real and metaphoric. Likewise, both reading and writing create, or forge, the same kind of interiorized rooms. Woolf needs privacy in order to make public, to publish, her ideas. Reading, too, requires privacy in which to consider ideas that will later be brought into a public setting through discourse. Those tiny characters on the page—a carefully inscribed blueprint—really work a kind of hallucinatory magic. In silent contemplation of the letters, a reader in an incantatory way lifts the words off the page and ingests them, taking

*Ibid., p. 130.

in the grammatical space, the relationships and hierarchy that verb and noun occupy on the paper. Drained of their meaning, sentences describe a geometry of articulate space, a tracery of lines that holds, like an ethereal suspension bridge, the weight of ideas.

In framing her discussion of literature in terms of architecture, Virginia Woolf draws on an ancient and important tradition. Classical orders of architecture, from Vitruvius on, exploit the belief that the microcosm reflects the macrocosm—in the case of architecture, a correspondence between proportionality and form—located in the human body and traced onto buildings. Vitruvius establishes, in the beginning of his third book of architecture, the rationale for drawing on the human form: "It is not possible for any building to be properly designed without symmetry and proportion, that is, without an exact relationship of parts, as in the figure of a well-made man." Vitruvius then goes on to list all the commonplace ratios that the Greeks took from the human form: *orygia* (the handstretch), *braccio* (top of the nose to the end of the fingers), and *uncia* (a division of the foot, the modern *inch*).

The circle, the square, and by extension, the triangle, the basic Platonic forms, can also be derived from the outstretched body, so that, using the human figure as a template, the architect in*corp*orates the body's proportionality into each building:

Nature so has it that the center of the body is the navel; were you to lie a man supine on the ground, with his arms and legs akimbo, and set the point of the compass on his navel, the circumference of the circle you could draw would touch his outstretched fingers and toes. Moreover, as the circular scheme may be found in the body, so also may the square. For if you take the measurements (of a man) from the feet on the ground to the top of his head, and compare this measurement to the full spread of his hands, they will be found to be exactly equal. . . . What is more, [famous painters and sculptors from antiquity] derived from the members of the body the standards of measure which seemed necessary for all their work.*

---

*Pollis Vitruvius, *De architectura* (Munich: Fink Publishers, 1969), Book 3.

116

THE
PRIVATE
DEATH
OF
PUBLIC
DISCOURSE

This body symmetry, the ancient guide to human proportionality, Vitruvius calls by a term already well known to him, the *kanon*. I quote here from a most remarkable book on ancient and classical architecture, *The Dancing Column*, by the architectural historian Joseph Rykwert: "[*Kanon*] seems originally to have meant a straight rod or stick, such as a cane, which by metonymy came to mean a measuring-rod in classical Greek—or a ruler, even a carpenter's square, a mason's level and the beam or tongue of a balance; its assumption into musical theory—which inevitably also meant number-theory—is perhaps more important in this context. *Kanon* came to mean a monochord, on which the pitch of the plucked string could be altered by moving the bridge."* Since the Greeks derived so much of their number theory from the body, the canon (*kanon*) enfleshes in every person Pythagorean number theory, proportionality (in the musical sense of space), and the idea of "the golden mean." This immutable proportion guided behavior by setting absolute standards. A person reshaped reality guided by the rhythmic proportionality of the *kanon*, and arrived at meaning through such negotiations:

By a further metaphoric extension, *kanones* came to mean any rule of standard or excellence. The notion was applied to literature: So Herodotus was thought to be the canonic writer of the Ionic dialect, as Thucydides was of the Attic. Many artists were interested in finding a rule for achieving excellence; and inevitably the human body was thought to hold the key to it. The word *kanon*, therefore, became a technical term for an account of its proportions. In late imperial and into medieval times the Latin transcriptions of the word, *canon*, signified anything that must remain unchanged, such as the text of scripture or the canon of the Latin mass.†

In the *Timaeus*, Plato calls the Creator the "Architect of the Universe," and later a *tekton* ("craftsperson" or "builder"). An *arche-tekton*, our modern *architect*, referred to a master builder, the highest order of all craftspeople. The supreme architect, the master mason, crafted the world

---

*Joseph Rykwert, *The Dancing Column: On Order in Architecture* (Cambridge, Mass.: MIT Press, 1996), p. 96.
†Michael Baigent and Richard Leigh, *The Temple and the Lodge* (New York: Arcade Publishing, 1989), p. 132.

through geometry. In the thirteenth and fourteenth centuries, illuminated manuscripts showed Christ as the Divine Architect, compass in hand, inscribing on Chaos the circumference of the Universe.

Since God was One, the Supreme Unity, He could be found not only *in* all things, but *as* all things: "God was to be discerned in the principles of shape—determined ultimately by the degrees in an angle—and by number. It was through shape and number, not by representation of diverse forms, that God's glory was held to be manifest. And it was in edifices based on shape and number, rather than on representational embellishment, that the divine presence was to be housed."*

Master masons of, say, cathedral projects understood the requisite technology. A few, however, held knowledge of a more metaphysical or spiritual order—knowledge of the sacredness of geometry, which came to be called in its most arcane form speculative Freemasonry. The Freemasons had access, it appears, to Pythagoras and Hermes, to the teachings of Vitruvius, to Neoplatonic thought before its popularization in the Renaissance.

Their immersion in number, proportion, and pattern even carried them beyond architecture to another, highly abstract and sacred art— music. Words like *harmony* and *unison*, vibrations of line length in musical instruments and in poetry, patterns of dance steps, characterized the raising of buildings in the Middle Ages, as well as the raising of young people during the period: "For such masters [masons] a cathedral was more than a 'house of God.' It was something akin to a musical instrument tuned to a particular and exalted spiritual pitch, like a harp. If the instrument were tuned correctly, God Himself would resonate through it, and His immanence would be felt by all who entered."† In this context, *decadence* speaks of souls out of step, out of harmony, out of tune with the world and the will of God.

Freemasonry grew during the sixteenth and seventeenth centuries

118

THE
PRIVATE
DEATH
OF
PUBLIC
DISCOURSE

---

*Ibid., p. 164.
† Ibid., p. 134.

in Europe, particularly in France and England. Groups of masons organized into small societies, called lodges, just as Vitruvius had recommended that builders organize into *collegia*. Certain Freemasons—scientists and philosophers—formed an "invisible college," placing themselves in a progressive vanguard that had as its mission the uncovering of the sacred geometry of the world. That group included two seventeenth-century figures crucial in our earlier discussions, John Locke and Robert Boyle. More important, under Stuart patronage the invisible college was transformed into the Royal Society of London for Improving Natural Knowledge.

To see that the tradition of linking body with building still lives, at least in the language, we need only think about the word *story*, which comprises both fiction and architecture, the two senses of which originated in ancient Greece but entered English at the same time, in the thirteenth century.* Ancient rhetorical theory also linked body and building. A mnemonic rhetorical aid, from the ancient world well into the Middle Ages, required one to construct a castle or a temple in the mind. Such imaginary buildings went by the name "memory palaces." To become truly accomplished in rhetoric, one had to master this practice. Thus, to remember a list of subjects or ideas in a speech, you would conceive of your mind as an elaborate palace complete with many rooms and would place in each room one of the items from the list. You would then deliver your narrative as you roamed through the imaginary palace, making a mental stop in each room to gather up the separate items.

Medieval monks continued this strategy by laying out certain manuscripts with both stylized letters and decorations, to emphasize the

---

*The conflation of these two meanings of *story* may derive from the inscriptions on the friezes of ancient buildings, fiction collapsing onto facade. The *Oxford English Dictionary* gives as a sixteenth-century definition of *room*: "A place in a series, narration, or logical sequence."

Only one room in the house is both verb and noun, place and activity—the study. It does not need the word *room*, like living room, dining room, bathroom, or sewing room, to complete its designation. The study collapses activity into location, which may happen because studying—reading and reflecting—is the most interiorized, most architecturally conceived, of all household activities. Room and activity collapse into each other; the person, in a sense, becomes the room by internalizing it.

All through the nineteenth century, and certainly until the 1950s and maybe even today, architects designed the study exclusively for men.

visual aspects of memory and to underscore the importance of architectural imagery in learning and understanding. Manuscript leaves in many instances resemble verbal diagrams that organize written material as a mental picture, a template for the imagination, laying out and organizing subject matter to make it all the more easy to memorize. In many cases, a central room on the page radiated out into smaller rooms around the margins of the manuscript. All manner of medieval texts—psalters, visionary poems, books of hours, bestiaries—followed this architectonic plan.

Saint Teresa of Avila, an unschooled Carmelite nun living in sixteenth-century Spain, when directed by her superiors to write about the journey of the soul from sin to divine grace, composed the profound *Interior Castle*. Cloistered nearly her entire life, the idea of enclosure, reinforced by privacy as an architectural phenomenon, suggests the central metaphor for her description of the soul: "I began to think of the soul as if it were a castle made of a single diamond or of very clear crystal, in which there are many rooms, just as in heaven there are many mansions."* Since the soul resided in the body, each person had to be vast enough to hold the enormity of such a many-roomed structure, and sturdy and upright enough to support such an imposing edifice. *Bearing* is a religious term freighted with significance. The spiritual life depends (hangs and rests) on it.

Like the radiating building plan of many medieval manuscripts, the castle that Saint Teresa asks her readers to imagine "contains many mansions, some above, others below, others at each side; and in the centre and midst of them all is the chiefest mansion where the most secret things pass between God and the soul." Without any formal schooling, but inspired by God, Teresa tries to imagine the space inside each person—the "interior castle" of the book's title. The real work of life involves diligent religious con-

120

THE
PRIVATE
DEATH
OF
PUBLIC
DISCOURSE

Mansion here does not refer to some palatial estate, but rather to its early meaning of "dwelling place" or "resting place," particularly after a long journey. Given this meaning, a home or palace could have many mansions. Quotations from *The Interior Castle* are from the 1989 Doubleday edition edited by E. Allison Peers.

centration to undertake the painstaking journey to the center of the center, the most secure redoubt of the soul.

So Saint Teresa describes the passage of the soul from its imperfect, sinful state to divine proximity, culminating in a sublime, spiritual marriage as the bride of God. To make its way, the soul must move, room by room, from the first mansion all the way to the seventh and last, to its very interior. As the soul moves from room to room, the person fills out as well, to accommodate the fully realized soul. Entering—sometimes reluctantly—the mansion of humility, at the start of its monumental journey, the soul "must be allowed to roam through the mansions and not be compelled to remain for a long time in one single room." The soul starts small, but begins building in size. What sends it home is meditative prayer, the chance for every person to turn inward and to find rest from worldly woe, in that last mansion, the heart of the interior life.

The connection between architecture, narration, and an interior space, variously construed as memory or mind or imagination, continued throughout the rest of the Renaissance, and persisted well into the seventeenth century. In the eighteenth century, all three—architecture, narration, and the imagination—coincided in a discrete literary genre. In France, male aristocrats erected small houses on the outskirts of the city as very private retreats for their secret trysts. Furthermore, their architects supposedly designed seduction into these *petites maisons*—architecture traditionally being a male profession—one room enticing the young woman into another, deeper and deeper into the building, until she wound up (surprise!) in the bedroom. These structures stand as a cruel parody of Saint Teresa's spiritual metaphor.

Jean-François de Bastide tells the story of one of those trysting places in a novel, first published in 1798, suggestively titled *The Little House: An Architectural Seduction*. The reader enters the novel by passing through the front door of a house owned by the Marquis de Tremicour, the story's narrator. The novel forces the reader to re-create the house, with all its erotic charge, in the imagination, as the author traces the plot onto the floor plan.

More than in most novels, the reader turns architect, becoming slowly aware that space appears in the novel as one of the key characters. Indeed, private space takes over as the most powerful character in the novel, time the suavest seducer. I quote here from the introductory essay to *The Little House*:

In the task of establishing a world apart, the role of space is crucial. In the first place, space operates to set boundaries, establish limits, and resist encroachment; in the more fundamental sense of the erotic narrative, space suspends the supreme moment for an infinity, defending the all-too-transitory act of love from time, day-to-day routine, and, of course, the inevitable process of aging. Space offers a place in which to escape from history. Such a role for space, implicit in the very form of "no-place," was to be explicitly noted in an erotic story written by a younger contemporary of Bastide, the archaeologist and writer Dominique Vivant de Non, whose *Point de Lendemain (No Tomorrow)*, published in 1777, carried the message in its title. Indeed, in this short tale, the place of eroticism in architecture and architecture in eroticism is suddenly reversed, as when, intrigued by the description of his lover's secret room, the narrator bluntly avows: "I was very curious: It was no longer Madame de T that I desired, but her *cabinet*," thus reinstating architecture as the primary object of eroticism.*

122

THE
PRIVATE
DEATH
OF
PUBLIC
DISCOURSE

In Germany, nineteenth-century coming-of-age novels comprised a genre called the *Bildungsroman*, explorations of the "building," the foundation and construction—the architecture, that is—of young people's lives.† Nineteenth-century educational theory in Germany, which shaped educational trends in this country as well, continued the architectural connection between raising young people and raising buildings. These theories also continued the idea of Vitruvius's *kanon*, as the Greeks extended the concept to mean any template, like education, through which human proportion and harmony began to trace itself out in the world.

Thus, classical education, *paideia*, emphasized rhythm, dance, number (theory and poetic)—what the Greeks called *mousike*. For the Greeks, as Werner Jaeger, the author of a three-volume study of education in the ancient world, points out, "the words for *education* and *child-rearing*, which originally were almost identical in meaning, always remained closely

---

*Jean-François de Bastide, *The Little House: An Architectural Seduction*, trans. Rodolphe El-Khoury (Princeton: Princeton University Press, 1996).

†To pursue the idea of education in the Middle Ages, one must look under the rubric *edificatio*, whence "edification" and "edifice." In modern English, we "frame a notion" or "build character."

akin."* In Greek culture, and hence in education, poetry and music were the "blest pair of sirens." For Plato, music provides "the most important nourishment" (*The Republic*, 401d) in the *paideia*. Rhythm and harmony, Plato instructs, "sink furthest into the depths of the soul and take hold of it most firmly by bringing it nobility and grace" (*Rep.* 401e).

Schools for teaching teachers in this country were called "normal schools," after one of the principal architectural templates, the *norma* (one more part of Vitruvius's *kanon*), used for projecting precise ninety-degree angles into space. Applied to human behavior, this particular template revealed in one's posture the proof of a job well done: someone raised well will not just act but will also look upright—no slouching, no drooping, no stooping. Good posture reflects a foundation of solid character. The well-behaved walk through the world with straight spines, heads held high, eyes lifted toward heaven. Teachers, as architects of inner lives, emphasized citizenship and deportment, along with the proper reading material, so that the *kanon* would inform their students' daily lives.†

This educational theory was more than a linguistic movement, more than just a collection of cute and colorful terms. That the remote architectural language of the ancient world could begin to drive educational theory in this country in the nineteenth century represents a conceptual shift of the greatest importance. It meant that nineteenth-century educators had turned their attention to the in-dwelling life of each child— "into the depths of the soul"—to a youngster's moral development, suggesting, for the first time in the literature, something quite sophisticated about young people: One, that they indeed possess an interiority; two, that they might be as important as adults; and three, that education, primarily through reading and writing, could shape their lives. Drawing on the *norma* suggested that the old *kanon*, the sense of life as a harmonious dance, still counted. It suggested above all that young people occupied their own separate category called childhood, that they needed nurture and

---

*Werner Jaeger, *Paideia: The Ideals of Greek Culture* (New York: Oxford University Press, 1939), 1:69.
†Recall that for the Puritans proper posture was one indication of possible election.

attention. The two most contentious political movements in America in the middle of the nineteenth century divided between those who advocated abolishing slavery and those who advocated abolishing corporal punishment for children (two themes that drive Mark Twain's *Huck Finn*). Educators wanted to shift attention away from the body and onto the soul of the child.

This conceptual shift coincided with a tremendous rise in literacy in this country. Reading became less of a chore. For one thing, reading material became more accessible in the nineteenth century. Because of cheap paper and printing innovations (the rotary press appeared in 1845), pulp magazines proliferated, and people read novels serialized in those magazines. Transcontinental rail provided cheap, efficient, and fairly fast distribution of reading material, especially important since book distribution from its inception followed the rail lines rather closely. The manufacture of reading glasses on a large scale began in 1833. In the next decades, new steel spectacles—as opposed to the earlier ones made of precious metals— allowed many more middle- and even some lower-class Americans to become readers.

Toward the end of the century, reading got its biggest boost: Illumination changed. Readers no longer had to struggle to see the page in cavelike darkness. One might say that reading in America just after the Civil War was in its Cro-Magnon stage:

In a time of sunup to sundown labor, readers required adequate illumination for reading during the few moments of leisure at night. Like many other facets of antebellum life, illumination was socially distributed. The whale oil lamps of the period gave but an inferior light; camphene, which came into use in the 1830s, gave a more brilliant light, but the fluid cost so much for working people that it could be used only for special occasions, if at all. Even whale oil was so expensive that the most popular glass lamps became miniature sized, giving off less light than a modern 60-watt bulb and making the reading of book-length materials impossibly trying.*

124

THE
PRIVATE
DEATH
OF
PUBLIC
DISCOURSE

---

*Ronald J. Zboray, "Antebellum Reading and the Ironies of Technological Innovation," in *Reading in America: Literature and Social History*, ed. Cathy N. Davidson (Baltimore: Johns Hopkins University Press, 1989), p. 196.

Then, in 1879, Thomas Alva Edison pushed the boundaries of daytime further into the night with a single invention: the carbon filament light bulb. The world came to light and luxury.

People read. And educators began to assume something new about their students—that they could read and write. This assumption proved true to such a degree that in 1883, only four short years after the invention of the incandescent light bulb, the *New England Journal of Education* coined a new word to characterize those who now embodied the activities of reading and writing. That word, *literacy*, referred to the state, the condition, of knowing letters.* This new category, notches above the already-existing category of *illiteracy* in prestige and power, suggested that letters had the ability to fashion the interior life of a reader and to turn that reader, almost overnight, into a totally intelligent creature. Moreover, like character training, reading and writing "in-formed" young people— changed their posture (attitude), their stance, their entire approach to experience. Indeed, the *Journal* impressed the new term into discussions, at a theoretical level only, of course, to determine which residents of Massachusetts were truly qualified to vote. This seemingly innocuous word, *literacy*, permitted the State of Massachusetts to keep immigrants, blacks, along with many artisans and women—the Other of various kinds—out of that elite category and to confine them, linguistically, as *illiterates*.

For schools to concentrate on literacy practically guaranteed that young people could acquire at least the possibility of enjoying a lively interior life. It also meant that discussions of morals and character could take place, not at some abstract level, but reaching deep into the daily lives of youngsters. Like a building being framed, character could be built from the inside out. This belief carried over into the penal system. Thus more humane prisons, like Auburn State, in New York, started by Quakers, were

---

*The Colony of Massachusetts concerned itself early on with reading. It enacted legislation in 1642 that empowered the colony's elected representatives, the selectmen, to ascertain "the calling and employment" of all children, "especially of their ability to read and understand the principles of religion and the capital laws of this country." Concern for writing only came later. Reading, 'riting, and 'rithmetic became the deliberate order of education in the colonies. Schools first taught reading, independent of writing. Arithmetic, which depended on both reading and writing, teachers took up last.

organized on the principle of rehabilitation, specifically, rehabilitation through education. Belief in the efficacy of literacy goes a long way toward explaining why Auburn authorities considered solitary confinement the most humane treatment; a man in a cell with nothing more than a Bible— a literate man, that is—was handed the most privileged opportunity of confronting his own soul in absolute privacy. For Puritans, literacy meant election. For prisoners, literacy meant redemption.

But it also meant something more. Literacy forces a new cultural distinction between the public and the private. People in orality have little opportunity for exchanging secrets with those inside or outside the family except in out-of-the-way places. To be intimate in orality means talking to another away from the rest of the group, or requires whispering surreptitiously in front of the group. No one passes notes; no one writes letters. The two modes of interaction in orality, speaking and listening, usually take place in plain view of everyone: Every person within earshot can overhear. Orality is noisy, public, near communal. Silence—a personal silence, achieved in the luxurious space of thinking and planning (even in the midst of a bustling crowd)—rarely if ever happens in orality. That's one reason oral peoples do not generally use the future tense. The future begins as an abstraction; it lives only in an eerie, silent anticipation in the head. The present bangs and rattles, pops and explodes in our faces each and every minute. Everyone who can hear the here-and-now participates in it. Eavesdropping comes into being only when the group adopts a clear definition of privacy, and someone violates it.

Reading and writing are, by nature, private acts—so private that they exert an architectural force by demanding their own protected spaces. One immediately thinks of libraries; but centuries before libraries, in England and Europe of the Middle Ages, monasteries accommodated reading and writing in specially designed rooms: *carrels* for the mumbling of monks who could only read by sounding words aloud, and *scriptoria* for monks taking dictation from authors. In houses, architects designed sitting rooms lined with books, including sometimes a small desk for writing, in those shelters of silent activity I referred to earlier, studies. The book, the

126

THE
PRIVATE
DEATH
OF
PUBLIC
DISCOURSE

room, and the reader's mind meet in what I want to call the hieroglyphic of the reading experience. Readers internalize the metaphoric space produced in the act of reading, carry it around inside their very beings, and organize their inner lives around it. They have traded one volume (orality) for another volume (literacy). Like Ivan Illich, I too wish that outside the house and outside the school system there might exist what he calls "*houses of reading*, not unlike the Jewish *shul*, the Islamic *medersa*, or the monastery, where the few who discover their passion for a life centered on reading would find the necessary guidance, silence, and complicity of disciplined companionship needed for the long initiation into one or the other of several 'spiritualities' or styles of celebrating the book."*

A book almost begs for seclusion and furtiveness. It encourages secrecy and privacy. Soon after books began to roll off the presses in the late fifteenth century, printing houses started to make them very small so that monks could tuck them into the sleeves of their gowns and carry them about, pausing in out-of-the-way spots in the garden, say, to read far removed from all the other monks. Those early volumes, reeking of secrecy, also turned quite quickly to pornographic subjects, complete with startling graphic illustrations: privacy and secrecy promote titillation. Any book, of course, can be carried about virtually anywhere and read in seclusion. Roger Chartier, a French historian, claims that "each reading by each reader is actually a secret, singular creation."† Readers can shut a book, just like their eyes, whenever they choose and not read another page, or into a situation anymore. At that moment, the solitary and singular act of reading comes to an abrupt end. The ears have no flaps, no lids. Listeners have to put their fingers into their ears to stop the sound. In orality one always hears. One does not, however, always have to see.

Reading a book reinforces the idea of privacy. Reading a screen, however, blurs distinctions between the public and the private.‡ On that

---

*Ivan Illich, *In the Vineyard of the Text: A Commentary to Hugh's Dedascalicon* (Chicago: University of Chicago Press, 1993), p. 3.

†Roger Chartier, *Lectures et lecteurs dans la France d'ancien régime* (Paris: Seuil, 1987), p. 18.

‡The V-chip tries to address the problem of making public access a private event in the home.

superhighway of information, someone could be reading over your shoulder and you would never know. Turn around: There's no one there, but they can read your thoughts. With computer technology, not only have the concepts *public* and *private* become confused, or worse yet, vanished altogether, but so has the idea of space itself. As private, interior space disappears from our lives, computers have rushed in to fill the need. The Internet and the Web, urging users to anonymously "drop in" on other people's typed-out lives, or to share some virtual intimacy in their "chat rooms," promote a new, heightened kind of voyeurism. One pulls off the information superhighway to pause and eavesdrop and play at intimacy. Cyberspace entices with its insistence on *entering*—just hit the *appropriate* key—but of course it can deliver only illusion. We enter into nothing. I doubt if Virginia Woolf could have composed, conceived of, *A Room of One's Own* sitting at a word processor. Miniaturized computers entice, too, with a suggestive name—laptop. How much more cozy can one hope to get with a machine. *Ergonomic* takes on new meaning. But people need little inducement to use computers.

128

THE
PRIVATE
DEATH
OF
PUBLIC
DISCOURSE

Having been denied the retreat into inner space, a good many people willingly throw themselves into the infinitude and quietude, the comfortable anonymity, of cyberspace—way out there, somewhere, in electronic nowhere. The computer program tries to induce a technological reverie, an electronic daydream on one subject or another; but after all is said and done, technology defines the experience and a program defines its movements: A button still turns it on and off.

Vice President Al Gore pushes another kind of space. On July 2, 1996, he announced that the government would let a $1 billion contract to the Lockheed Martin Corporation to build a new reusable spacecraft, with these remarks: "We set sail for the future. You don't have to be a rocket scientist to understand the importance of this moment." (A bit of Gore humor: The vice president delivered his remarks at the Jet Propulsion Laboratories, in Pasadena, where you *do* have to be a rocket scientist.) But one does not have to be a rocket scientist, or even a social scientist, to catch a glimpse of what's going on. Americans want space, and then more space. The highways are gridlocked, the tenements jammed, the prisons overcrowded, and the air polluted. Much more constricting, interior space has shrunk dramatically or disappeared altogether. We have run out of space, but space has also run out on us. Where can we go?

If cyberspace sells people on the possibility of unbridled freedom, then the idea of "inner city" accomplishes just the opposite. "Inner city" sounds as if it might refer to a deeper, more interiorized living experience, a place to dwell at the heart of things, an update of Saint Teresa of Avila. But if the inner city stands in relation to the city as inner life stands in relation to the person—both face terminal illness. During the 1996 Democratic Convention, a reporter for the *Chicago Tribune*, David Lynch, tallied up the numbers for the inner city on Chicago's West Side: Joblessness had risen to over 50 percent, the highest level in the twentieth century. The fifteen-square-mile area contained not one movie theater, and just a few scattered banks (the jobs taken over by check-cashing outlets). Close to 60 percent of the housing lay abandoned and gutted, drop points for crack dealers. The average dropout rate for all the West Side schools hovered around 59 percent.

The West Side does not differ greatly from other American inner cities. While Chicago has lost 60 percent of its manufacturing jobs, Philadelphia has lost 64 percent, New York 58 percent, and Detroit 51 percent: "The hard truth is that the nation has not only withdrawn much of its federal support for inner-city services, we have also withdrawn our psychological support."* Cities have run out of space. Even the lowly fryer has been let out of the cage: chicken farmers advertise "free range." But not the poor, not the needy, not people of color. Let out of their cages, we do not call them free range. We refer to them as homeless.

New Age psychics and channelers have found some barely used space. True space, the only real space, exists for New Age frontiersmen and women in an alternative, mysterious, and opaque fourth or fifth dimension, where every square inch of the world teems with spirits of various

---

*David Lynch, "A Bridge to Nowhere," *U.S. News and World Report*, September 9, 1996, p. 64.

sorts. *Life* magazine devoted an entire issue in 1995 to the paranormal; *Time* and *Newsweek* followed suit, and each of the major television networks, as well, have recently produced special reports on UFO sightings, near-death experiences, visitations from ghosts, angels, aliens, Jesus, Moses, and for a growing number of the population, even God. For a long time, one of the most popular TV series, "Star Trek," took place in a fuzzy border between this world and one where the Vulcans live. More recently, "X-Files" and "Third Rock from the Sun" beam their signals from somewhere in the twilight zone.

Those devoted to the occult and the paranormal believe that they can discern life—writ with the largest imaginable capital *L*, pulsating life, we might say—*only* in moments of visionary ecstasy or hallucinatory excess. They come to understand their own lives through past-life readings, astrological prognostications, and other-world channelings of departed friends or celebrities. At the outer limits of such vibratory space, drugs like LSD (currently making a comeback on college campuses) and Ecstasy, mantras from various Eastern religions, guidance from clairvoyants, propel the most ordinary of citizens into some other dimension.

"Where we read truly, where the expectation is to be that of meaning, we do so as if the text (the piece of music, the work of art) *incarnates* (the notion is grounded in the sacramental) *a real presence of the significant being*"—thus George Steiner.* He goes on to declare, quite emphatically, that "these are not occult notions." The desire for meaning has been ingrained (the reference here, again, is to some transubstantive, sacramental ingestion like the wafer) in human beings for several millennia. Whether we "read" a piece of music or a work of art, the semiotic of meaning has been founded on the text, developed, nurtured, and rehearsed in the acts of reading and writing. The literate mind grabs for meaning. Today, the Word comes to us compromised, reduced to binary impulses in an endless series of electronic signals—bits of data. Communication passes

130

THE
PRIVATE
DEATH
OF
PUBLIC
DISCOURSE

---

*George Steiner, *Real Presences* (Chicago: University of Chicago Press, 1989), p. 147.

for language. Presence has escaped, slipped out of the Logos, to take up residence . . . somewhere else.

Unlike Steiner, I do believe the current obsession with things occult is directly related to the degradation of the word. Throughout history, people have read the world for any particle of the invisible. A divine presence has always driven myth and religion, and now it informs a good deal of popular culture. When Jerry Garcia improvised, Deadheads would report that he had "tuned into"—interesting phrase, here—another dimension: The guitar played itself; Jerry just moved his fingers. Inspiration came from, well, he knew not where. The Grateful Dead gave to millions of tie-dyed fans the music of the spheres. After all, the group had lifted its name from the *Tibetan Book of the Dead*, an ancient text for passing through the *bardos* of this world in anticipation of entering the supranatural.

That other world, however, has been nabbed by big business, packaged and delivered by televangelists, phone psychics, whole earth gurus, and shamans without shame. No one, of course, sells it better than Hollywood. What else could a powerhouse like DreamWorks conjure but the tantalizing stuff of dreams? That's Spielberg's metier. George Lucas suggests the same hallucinatory goal in the name of his company, Industrial Light and Magic. Hollywood's magic rests on the greatest technological trick of all time: transforming too, too solid flesh into glimmerings of light. Movies like *Poltergeist, Ghostbusters, Ghost, Ghost Dad*, and *Field of Dreams*, to name but a handful, merely give evidence of Hollywood's own realization of what it does best—making ghosts, eerie presences, of everyone and everything it touches.*

The real world is so constricting, so damned dull, but the world of ghosts and angels keeps the flame of mystery burning brightly—there, the unexpected and the downright surprising invigorate the ordinary and the average. There, God blesses the nonconformist and redeems the crazy. The

---

*Dan Ackroyd, who wrote a good deal of *Ghostbusters*, takes such subjects seriously. He went on to host a late-night television program exploring the paranormal.

world's all right again, because no one has any rights. They only have power. This other world suspends all rules, every bureaucratic boundary, in the name of sheer experience.

Like the New Age warriors, the New Patriots have found their own space. The Viper Militia in Arizona, the Freemen in Montana, the Michigan Militia, and the Idaho Militia all deliberately try to corral the freedom they so desperately want, in the most remote, wide-open spaces they can find.* It isn't just the vast distance between their tightly guarded compounds and the nearest courthouse or government outpost that so attracts these groups. What matters more, I think, is the exhilaration of freedom engendered by miles and miles of nothing but horizon. Raze all the buildings, dig up all the highways, take down all those damned billboards. If there's nothing out there, nothing can infringe on me. I command all that I see. But such thinking, of course, remains shortsighted. The widest horizon cannot rival the absolute enormity of space that Virginia Woolf taps into in *A Room of One's Own.*

Cyberspace, outer space, occult space, the wide-open spaces: People feel desperate for air rights. They're more than ready to fight for them—on the freeways, in their backyards, in court. They feel anxious, more anxious than they need to feel, because they experience no depth within themselves.† When interiority collapses, only Montana will do. The infinite universe of the imagination—unaided, that is, by a computer chip—no longer exists for many people. Only the boldest, broadest actuality of absolute space—unimpeded land and lots of it—will satisfy. Freedom can be measured in hectares. Or even, as we set sail with Al Gore, in light-years—witness the summer 1996 photographs of Ganymede, Jupiter's largest moon, taken by a camera aboard the spaceship Galileo, which started its journey toward that planet in 1989. Could it be that space exploration keeps a whole lot of people from feeling stifled, secure in the knowl-

132

THE
PRIVATE
DEATH
OF
PUBLIC
DISCOURSE

---

*Northern Idaho first attracted the Aryan Nation in 1990; then the Christian Identity Church moved in. And following that, in 1992, the nation learned about Ruby Ridge. We should not, of course, label every person in Idaho as a far right fanatic, but the state has attracted a lot of fringe groups.

†*Anxiety* and *anxious* derive from the Latin *ango, angere,* "to choke." Distress suffocates.

edge that NASA-trained astronauts are circling, in giddy weightlessness, over our heads?

Outer space has its weightlessness, the wide-open spaces its law-lessness, and cyberspace its boundlessness. All three defy expectations and laws, both natural and legal. A suspension of rules makes all three spaces places of exhilaration—a lifting of *gravitas*, in all senses of the word, "grav-ity," "heaviness," and "seriousness"—through defiance. But such freedom does not ground itself in promoting justice or decency for others, or in cre-ating a better society for the neglected and the enfeebled. Instead, it creates the kind of liberation a youngster thrills to when his parents go away for the weekend and leave him alone to have free run of all the rooms and spaces in the house, from the bedroom to the liquor cabinet.

In any case, I have been arguing for another, more precious space: the canon of proportion and harmony, of order and symmetry, the only space, it appears, in which society can be held together. I have been arguing for inner space, the golden mean of action. Throughout this chapter I have maintained that literacy builds the inner temple. I have also pointed out that reading—serious and analytical reading, in which people must follow the mazy paths of an argument—is on the decline. (I say this knowing full well that book sales have set records in this country for the past three or four years.) The passing of literacy also carries to its death analytical think-ing and the emotional life. Confronted with such a monumental collapse of interiority, people have little choice but to spend their leisure time on their bodies: pumping them up; filling them out with steroids, silicone injections, or collagen implants; tattooing them, piercing them, scarring them; buffing them up and thinning them down. Hulk Hogan or Kate Moss, both demand that we pay strict and admiring attention to the body. If you look tough, though, gangsta tough and guard-dog mean, you can expect a lot more attention and respect on the streets. People stay clear. They back off. You give off the no-nonsense look of substance.

Oddly enough, even though food manufacturers have rendered fat out of everything from meat to cheese—even, remarkably, out of fat itself, witness the Procter and Gamble $6 million gamble, Olestra—Americans on the average keep growing fatter and fatter year after year. We need bulk, as even fat turns virtual, to know we actually exist. Piercing has the same effect: I know I have some substance, the thinking must go, if I can draw on my skin, or put a piece of jewelry through my flesh, or scar my body somehow. The truly tough search for the places that hurt the most—public and private. Pain, of course, has always been a fairly good indicator of one's aliveness. In these unstated strategies of defying virtual existence, Hollywood must give special credit to Stallone and Schwarzenegger as actors of considerable substance.

In a marvelous piece about John Wayne's masculine march through a long string of Westerns, Garry Wills places Stallone and Schwarzenegger in the context of America's failure in Vietnam and the collapse of the Cold War:

134

THE
PRIVATE
DEATH
OF
PUBLIC
DISCOURSE

The ending of the Cold War should have been a comforting development, but it was also seen as the end of empire. America *lost* Vietnam, with a corresponding breakdown in its internal imperial discipline, which led to a sense of drift, a new awareness of crime as unravelling the social fabric. It is significant that gender studies of movie masculinity have added a third item to their treatment of naked gods and troubled boys: The "hard bodies" of the post-Vietnam era—men engaged in revenge fantasies. Rambo goes after the abandoned relics of empire in Vietnam. ("Do we get to win this time?") Rocky Balboa greets the Russian giant when Rocky's government has to confine itself to nuclear standoff. Dirty Harry goes after the punks who have made the city a jungle, using tactics forbidden to the ineffective police force. Citizens take up arms, alone or in private militias, since the government has failed its subjects, abroad or at home. Conan the Barbarian, created on the screen by John Milius (the same man who gave Dirty Harry his swagger), becomes an avenger when his entire village is wiped out. In Milius's "Red Dawn," teen-agers must fight for a government that adults have surrendered.

The sense of opposing tremendous odds, of standing against the whole of legitimate society, calls for a hypertrophy of the individual's musculature and weaponry. Stallone and Schwarzenegger are fitted out with bodies that are nothing but body armor. Stripped naked, they carry huge cannons and automatic firing systems. Dirty Harry's gun gets longer and longer, blowing away whole phantom structures of evil, not just single bad guys.*

---

*Garry Wills, "John Wayne's Body," *New Yorker*, August 19, 1996, p. 48.

Oversized pants cut off just above the ankles, gigantic shirts, baseball caps turned backward—a good many young people, scooting along on their skateboards, look for all the world like the characters in the comic books they read, or in the cartoons they watch. They make adolescence, or preadolescence, look like it could go on forever. Deliberately so, I think, as meaning is increasingly carried, just as it was in medieval iconography, through the body—in exaggerated gestures and clothes. Art Spiegleman, author of *Maus*, the comic-book rendering of the Holocaust, and a contributor to the *New Yorker*, says he loves comics because "you gotta boil everything down to its essence in comix." No time, that is, for details and complexities, a perfect medium, Spiegleman must believe, for an event as straightforward and simple as the Holocaust. TV offers very few, if any, characters with depth. And the great majority of films these days feature characters as thin as the movie screen on which they flicker. In fact, as I have said, the blockbuster stars of movies like *Independence Day, Mission Impossible*, and *The Nutty Professor* are not humans at all, but special effects—modern-day iconography as gesture, pumped-up versions of medieval art.

Thinness of character makes the perfect medium for meanness, for meanness is not a deeply anchored, subterranean phenomenon. Meanness has to be heard and seen, in loud and nasty voices, cruel language, and violent actions. Meanness does not dissemble. It reaches out, as the slang has it, and gets "in your face," a term that combines the verbal and the physical. Kids typically act meanly: They fight over toys and blocks. They hide things. They grow jealous and whiny. "I hate you," they scream, "I hate you!" When interior life collapses, grown people, too, act like kids, for the last emotion to disappear is anger. It requires little if any reflection. An angry person reacts.

Plotting and calculation require reflective thinking, in the way, let's say, that Raskolnikov carries out his designs of revenge in *Crime and Punishment*. A drive-by shooting does not, however, require Hamlet's ratiocination. Such random violence is the stuff of "Tom and Jerry" and "The Roadrunner," except with the direst consequences. A wilding in Central

Park is immediate and brutal. A vicious rape is of the moment. Without depth of character, in the literal sense I mean it, the aggressor cannot recognize a private life in anybody else. In the most dangerous sense imaginable, real life drops away.

At no time in our history has the idea of the private seemed so endangered; at no time has sheltered space become such a scarce commodity. So many people in America today—including families with children—live on the streets, or when we wish to describe them with a bit more compassion, survive as homeless people. In either case, those on the streets—in the open—some by choice and most by circumstance, live in the unhoused space of rousts by police, beatings by junkies, insults from passersby, disregard from the busy, contempt from the righteous, and a score of other indignities. For respite, they might spend a night or two in a shelter, though those spaces seem more and more marked by drugs and violence all the time.

136

THE
PRIVATE
DEATH
OF
PUBLIC
DISCOURSE

Gangs, too, conduct a good deal of their business and pleasure on the streets, in the "hood." Crips and Bloods identify their individual sets in South Central Los Angeles by street numbers: the Eight-Tray Crips, or the Eighteenth Street Gang. Street rap pounded out in the foulest of street language blares from their cars. Where do they go for shelter? For intimate, private time? *Nowhere.* A clean, well-lighted place does not exist. Crack houses do. Some Seven-Eleven convenience stores stay open, as they say, 24/7—around the clock, every day of the week. On the streets, one can only hang *out.* To go home is to go to a broken home. Or no home at all. All that remains is what we have grown used to calling the mean streets.

Think of it: to be without shelter. I read the spate of burnings of black churches as a recognition by racists, at some deep and perhaps unspoken level, of just how powerfully our innermost lives get shaped by sheltered space. I see in those acts just how desperately some people desire to destroy the Other, how fiercely they are determined to unhouse them. In the eradication of those churches, fire is not *like* anger; it does not burn metaphorically. That fire *is* anger—even rage.

Similarly, a church is more than a meeting place. It serves as a place to go for individual *and* group contemplation, a necessary, essential, and public place to entertain private thoughts, and for the noisy, soul-spanking joy of the clapped-out voices of church members. In either case, church space always offers sanctuary—a place to spend nourishing, solitary time. For a brief moment, a poor parishioner can leave the worries of the world.

To destroy a church is to destroy more than a building. It eliminates the possibility for sheltered space, for private, contemplative time. These fires go straight for the individual; they aim to burn out the chance for any black man, woman, or child to enjoy an interior life. Burn down one building, and you turn to ash and cinder the souls of hundreds of people. Burn down one building, and you can burn out solidarity. You destroy people at the most fundamental level. Without a community church, a parishioner moves from solitude to something more despairing: isolation.

More than at any other time, people, particularly poor people, need such invigorated spaces, quiet and private sanctuaries of their own where they can carry on conversations with themselves in silence, where they can contemplate their own moral beings, and where they can hear the harmonies of a room filled with human voices. The nonspace of TV or the movies, of video and the computer screen, even the infinity of cyberspace, offers no such refuge for the self. Only a room of one's own allows the relationship with self. Many poor people jointly own that room; they talk and pray and think in it. They go to it in time of need. They need church.

The time of symbols has passed. No need to burn crosses. The fire this time does not intend to intimidate; it does something more deadly than lynching. For a racist, worse than the existence of a black person is the possibility that someone black might be a person. So the new fire means to sear people and burn out all chance for community. Such acts of violence, as ultimate testaments of meanness, may give us an x-ray look at just how private the death of public discourse can be.

The internalized sense of privacy I describe no one can see. It is invisible. One can only imagine how it looks. Imagination concerns itself only tangentially with the way the real world looks. Imagination seeks its shapes instead in the infinite possibilities of the never-before seen. The ultimate re-former, imagination often suggests the way things *should* look. Out of the imagination comes hope.

In talking about distinctions between public and private, inside and outside, in pointing to borders and margins, categories and definitions, and even space itself, I am of course trying to describe a large chunk of that world toward which we grope. Because it is invisible, however, I do not find it less important than the tangible world. On the contrary, the whole of medieval society rested on the invisible—on the miracle of a savior who proves his potency by disappearing. For the medievals, Christianity renders itself immediate in the fact of the risen Christ, in the absence of his body in the tomb. All the modern, abstract concepts, from values and morals to religion, shimmer invisibly behind the gritty actuality of daily existence. That unseen world sustains and buoys, informs and fills out the quotidian life. What's invisible—love, friendship, the spirit—is what is most important, as it has always been.

138

THE
PRIVATE
DEATH
OF
PUBLIC
DISCOURSE

Virtual reality, the goal of the electronic revolution, pales before the invisible. The virtual promises, through electronic wizardry, to present an alternative reality to our disbelieving eyes. It replaces the work of the imagination with claims of more intense, hitherto undreamed of experiences. Virtual reality does not so much drain the material world of substance and vitality as, with more deadly intent, threaten to kill imagination. Just like the recent church burnings, virtual reality goes after the heart of lived reality—the invisible. Special effects in movies and on television serve as a transition, a bridge, to full-blown virtual reality. Soon, I assume, we will all be there. This end, however, will probably change our lives forever, like microwave technology, from the inside out. Under the domain of technology, the invisible world will lose its vibrancy; worse, it will lose its purpose.

I leave this chapter with a question: Can such a thing as the invisible—with no heft or substance, a shadow in the midst of material culture—can such a non-entity move toward collapse? I have tried to suggest the possibility of this happening and have maintained that we can now see the implications of such a disaster. When people lose the ability to conjure the invisible world, then discussions about issues like inside and outside, borders and margins, get recast and talked about in other, more concrete terms. Heated shouting matches, even those horrible point-blank shootings at abortion clinics, really represent arguments over insides and outsides. Is the interior of a woman's body her own domain—an issue of ultimate privacy—or merely one more area suitable for legislative control and reform? Do we all get to say what a woman does with her reproductive system, or only she?

The issue—a refusal to respect boundaries—slides over from abortion to education. Schools in most major cities have taken to reinforcing the boundary separating kids inside the school from guns and drugs outside the school, by restricting the number of exits and entrances, surrounding all the buildings with fencing, hiring guards who frisk each kid each morning, and installing surveillance cameras and metal detectors at every door to ensure children's safe passage in and out of the grounds. Students need identification cards to enter and, to leave before the end of the school day, signed permission slips. Even with all these safeguards, educators still measure the success of a school, in part, by its drop-*out*/stay-*in* ratio. But it proves more and more difficult to determine just when a youngster is actually *in* school. The fact of physical presence testifies to little more than another cipher in the daily body count of registered students.

Nowhere has this country—or the world, for that matter—faced the issue of inside and outside with more pain and anguish than in dealing with modern terrorism and AIDS. In the context of AIDS, the idea of penetration of the human body, either through sexual intercourse or with intravenous drug use, has to be confronted. The world has been hit by plague. No inoculations seem to work. The immune system cannot stand up against such an awful assault.* People scamper about for solutions. In this light, proposals about "English Only" can be interpreted as a linguistic inoculation, an attempt to strengthen, to make more solid and apparent the

---

*Note here that, in the electronic transfer of the virtual to the actual, users must not only stay healthy themselves, but they must also protect their computers against invasion by one or another strange strains of virus. The immune system cannot stand up under attack in either the real or the electronic world.

idea of an inside, the English language a stout defender of the body politic against foreign invasion.*

People feel the need to take such measures because the actual and the metaphoric borders keep falling away or being penetrated. The terrorist bombing of the U.S. military barracks near Dhahran, Saudi Arabia, on June 25, 1996, killed nineteen servicemen and injured over four hundred more. The explosion sheared the face off an eight-story apartment building in the military compound. No one penetrated the building in disguise and planted the bomb. "Breaking and entering" describes an old world. The truck bomb exploded more than thirty-five yards from the apartment. More powerful than the Oklahoma City detonation—also set off *outside* the building—the bomb exploded with such force it blew the windows out of buildings at least half a mile away, wounding people at that considerable remove from the epicenter.

140

THE
PRIVATE
DEATH
OF
PUBLIC
DISCOURSE

Arguments over Proposition 187 on the California ballot are not just about keeping immigrants out, but really mask discussions over what it means to live inside the borders, what it means to be at home as an American. When Pete Wilson, the governor of California, proposes erecting steel fences to separate California and Mexico, he speaks to the need for making concrete and tangible the outlines of the state. But steel or even chrome-molybdenum fencing won't do much good. The problem lies elsewhere—in the idea of a "homeland." Without the metaphoric, highly invisible sense of place that we have been exploring, no one can ever really "enter into," can ever really take inside themselves, the secure sense of being *home.*†

When Yeats wrote that the "centre will not hold," he was referring to the failure of all the old familiar social, political, and cultural guarantees and forecasting chaos with the awful vision of a Second Coming, lumbered in by that "rough beast, its hour come round at last / [that] slouches

---

*Some members of the Oakland school board would make the same argument about black English, or what has come to be called Ebonics.

†Notice that people "enter into" arguments with each other, as they begin to share some invisible space.

towards Bethlehem to be born." Institutions had cracked open. The First World War had changed everything. But I mean something quite different from the dislocations Yeats described. To be sure, today's definitions and categories, like gender, also stand on shifting ground, and that confuses and angers a good many people. Gays, lesbians, transvestites, cross-dressers, all those who refuse to stay in their place and who prefer to take up life at the margins, upset those who crave stability. But it is really the *internal* center that will not hold. It is the utter lack of an inner life that makes every social and cultural change—same-sex marriages, gays in the military, welfare for unwed mothers, health care for illegal immigrants—seem so overwhelming to so many Americans.

When people cannot project anymore the architecture of their inner lives back out into the world, the web of invisible relationships rips and tears. Once the computer and the TV get under the skin of a culture and replace the text with a screen on which permanence lasts but briefly, interiority cannot hold. A room of one's own makes no difference if its main appliance is the screen. The ancient *kanon* of proportion and harmony—the human as measure for the rhythm of the world, for the order of social interaction, makes sense no more. We Americans suffer from arrhythmia. You can hear it on rap CDs; you can see it on EKG printouts. *Decadence*, as we have seen, is a musical term.

The *kanon* has collapsed. No coincidence that some people want desperately to hang on to the old literary canon. No coincidence, either, that people mistake the power of the computer for their own, and feel no discord in—indeed, feel comforted by—the use of human terms, like memory, language, neural networks, virus, cellular automatons, for the machine. People need to sense their own power, not in the exercise of authority over others, but in feeling fully invigorated, able to articulate ideas, to step into that continuing stream of history called public discourse and at least think about the possibility of affecting its course. In "Second Coming," Yeats says "the best lack all conviction, while the worst / Are full of passionate intensity." A very thin line, an invisible thread, separates such passion from the stepped-up meanness I describe in this book. One might even call it a misdirected passion that needs to be wrenched back on course.

None of the abstractions I have mentioned—inside/outside, margins, boundaries, private/public—can actually work unless those with powerful interior lives sustain them. It is people who keep them aloft, like so many juggled balls, with their belief, a belief capable of ensuring the very DNA of the invisible world. Alas, the web of the imagined world cannot match the fascination and the power of the World Wide Web. Computers pull on our attention, promising to satisfy all that we have lost of human interiority.

The indwelling life exists in a dynamic tension with the outside world. If the infrastructure of the lived life stands in need of repair, then we can expect the built environment to suffer as well. They depend on each other. Holes in our lives, potholes in the streets: The collapse is thoroughly systemic. If we don't—or can't—care about ourselves, why care about our surroundings? In Los Angeles County, according to the city council, it will take seventy years to make a complete round of the city to repair all the streets. And then it will be time to begin again. As a consequence, the county has closed certain bridges and shut down certain streets. Without interiority, abstract ideas no longer sustain and reassure; they move and shift and eventually collapse. Some people, of course, can adapt to enormous change. Others grow angry and nasty, watching their world go to pot.

Anger bypasses the inefficiencies of mulling and reflection, of life deep in the self, and goes straight for the action. Living inside anger for a time, one might not even notice the absence of every other emotion forming inside oneself. Unfortunately, anger shuts out discussion, especially when discussion is most needed for serious and complicated political and social issues. In deep personal relationships, anger unties every close bond.

I close with a contemporary poem by Cheryl Savageau, an Abenaki Indian, who captures all that I have been trying to say in a simple incident: A young boy (her own brother, it turns out) is thrown out of class— tossed out of one space, suspended in another (the hallway), unable yet to

142

THE
PRIVATE
DEATH
OF
PUBLIC
DISCOURSE

find solace in inner space. Savageau writes beautifully about letters and literacy, about outsiders (Indians) made insiders (students) turned outsiders again (misbehaving students). The hallway space becomes a reconfigured hospital space, the boy's aloneness reminding him of his sick grandmother. A spider weaves all those invisible gestures together—the imagined world conjured in fear and idleness—in a web on a window that offers the boy a view of the outside, of escape, of freedom. The poem closes, however, with that Woolfian declaration of internal power and persistence, the great song of literacy that even "the teachers can't silence":

First Grade—Standing in the Hall
—*for my brother, Ed Savageau*

Because he can't read
the teacher makes him stand
in the hall. He can sing
all his letters, knows
what they look like. He knows
that out of books come stories,
like the ones his Gramma told him.
Now she is in the hospital.
He wonders if she is sleeping,
when she will come home.

The letters do not
talk to him.
They keep their stories
to themselves.

He is hopeless, he is stupid
he is standing in the hall.
He is waiting in the hall
for the principal
to see him, for the bell to ring,
for the teacher
to call him back inside.

After awhile
when no one comes
he stops crying.

A spider is webbing
the pie-shaped window pane

and outside,
the sun is making fire
in the yellow leaves.

If he listens closely
a song will begin in him
that the teachers
can't silence.*

---

*Cheryl Savageau, *Dirt Road Home* (Willimantic, Conn.: Curbstone Press, 1995), p. 46.

5

Benjamin Spock, the wildly influential baby doctor, radically changed the way parents raised their children in the fifties and sixties in this country, primarily through a book he published in 1946 titled *The Common Sense Book of Baby and Child Care*.* The book carried a simple premise: Instead of training infants to conform to precisely scheduled feeding times, mothers should respond whenever babies seem fussy or hungry. Spock never pushed hard for his plan. Rather, he worked his particular philosophy gently and evenhandedly through the book, a philosophy that argued for the essential humanness and integrity of the baby. Speaking about the newborn infant, Spock casually dropped in startling but commonsensical suggestions:

He isn't a schemer. He needs loving. You'd think from all you hear about babies demanding attention that they come into the world determined to get their parents under their thumbs by hook or crook. This is not true at all. Your baby is born to be a reasonable, friendly human being. If you treat him nicely, he won't take advantage of you. Don't be afraid to love him or respond to his needs. Every baby needs to be smiled at, talked to, played with, fondled — gently and lovingly — just as much as he needs vitamins and calories, and the baby who doesn't get any loving will grow up cold and unresponsive. When he cries it's for good reason — maybe it's hunger, or wetness, or indigestion, or just because he's on edge and needs soothing. His cry is there to call you. The uneasy feeling you have when you hear him cry, the feeling that you want to comfort him, is meant to be part of your nature. A little gentle rocking may actually be good for him.†

---

*In a survey of 1,000 adults conducted by BARNA Research, those polled ranked the Bible as the most influential book in history (presumably, BARNA asked only about the West), followed in second place by Spock's book of common sense.

†Benjamin Spock, *The Common Sense Book of Baby and Child Care* (New York: Duell, Sloan and Pearce, 1946), pp. 19–20.

For Spock, feeding clearly belongs in the category of common sense. Spock reverses the usual ideas about the all-knowing mother and the utterly helpless, ignorant babe. Listen to the baby's inner wisdom, Spock urges. Mothers—especially nervous mothers—must allow their babies the opportunity to teach *them*, which they can do once they relax and learn how to listen properly. It is not necessary to give the baby exactly four ounces of formula every three hours, for instance (or to fret when all of it is not finished), because "the baby is the one who knows how many calories his body needs and what his digestion can handle. If he's regularly not getting enough, he'll probably cry for more. Take his word for it. . . . If there's more in any bottle than he feels like, let him stop when he wants to."*

In his concerns, in his radical drive to see the baby as an individual capable of articulating needs, Spock expanded his advice and asked parents to treat all young people with the same seriousness. In fact, in 1970 Spock published another book, *Decent and Indecent: Our Personal and Political Behavior*, in which he explored adolescence as a wonderful period. In a significant way, the dedication inscribed in that book reveals Spock's deep affection for and belief in young men and women: "To the young people, black and white, who are being clubbed, jailed, and even killed for showing us the way to justice."

Although Spock later came to question the impatience of the young people he praises, he cannot take all the blame—or the credit—for a generation bent on change. As most often happens, change occurs through a convergence, sometimes only coincidental, of several key innovations or ideas, and what newspapers would eventually call the New Left must be seen in its political context. Some recent historians have argued for the influence of radical pacifists of the thirties and forties on the emergence of the antiwar movement. More immediately, the organizing strategies of the Student Non-Violent Coordinating Committee (SNCC) and the Congress of Racial Equality (CORE) during civil rights actions of the early 1960s

146

THE
PRIVATE
DEATH
OF
PUBLIC
DISCOURSE

---

*Ibid., p. 23.

directly influenced, for example, the free speech movement in Berkeley. Other historians cite the history of this country as one of political dissent and see the student rebellion of the sixties as just another phase of that continuing tradition of protest.

Nonetheless, Spock worried that the demands of the student generation reflected a desire for immediate gratification, a pattern he found disturbing and that he linked to another trend in modern American society. At about the same time that Spock started making medical house calls, TV made its own dramatic appearance into the living rooms of American families. TV instrumentalized gratification and immediacy: Just flip the switch, sit back, and in no more than a second or two—voila!—sound and sight and plenty of dazzle provide excitement and action. (Most TV sets now have a low current running through them all the time, so the picture instantaneously appears, like an electronic pop-up book.) More important, the screen flashes image after image of the latest products and appliances. J. Fred MacDonald, who has surveyed the rise and decline of network television in America, reports that in mid-1949 "the U.S. Department of Commerce confirmed . . . that TV soon would become the nation's leading sales tool. The department emphasized that the effectiveness of 'television's combination of moving pictures, sound, and immediacy produces an impact that extends television as an advertising medium into the realm of personal sales solicitation. Television makes the home the location of the point-of-sales presentation and reduces follow up personal selling to a minimum."*

Very few TV commercials mention price; none mention the labor it takes to purchase shiny appliances and sleek automobiles, but those commercials enable viewers to see gratification in action. No commercial carries a warning that the product it advertises may be beyond one's reach. Instead, TV offers images of happy, usually young people enjoying their brand-name abundance. In fact, those people have found happiness because of their new gadgets and goodies. Early viewers wondered, Why

---

*J. Fred Mac Donald, *One Nation under Television: The Rise and Decline of Network TV* (New York: Pantheon Books, 1990), p. 51.

can't I do the same? A lot of them obviously believed they could: By the end of 1949, TV sales had reached a whopping 60,000 sets a week in America. By the end of 1950—just four short years after its introduction, and as unbelievable as it sounds—10 million American homes had television sets. By 1955, American business had introduced a concept to help people, especially poor people, extend their economic reach. Called "easy payment" or "installment buying," credit very quickly turned TV images into reality. A bit of money down, followed by small monthly payments, and you theoretically could own whatever you desired. That same year, perhaps to help those who still could not afford to buy whatever was being pitched most recently on the major networks, the medical industry came to the rescue and promoted instant calm. Almost overnight, pharmaceutical companies spoke about a new category of drug called tranquilizers, and Americans downed a new miracle pill, Miltown.*

148

THE
PRIVATE
DEATH
OF
PUBLIC
DISCOURSE

I dwell here on TV's effect on ways of living, particularly on perception, because TV made factory *production* so immediately and forcefully visible. Advertisers used TV as a conduit for moving products from their source to the living room of the consumer. Far from an intrusion, production took on a certain air of intimacy as cars and Camels and Coors came tumbling in never-ending profusion for a few moments' stay inside our homes.

Earlier, I talked about the fine meshing of the Protestant work ethic with the spirit of capitalism: amassing wealth stood as one possible sign of election. I know God has looked favorably on me and my way of life, the reasoning goes, because he has rewarded me with great wealth. I must be special. TV speeded up the process of acquiring goods by creating (in some cases, actually reinforcing) a need for more and more products. People worked harder, put in longer hours, took on extra jobs. With its electronic trickery, television broadcast images of election to hungry audi-

---

*It was impossible to speak about someone "being tranquilized," before 1955. *To tranquilize*, first used in the seventeenth century as part of the vocabulary of the newly opened interior of the body, was an intransitive verb: it could only be done *by* oneself *to* oneself and referred to a state of being—free from agitation, calm and serene. Medical intervention made the verb transitive—the object of the verb, a pill.

ences. As I say, it not only speeded up production, much more important, it elevated production to the highest goal of a free society. Everything visible, concrete, and material was suddenly a crucially valuable commodity. The invisible world of the spirit faded far away. TV made desire palpable, right there on the screen.*

Of course, no television viewer could touch or smell those objects of desire. No one could reach out and grasp them. They remained, quite literally, out of reach. TV offered only an illusion. To possess those things, you had to *do* something—namely, go to work, no matter how hard or long, no matter how stifling or backbreaking, to earn the money to buy them. In that sense, we might consider TV, in a perverse way, inspirational, a goad to work. But as the gadgets and appliances grew more expensive, TV sent both parents out to work. Parents placed their children in something called preschool, in day care, in after-school care.†

In our competitive world, people get sorted into winners and losers. Even with the help of credit, not everyone can afford to buy their heart's desire. They not only remain out of the winners' circle, they go through life filled with frustration and despair. Lots of them—families with children—wind up on the streets. We have to remind ourselves just how democratic television can be: poor people in the ghetto get the same reception, see the same commercials, as viewers in Beverly Hills or in Hyannis Port. A recent bumper sticker reads: "Whoever dies with the most toys wins." These toys have been distributed in a very uneven way: The top 1 percent of the wealthiest Americans own as much as the bottom 95 percent—the most radical inequality since the twenties.

How can those locked out of the system get what they want? One way, an option seized on by more and more people, takes them to Reno or Vegas, on a riverboat in the South, or to a dozen or more Indian reservations, for poker, blackjack, or craps; or to hundreds of thousands of liquor

---

Production derives from the Latin verb *producere*, "to stretch," "to prolong," and also "to draw into visibility."

†In some families today, of course, both parents must work just to meet basic living expenses.

stores and convenience stores in various towns and cities to play the state lottery. Others, more frustrated, perhaps, or more desperate, resort to robbery and burglary to get cash or "stuff." And thus we have the two major growth industries in late-twentieth-century, postindustrial America: prisons and gambling.*

In an essay in the *New York Times*, "What Will Gates Give?," Michael Lewis suggests what the richest man in the world—he pegs Gates's personal wealth at $18.5 billion—might underwrite to transform America. He does not recommend first what one might expect—jobs or education or even financial assistance programs. Lewis asks for Gates to spend his fortune on the creation of one thing only, public space, and makes the following important political observation: "The decline in the number of places where all social classes mingle is one of the more noticeable trends that goes hand in hand with the widening gap between rich and poor."†

In an eerie distortion of what Lewis means by public space, a leveling, democratic piece of turf, where "mingle" means social intercourse, both casinos and prisons welcome everyone. Indeed, they each make it easier and easier for folks to enter their inner sanctums. They each pretend that money is not an issue, that rich or poor, once inside, face the same

150

THE
PRIVATE
DEATH
OF
PUBLIC
DISCOURSE

---

*Some states have turned to gambling as a way to balance their budgets. Twenty years ago, only Nevada allowed commercial casinos and only thirteen states sponsored lotteries. By 1996, thirty-seven states had lotteries, and twenty-three states allowed some form of casino gambling (riverboat or Indian reservation gaming houses), with full-fledged gaming meccas operating in Las Vegas, Atlantic City, and along Mississippi's Gulf Coast. In 1975, Americans wagered $17 billion on legal gambling. By 1995, that amount had soared to $550 billion, a figure that includes lotteries, horse races, bingo and casinos. Gambling companies showed revenues of $44.4 billion in 1995 (Herbert Muschamp, "Animal Phantasmagoria Not Just for Gamblers," *New York Times*, October 28, 1996, sec. B, p. 1).

Other states have found wonderful sources of additional revenue in opening prisons in their communities. In California, for example, the prison industry has been the *only* growth sector in the nineties. In one California community, Chino, about forty miles east of Los Angeles, the California State Institute for Men has added $70 to $75 million a year in salaries to the local economy. In addition, the prison contracts for a good deal of its goods and services from the community.

California's budget for prisons went from $300 million in 1980, to $3 billion in 1994. From 1984 to 1994, prisons have accounted for 45 percent of the growth in California for all jobs. The correctional officers union in the state, the CCPOA—California Correctional Peace Officers Association (they reserve the term *guards* for stooges at the front door of K-Mart or the Bank of America)—collects over $8 million in dues a year. According to the *San Francisco Examiner*, CCPOA contributes as much as the California Teachers Association, although it is only one-tenth its size. CCPOA's PAC is second only to the California Medical Association in political contributions. Don Novey, the head of CCPOA, boasted in 1994 that the union's political contributions had resulted in thirty-eight victories out of the forty-four bills introduced under the last three governors of California.

†Michael Lewis, "What Will Gates Give?" *New York Times Magazine*, February 19, 1996, p. 28.

odds, the same sentences. Many casinos use chips or silver dollars instead of the usual currency, and prisons virtually abolish all cash. Casinos make a visit to exotic places like Egypt (the Dunes) or ancient Rome (Caesar's Palace) a possibility for even the most impoverished players. They pull people out of space; they deliberately disorient. At the Chino Men's Institute, prison officials call cells dormitories and give them names like Cypress, Cherry Cove, and Willow Springs—a congenial campground really. To enter prison, like entering a casino, is to leave the known and familiar world behind.

Statistics and numbers control both casinos and prisons, in odds and playoffs, years and paybacks: Every player, legal or illegal, wants the same thing—immediate and abundant pleasure, measured in cash, the most liquid of things. Both in-laws and outlaws try to catch a break in a world that seems so crushingly unfair.* Rollers in Vegas and players on the street both try to beat the same system, to "break the bank." For gamblers and gangsters, the normal rules simply do not apply; they stifle and suffocate. Only a sucker would get sucked into such a rule-bound world. For each group, Lady Luck spins her lazy wheel—all bets down on roulette or fortune—and shines her countenance on a chosen few. In an instant, she transmogrifies the average citizen into a millionaire. In a flash, she bestows respect. Alas, on the vast majority of others, she casts her long and sorry shadow. Them's the breaks.

Prisons and casinos can be seen as culminating points in that long history of instant gratification, to which I now want to return. The explosion of fast food restaurants—led by the now ubiquitous McDonald's—during the early to late fifties also helped to satisfy, almost instantaneously, America's hunger pangs.† Rather eat at home? You could buy a complete meal in 1954,

---

*No wonder one out of every four males in this country has an arrest record. No wonder, also, that 50 percent of inner-city children have at least one parent in jail, on parole, on probation, or on the lam from the law. (See the report from the National Criminal Justice Commission *The Real War on Crime*.)

†The first McDonald's hamburger stand opened in Downey, California, at the intersection of Lakewood Boulevard and Florence Avenue, in 1953. It opened with a sixty-foot sign of Speedee, the company's earliest logo—a chef who could deliver a burger upon demand.

frozen in its own plate, by simply asking your supermarket clerk for a Swanson's TV dinner: turkey, gravy, cornbread, peas, and sweet potatoes. Want coffee? It's yours in an instant in 1955, by adding boiling water to a spoonful of dessicated powder from Maxwell House.* To appeal to yet another basic drive, the birth control pill eradicated the fear of pregnancy, permitting a more spontaneous, carefree, and immediate kind of sexuality. Even though critics of "the Pill" protested that it would foster lives of moral depravity and promiscuity, the FDA approved the first public sale of an oral contraceptive, Enovid, on May 9, 1960. If any single event can be said to have ushered in the sixties, we have to consider the introduction of the pill as a serious candidate. It even prompted a new phrase to describe the offspring of Doctor Benajmin Spock: "The Free-Love Generation."

152

THE
PRIVATE
DEATH
OF
PUBLIC
DISCOURSE

One of the bibles of the sixties, a manual for reaching the supreme clarity of enlightenment, written by Baba Ram Dass (born Richard Alpert), commanded its readers: *Be Here Now*. Alpert's former colleague in the psychology department at Harvard, Timothy Leary, coined his own monosyllabic mantra in pursuit of pleasure, "Tune In, Turn On, and Drop Out." The "turn-on" came from the most powerful stimulus for grabbing pleasure in the heat of the moment: drugs—LSD, marijuana, hashish, cocaine, speed, PCP ("angel dust"), Ecstasy; for the hard-core, heroin, and later, the super instant gratifier, crack cocaine.

To postpone pleasure, to push it somewhere into an opaque space called "some later time" (a vaguely future tense that makes most people tense) requires, among a host of other things, a mind that can abstract—a mind, that is, that can conceive of such a highly metaphoric space as *later*. It takes a person who has internalized a degree of self-discipline along with a sense of moral responsibility. The ability to postpone pleasure means a person has really reached a maturity, an inner sophistication. I am of course describing the literate human being. In discussing what he calls "personal

---

*Beginning in the fifties, the instant became the coefficient of satisfaction. The instant touched everything. If a product was not "time-saving" or "labor-saving," it had no place in the modern, liberated household. On May 11, 1949, for example, Polaroid announced the Land Camera, which could produce a developed picture of family fun almost instantaneously.

autonomy," the philosopher Thomas Nagel draws a picture, without naming it, of a person who has not passed into literacy: "If someone reaches adolescence without a conscience or the ability to postpone gratification, rational persuasion or education are not going to make up for it, and social control will have to rely on force."*

How can one hold up under such enormous pressure, when every message says, "Buy this now. Do what you have to do, but just get it," and the authorities counter with "Do it legally, or we'll bust you?" "Just Do It," Michael Jordan insists, his $300 Nikes high above the hardwood floor. "Just Say No," the drug fighters insist. "Dream," say the commercials. "Don't daydream," say the teachers. Such mixed messages can drive anyone to the far edges of frustration. Someone, in particular someone poor with little chance to own very much, might just decide to take on the law, try robbing and stealing to get a share. To hell with the consequences, poor people reason, life is hard enough as it is, what do I really have to lose? Not much of a choice: life in the ghetto or life in prison.

Only by weighing situations and deciding between different courses of action can one begin to feel the stirrings of something called autonomy. What price do I pay for acting now? How long can I wait? What's the payoff? What's my plan? In literacy, the surest training for the experience of postponed pleasure is reading, and in particular reading novels. In novels, one must work diligently through pages and pages of plot intrigues, of character development, reversals and betrayals of all kinds, before reaching the singular pleasure of resolution or culmination that arrives only near the very end of the narration—at the climax. In the process, the reader has to suspend judgment for many hours and postpone the ultimate satisfaction of closure.

To judge by bookstores and newsstands, the reading matter of choice these days is something quite different—we love our magazines. One can pick up a magazine on virtually every topic imaginable, from

*Thomas Nagel, "The Cult of the Individual," *New York Times Book Review*, September 8, 1996, p. 24.

cigars and seasoning, from fashion to football, from marriage to money, as well as on more arcane subjects, like Asian martial arts, tattoos, and even tatting.* In addition, a whole new genre of magazine-cum-newspaper has recently come onto the market. Self-published and self-distributed, these "zines" report all the latest news on every aspect of alternative lifestyles.

Slick, glossy objects, easy to hold and easy to digest, magazines satisfy desires with little or no effort from their readers. If you don't like one article, you can move quickly to the next. If you don't like one magazine, toss it and grab another. Can't stand this issue? Wait for next month's. Magazines are easily disposable, even recyclable, and still cost far less than the overwhelming majority of hardcover books. Finally, reading a magazine article requires but a few moments, no more time then it takes to consume a Big Mac and fries. The prose runs in such narrow columns that you merely have to run your eyes down the center of the page to catch the meaning. Magazines invite skimming.

154

THE
PRIVATE
DEATH
OF
PUBLIC
DISCOURSE

With literacy no longer providing a filter of analysis and abstract reasoning between individuals and their experience, a good many people exist in a perpetual *now*, driven by an insatiable hunger for sensation, and more sensation—for heightened sensation. Without literacy, people have no inkling of a detailed, desirable future. Street kids, say, find themselves either in a gang or out of a gang. They do not say—cannot say—I think I'll quit next week or, if the weather turns warm, maybe I'll leave the gang in the summer. They cannot, as we say, stand back from situations and imagine the consequences of their actions. They have not ingested social constraints, and so come alive only in acting, in doing. As Thomas Nagel warns, without a conscience the future falls away. Without guilt and shame, the social contract falls apart as well. Gratification knows only one tense, the present.

A large chunk of the population craves—*demands* actually comes

---

*According to Samir Husni's *Guide to New Consumer Magazines*, in 1995 the total number of new magazines reached 838, a fourfold increase from the year 1985. The survival rate for new magazines increased to 30 percent, from 20 percent in 1985. The editors of the Publishers Information Bureau report that from January through September 1996 advertising revenue hit $7.8 billion, up 8.5 percent for the comparable period in 1995.

closer to the truth—fun and titillation. Even literate viewers have been taught by TV to desire things now, rather than later. The computer reinforces that desire to have it—information, solutions, data, answers—now. Computer manufacturers measure user satisfaction in fractions of seconds: more power, more speed. Gun manufacturers brag about rounds per second. The Cobray M11/9 fires an astonishing thirty-two rounds of 9 mm ammunition in one and a half seconds. Even with speed limits averaging around 35 miles per hour, most car manufacturers still report their cars' performance in seconds required to go from 0 to 60 miles per hour, as if that could ever matter for normal driving. It may not, but that misses the point. Potentiality means that I can always punch the gas pedal and get results *now.*

For the past several decades, Americans have been cajoled into viewing time as the most ferocious of enemies. *Now* is when we want things—food, objects, memos, affection, a good dose of recognition and, if at all possible (please, Mr. Warhol) fame. *Now* is also when we want things fixed and problems solved. Most of us currently operate on emergency alert. We have been conditioned into a state of 911 frenzy. We face crisis after crisis in international and domestic politics, as well as in our own lives. The 911 hot line has become so overcrowded in many cities with people calling in what they perceive as emergencies—car problems, cooking disasters, even checkbook overdrafts—that some lawmakers have proposed a 912 line for real emergencies. One can now purchase an "SOS phone" to speed dial 911 or a local towing service. Commercials scare us into believing that without Intel or Windows 97 we won't be able to cope. We won't matter. Parents of kindergartners believe that if their children do not achieve something called "computer literacy," there will be no hope for them, no jobs, no future. Actually, the most popular phrase—the most frightening worry—that parents mention is that their children "will be left behind," abandoned, I suppose, to some desolate off-ramp on the superhighway. The sirens scream "NOW NOW NOW."

The more time we take in acquiring objects, the less substantial we appear to the rest of the world. Of course, some things, like Rolls Royces and mansions, will always remain beyond the reach of but a very few. But the vast majority of other things, even outlandishly expensive production cars, must be obtained—the message comes to us repeatedly—*quickly*. Very quickly. Every advertising line, every brochure headline, insists that cost should not stand in the way of our desire: Money should not present an obstacle. If it did, the reasoning goes, very few people would live in large houses or drive fancy cars. And there would go the American Dream.

Credit, at incredibly high rates, removes with the stroke of a pen the debilitating frustration of postponement. Like a magic telescope, credit brings every distant desire into immediate and sharp focus. Advertising creates the need; credit helps satisfy it. Capitalism, however, abhors a sated customer. So advertisers face a daunting task. They must create more and more deeply felt needs. How utterly efficient when, as a consequence of its built-in obsolescence, the product itself can create a need for more advanced models—just a bit better, just a bit more powerful, faster, and probably just a bit more expensive. *Now* goes by so swiftly that advertising strategy keeps every man, woman, and child focused forever on the future, on the next generation of products. By permitting them to buy things on time, credit enables consumers to turn that future time into immediate pleasure.* And the cycle goes on and on, the wheel eternally turning in the Dharma of Consumption.

The most powerful engine of instant gratification, however, has nothing to do with credit or crack, has no connection with TV or tranquilizers. If the Pill helped characterize the sixties, the chip surely gives the nineties its particular character. Personal computers work with dazzling speed and promise to bring an entire universe of information into the expectant hands of the user. The PC is every time-saving, pleasure, and power provider rolled into one. *Ergonomic* does not come close to describing it. One

156

THE
PRIVATE
DEATH
OF
PUBLIC
DISCOURSE

---

*Savings trade time in the opposite direction—a person pulls money out of circulation now for future needs. Every study indicates that Americans do not believe very strongly in such behavior—savings in America has never been a very high percentage of income, averaging currently about 4 percent of net income. In comparison, the Japanese save about 20 percent, and the English about 10 percent.

exercises mastery over the machine and thus over the world. The Internet takes the most unassuming, average citizen anywhere; the superhighway knows no speed limits, recognizes no territorial boundaries, and everyone rides first class. The chip spins its Web worldwide. Though we can recite the numbers and know those numbers somehow mean power, few of us have a grasp of megahertz or megabytes. Even young children understand, however, that the bigger the numbers, the faster the ride—and the greater the thrill. Instant gratification in the late twentieth century has more to do with power than pleasure—or, rather, with the pleasure that power induces.

There's another way, however, to view the computer. That mighty box, hooked up by tiny optic fibers in a global network, like some international syndicate, testifies to a grand failure. The computer rests, on virtually every office desk, as an electronic carcass of a culture once humanly powerful, a culture that not so very long ago talked and argued itself into being but then, yelling and shouting, began to fall apart in the rat-a-tat-tat of discord and disharmony. The PC culture has failure written all over it. Only the Net and the Web, like so much packing twine, seem to hold it together. Like the images on the screen itself, the assemblage is illusory; the ties only appear to bind.

Diana Trilling once observed, "I think the life of significant contention no longer exists. We have enormous division in our society on sectarian and ideological lines. But we don't have any discourse."* Images cannot carry on discourse. Discourse is itself as deceptive as any TV or PC image: It only appears to come out of the mouth. In reality, it bubbles and gurgles up from far below. Its preparation takes years and years, beginning in early life. It starts in infancy, in orality, in the immersion of youngsters in talking, talking, talking. Even scolding has its beneficial effect: Do I deserve it? What did I do wrong? Should I change? On and on, the questions keep coming, far less sophisticated than Trilling's "significant con-

---

*Diana Trilling, "On the Steps of Low Library," in *We Must March My Darlings* (New York: Harcourt Brace Jovanovich, 1977). Trilling wrote the Low Library piece in 1969.

tention"; but who knows—who really knows—when mature thought has been achieved. Each of us runs on a different schedule. One has to be ready, however, to make it possible at all.

The technological failure I describe gnaws away at the very heart of modern culture. It is the failure of society to nurture decent and dignified face-to-face relationships through reasoned public discourse. In an Amos Oz novel, *Don't Call It Night*, an Irish traveler observes, "Anyone who has some good will can find good will everywhere." We have allowed microprocessing to take over the delightful task that we all once carried out in our interior selves. Now, *it* makes the connections; *it* carries the weight of human interaction. But *it* knows no tenderness or compassion. The PC treats everyone exactly the same, with the same cold dispassion dealt out by prisons and casinos. Goodwill has become scarce these days: efficiency and speed guide our lives. The computer does not reinforce or even validate goodwill. That's not what Apple and IBM mean by *ergonomic*.

Even if I arm myself with the very latest in electronic wizardry, I can only send and receive printouts of what the machine can handle about me. Communication means booting up and downloading data. To transact with other users—to interface without my face—my innards must be concentrated and summarized, my personality confiscated. That process is well under way. Somewhere, some government or corporate computer stores my health history, credit history, educational history, military history, financial history, employment history, criminal history, and travel history (air travel nowadays requires photo identification). The stroke of a key, by someone, somewhere, reveals my age, sex, weight, height, race, address and previous addresses, marital status, health status, telephone numbers, social security number, number of children, make and year of car(s), insurance information, retirement fund information, mortgage or rental status.

Computer files can trace my every cash withdrawal from any automatic teller machine; keep track of all the magazines to which I hold (or have held) subscriptions; record the time, dates, and numbers of all the telephone calls I both make and receive. All electronic mail, voice mail, and

158

THE
PRIVATE
DEATH
OF
PUBLIC
DISCOURSE

every site I might visit on the World Wide Web leaves a record somewhere.* Charge cards issued by supermarkets will permit market owners to monitor what customers purchase, in what quantities, and when. In essence, they will know what their customers ingest. One can only wonder if some agency knows our toilet flushes. Well, the Department of Water and Power certainly knows how much water we use.

Beyond all these pieces of data, James Gleick, the science writer, notes a more wide-scale snooping: "If you use a computer at work, your employer has the legal right to look over your shoulder while you type. More and more companies are quietly spot-checking workers' e-mail and even voice mail. In theory—though rarely in practice—even an on-line service or private Internet service provider could monitor you. 'Anyway,' advises a Web site, at naturally, paranoia.com, 'you should assume that everything you do on line is monitored by your service provider.' "†

The insidious reach of the computer should sound a warning: We all live under electronic house arrest.‡ At the bottom of the top of the line,

---

*Police cars in every major city have on-board computers, with data files on everyone holding a driving license or an identification card issued by the Department of Motor Vehicles. In South Central Los Angeles, computers hold identifying gang profiles—officers can download items such as dress, tattoos, and lists of known or alleged gang members. Young black males have been routinely busted by the computer: the suspect may be wearing, for instance, an article of clothing that matches gang colors; or a suspect may have been stopped for talking with a gang member, or just with some notorious character; or, according to police definitions, a suspect may just be a well-known nuisance, agitating in the community against such police practices. The police do not have to catch the suspect doing anything illegal. They arrest and leave it to the courts to decide whether they have violated civil rights. The American Civil Liberties Union has filed many actions in LA courts against such police action.

†James Gleick, "Big Brother Is Us," *New York Times Magazine*, September 29, 1996, p. 131.

‡I am suggesting here the way that we all submit to a virtual imprisonment, arrested not in any obvious way, but like Kafka's Joseph K., petrified in a bureaucratic entanglement we can neither make sense of nor touch.

That other growth industry, gambling, once it moves onto the Internet, will begin to function more and more like a prison. Indeed, the virtual casino will soon arrive: "The reach of the World Wide Web is erasing not only borders but the ability of the authorities to control wagering (not to mention their ability to tax it). And gambling over computer networks is still new enough that it remains unclear exactly what is legal and what is not." Anyone with a PC will be able to play blackjack, poker, slot machines or baccarat for money "at almost completely unregulated virtual casinos" (James Sterngold, "Virtual Casino Is Coming, but Regulation Is Still a Big Question," *New York Times*, October 21, 1996, sec. D, p. 1).

One currently active on-line casino, Virtual Vegas, has modified traditional games to resemble video games more closely so that a user can play Turbo Black Jack and Assault Poker, a combination, they advertise, of Doom and five-card stud. In essence, since most video games allow players to kill with impunity—dusting and wasting and whacking enemies just as real people do on the streets—gangsters and gamblers, prisons and gaming houses, slide into each other.

The final word about the new bed partners may come from John Kindt, who teaches economics at tangled somewhere in the mazy fibers of the Web, someone, some authority, believes that by punching the correct command key he has uncovered *me*. But the essential self of me, *Barry*, no one can feed into the computer; the thought and feeling of me, *Barry*, no one can stuff into microwiring. The problem, however, is that people begin to conceive of themselves only as data, to project themselves merely as information. In daily intercourse, the inconsistent, messy *me* that defines people has slowly seeped out of their fleshy encounters with others, leaving their meetings as virtual and evanescent events—neat and clean e-mail messages, falling far short of what we know as human interaction. The erasure of my private life, however, is matched by an erasure of something more private and precious— my interiority. The computer has erased the metaphors by which I contact and understand *me*. Tom Wolfe's self-absorbed, selfish and attention-grabbing *me*, the loud and brash egomaniac that prompted his phrase, "The Me Generation," I see as a perversion, a perception formed not in community but in acquiescence to consumerism driven by advertising and learned in front of a TV set.

Not so long ago, one could mine that *me*—the essential self—in the most secure privacy conceivable, in the dark depths of solitary contemplation, where one learned to prepare, in prolonged periods of analysis and reflection, for that journey back into light, toward speech and action, toward free and easy public discourse. People "collected" their thoughts, rehearsed their arguments, or just plain figured out how they felt about a subject. In that subterranean space, one discovered the swirl of the indwelt life, the tidal pulse of emotions. Under the domination of the chip, however, one's most potent and immediate feelings seem, at times out of total desperation, to be those that ignite, that simmer and stew, persist like a stubborn brushfire—in a word, feelings of anger.

160

THE
PRIVATE
DEATH
OF
PUBLIC
DISCOURSE

---

the University of Illinois and who fears the new kind of gambling. He talks about the incredible temptation of, and fascination for, the screen: "People will be trapped. They won't be able to get away from it" (*New York Times*, October 28, 1996, sec. D, p. 6). The nineteenth-century "poorhouse," a prisonlike institution where those on the dole could perform menial work, might, in the late twentieth century, find a counterpart in our own living rooms.

Electronic technology, by blasting a hole in our interiorized meta-phors, has totally restructured the emotions, rendering them for the most part unnecessary, or even beside the point. The computer leaves people with an impulse, a primitive reflex—anger—that defies the binary signaling system because it stays both on and off at the same time, inclining one to act while stifling action. The angry person feels choked and con-stricted—recall that its etymology points to reduced air—and wants to make an opponent feel the same discomfort by reaching out and throttling him or her. Of all the emotions, anger knows how it feels to try to survive within reduced space.

I refer here to nothing short of a human condition so altered that people, in a completely unconscious, reactive way, must go to great extremes in order to break free from the clutch of technology, in order to feel alive. How ironic, how odd—how distinctly cruel—that love no longer reigns as the most electrifying emotion. Today, anger crowds out all other feelings. As I hope to show in the rest of this chapter, that was not always the case.

In the early seventies, Benjamin Spock began to make public his growing concern that his advice to parents had produced a generation of young people who expected to get what they wanted—and who wanted it *now*. How could society hold together when its young people could not take no for an answer? In *Raising Children in a Difficult Time: A Philosophy of Paren-tal Leadership and High Ideals*, which he published in 1974, Spock even won-dered whether indulging them as infants in their cribs, whenever they demanded a breast or a bottle, had helped to lead young men and women into the streets, still demanding—not food, this time, but justice for blacks, the right to speak when and where they chose, and an immediate and unconditional end to the war in Vietnam.* "What do we want?" antiwar

---

*Along with the Reverend William Sloan Coffin, chaplain of Yale University, Spock and two others were convicted, on June 14, 1968, not just of counseling draft evasion, but of aiding those who evaded the draft. Spock may have felt responsible for some of the demonstrations against the war in Vietnam, but he him-self participated at the most fundamental level of outrage.

demonstrators chanted; and before anyone could answer, they snapped out their own reply to the question: "Peace!" "When do we want it?" they asked in a second round. Again, without waiting, they supplied their own answer—a single syllable that closed out all compromise, a simple and direct, no-nonsense embrace of the present: "NOW!"

The children raised on Spock had reached college age around 1964. I want to turn now to that year, and to a particular campus, to observe Spock's children in action. At the intersection of Bancroft Way and Telegraph Avenue, in front of Sather Gate, the official entrance to the University of California, Berkeley, several hundred young students experienced instant gratification in its most tantalizing, self-affirming form: Young men and women speaking their feelings, their minds, in total awareness that authority and convention stood solidly opposed to them. Some critics likened their actions to outbursts of angry petulance; but if so, their anger had shape and direction, a trajectory and a purpose—not to destroy, but to reform. The protestors utilized no electronic technology to enhance their message (except for a feeble portable PA system), no easy euphemisms or packaged sound bites to make their ideas more digestible. Through making speeches and organizing rallies, through sit-ins and protests of various kinds, through passing out leaflets and crafting placards, hundreds, eventually thousands, of young people accomplished something extraordinary: They created their own convivial space.

Students knew full well the consequences of their actions; the university published its position in letters and memos, sometimes hourly, but certainly day after day, complete with a list of ultimatums and possible punishments. When things got out of hand, the administration called in the Alameda County Police. The students persisted. In the most exhaustive account of those events, *The Spiral of Conflict: Berkeley, 1964*, Max Heirich details the opening moments of the protests:

On October 1 and 2, 1964, several hundred students at the University of California's Berkeley campus held a police car captive for thirty-two hours, until administrative leaders of the university agreed to negotiate a series of grievances. The

162

THE
PRIVATE
DEATH
OF
PUBLIC
DISCOURSE

prolonged conflict that emerged from the encounter of the newly formed "Free Speech Movement" with the university administration convulsed the campus for most of the year, leading to mass arrests of students, a general strike, the involvement of the entire faculty in the dispute, the removal of some administrative officers, and a continuing atmosphere of crisis and distrust. Perhaps more significantly, it saw the emergence in student circles of massive civil disobedience as a strategy for carrying on conflict, making the "philosophic" problem of the basis of law and order a matter of practical daily concern to the entire university community.*

The students continuously demanded their rights and they continuously insisted on immediate negotiation.

The free speech movement erupted during a strange, paradoxical time. It should have pleased Benjamin Spock. While the marketing strategies of the period focused on satisfying every conceivable need as fast as possible and so encouraged a deep self-absorption, the civil rights movement pulled people—some of those same people—out of their selfish concerns and persuaded them to direct attention to the plight, not just of others, but of the outcast, forgotten others. Students participated in something called a civil rights *struggle*, a *movement*, a commitment they knew might take some time. They preferred, however, to change the awful condition of blacks right away. To effect such monumental change—change nationwide—they seemed prepared and willing.

Civil rights activity began at a far remove from the elite, sequestered campus at Berkeley. On February 1, 1960, four black college students in Greensboro, North Carolina, sat down at a segregated lunch counter in the local Woolworth's expecting to be served and refusing to leave until someone waited on them. In the midst of the fast food revolution, those students confronted the racist response of slow food—or more flagrant yet, no food. The store manager could not serve them, he said, because Woolworth's adhered to local segregationist customs. The four students stayed seated until the store closed. Over the next couple of days, more black stu-

---

*Max Heirich, *The Spiral of Conflict: Berkeley, 1964* (New York: Columbia University Press, 1971), p. 1.

dents, along with a few white students, joined in. At week's end, in an atmosphere of violence driven by the Ku Klux Klan, Woolworth's temporarily shut its doors to any further business.

The students' refusal to take no for an answer quickly spread to fifteen cities in five southern states, culminating in the arrest of 350 students, on March 15, in Orangeburg, South Carolina, during more lunch counter protests.* Those initial absolutely courageous four students had launched what came to be known as the "sit-in movement" for civil rights.

Several historians have with meticulous care documented virtually every nonviolent direct action that took place, day by day, throughout the sixties.† One sometimes forgets, however, the heavy price black students paid for their commitment. Local police officers and sheriff's deputies not only arrested young people in great numbers, but attacked them with dogs, cattle prods, and fire hoses.‡ Southern black students got national recognition in part because they very early forged a remarkable victory: On October 17, 1960, four national chain stores announced the integration of their lunch counters in 112 southern cities. That astonishing record enabled the Congress of Racial Equality and the Student Non-Violent Coordinating Committee to spread out across the country and into the North, gaining the attention of sympathetic students in predominately white colleges and universities.

Founded in Raleigh, North Carolina, in April 1960, SNCC espoused nonviolence and aimed at linking civil rights groups into a close-knit network for strength and leadership: "These young militants also

164

THE
PRIVATE
DEATH
OF
PUBLIC
DISCOURSE

---

*Civil disobedience—breaking rules and boundaries—aimed at upending the status quo. Blacks, who had traditionally been kept out of the food section of the five-and-dime store in Greensboro, penetrated that invisible boundary and, interestingly enough, took on as their cause the most basic need—food. In a period that revolutionized food—making it faster, more concentrated—these students took their own sweet time. They would wait as long as it took, not just to be served, but to be heard—to be taken seriously as full-fledged human beings. They reversed Ghandi's strategy of fasting for change; they demanded food in order to force change.

†By April 1960, an estimated 50,000 people had participated in sit-ins or support demonstrations in over 100 southern cities, with police arresting at least 3,600 people. See Clayborne Carson, *In Struggle: SNCC and the Black Awakening of the 1960s* (Cambridge: Harvard University Press, 1981), p. 11; and Howard Zinn, *SNCC: The New Abolitionists* (New York: Alfred A. Knopf, 1965), pp. 16–17.

‡Attacks on black churches began with deadly seriousness on September 15, 1963, in Birmingham, Alabama, when a church bombing killed four young black girls.

wanted to protect their organization from domination by the older, patriarchical, church-based civil rights groups led by the prestigious Dr. Martin Luther King. . . . the Student Non-Violent Coordinating Committee was inaugurated in an atmosphere of generational revolt."* Perhaps here, again, Spock should have been pleased: Those students no longer needed their parents; they knew what they wanted and set out to get it in the boldest possible way, moving into the Deep South and confronting the toughest of white supremacists. But always, as if they had Spock in mind, when they undertook voter registration or literacy programs, the leaders of SNCC refused to choose for others. They lived by the rule "Let the people decide."

A network of concern thus wove itself throughout college campuses, a powerful union of fellow students tied in particular to the civil rights issues of black students in both the South and the North. Northern students set up picket lines outside chain stores that enforced segregation in several cities across the United States. CORE, relatively unknown in the opening years of the sixties, began organizing around civil rights issues on campuses beginning in 1963 and 1964.

In 1964, only eighty years after the publication of *Huckleberry Finn*, "civil rights" referred to more than a string of legal articulations drafted on some document. It meant acting decently and humanely toward all people, and especially toward those who had for so long gone unnoticed. It meant real people demonstrating to the world that they suffered from different protections under the law than their white counterparts—"Nigger Jim" still lived, and Miss Watson still held him strongly by the neck. The difference now was that all those wide-eyed Hucks decided to stay put, to demonstrate also, and not light out for another territory—either real or imagined. Southern blacks had brought "the territory" home to the North. The invisible web that I have described throughout this book began to connect student to student, demonstrator to demonstrator, black to black, and most important, black to white.

---

*Judith Clavir Albert and Stewart Edward Albert, eds., *The Sixties Papers: Documents of a Rebellious Decade* (New York: Praeger Special Studies, 1984), p. 8.

A great deal of *groundwork*, in the most literal sense of the word, went into the creation of the free speech movement. The movement, that is, could not have developed so swiftly or so effectively without the particular configuration of students, authorities, and buildings that the University of California had only a few years before overlaid onto the Berkeley campus. This web of relationships was made concrete and visible in a surround of buildings that would ultimately define, not only the shape of space, but the shape of speech itself. The organizers of the protests drew up a blueprint of action every day, sometimes every hour, unconscious of how those plans had been informed by the campus grid in which they worked and operated.

The struggle for speech, or more accurately, "voice," really took shape in a small area in front of Sather Gate, the entrance to the university. Since the 1930s, politicians had delivered speeches on that spot. In 1952, the university built a new building, Dwinelle Hall, just west and north of Sather Gate. A huge complex, Dwinelle had classrooms, lecture halls, a theater, and offices, all devoted to the humanities. Then, in 1960 and 1961, university officials moved the cafeteria, book store, and student union just south and west of Sather Gate. These two moves created new boundaries by shifting "the gathering point for coffee and conversation downhill to the natural territory set aside for political recruiting." Finally, in 1964, social science students got a new, eight-story classroom and laboratory building, located just east of the student union. All these new buildings effectively surrounded the major political gathering place with a concentration of humanities and social science students, traditionally the most politically and socially liberal and active students at the university.*

Telegraph Avenue, a fairly busy commercial street lined with small shops—boutiques, coffee houses, restaurants, bookstores—and one of the main arteries of the town itself, dead ends at Sather Gate. Beginning in the sixties, street vendors began setting up makeshift booths or laying out blankets from which to hawk handcrafted bracelets, belts, jewelry, macrame,

166

THE
PRIVATE
DEATH
OF
PUBLIC
DISCOURSE

---

*Heirich, *The Spiral of Conflict*, p. 16.

candles, incense—all the paraphernalia of the burgeoning hippie movement. That atmosphere of friendly gathering and bartering prompted
unsuspecting school officials to transform the block between the new student union and the administration building into a mall. Sproul Plaza, as
the new area came to be called, created a quite large open space that very
quickly filled with students lounging around, talking, reading, smoking,
eating, or just drinking coffee. They bought and sold things and exchanged
bits of information and gossip, class notes, and test results. Some passed out
leaflets; a few—a very brave few—smoked dope. They tossed frisbees to
each other or to their dogs. Conviviality flourished; camaraderie flourished. I call school officials "unsuspecting" because Sproul Plaza played a
role in stimulating public discourse in a way that surprised most everyone:
It obliterated the boundary between campus and community. Distinctions
between inside and outside disappeared. And the student protest movements of the sixties were not about anything if not boundaries—between
black rights and white rights, between Vietnamese peasants and American
students, between North Vietnamese and South Vietnamese, between the
North and the South in the states—boundaries between us and them.

The area also served as a kind of commons, a piece of turf owned
by everyone together, entered at will by anyone without question or
restraint, a shared space that by its very nature fostered free expression. Traditionally, each person has equal access to a commons, but each person
must likewise take equal responsibility for maintaining its continued and
lively existence. When we say in casual conversation that with a rival we
have reached "common ground," we draw on metaphor; but such an understanding comes about best when rivals in fact face each other on such a commons. Two people can "stand their ground" without rancor when they feel
they possess the ground in common.*

The idea of the commons, an agrarian institution that dates from
the Middle Ages, made it possible for landless peasants to survive by utiliz-

---

*You move off common ground when you cannot "stand" the other person.

ing a share of the arable fields in a village. The nobility thus promulgated a spatial solution to a feudal problem. From the Middle Ages through the middle of the seventeenth century, England put into practice, quite literally grounded in the native soil, the idea of freedom through sharing. The commons provided "grazing pastures for the animals of established peasant communities, timber and stone for building, reeds for thatch and baskets, fish and fowl, berries and nuts for food. Those areas supported large numbers of small peasants by means of those common rights. And these areas received the poorer and landless peasants who migrated from the overcrowded field villages of the corn-growing districts."*

Poor people share the commons not in any legal sense but in a much more powerful way. They incorporate the commons into their imaginations; they appropriate it for their myths; they use it as an image for their stories. The land diffuses its benefits in different ways among all the people, much the way sunlight shines on some at one hour and on others at a different hour. To own the commons means very little except for those who desire power:

A commons is not a public space. A commons is a space which is established by custom. It cannot be regulated by law. The law would never be able to give sufficient details to regulate a commons. A typical tree on the commons of a village has by custom very different uses for different people. The widows may take the dry branches for burning. The children may collect the twigs, and the pastor gets the flowers when it flowers, and the nuts from it are assigned to the village poor, and the shadow may be for the shepherds who come through, except on Sundays, when the Council is held in the shadow of the tree.

The concept of the commons is not that of a resource; a commons comes from a totally different way of being in the world where it is not production which counts, but bodily, physical use according to rules that are established by custom, which never recognizes equality of all subjects because different people follow different customs. Their differences can be recognized in the way they share the commons.†

168

THE
PRIVATE
DEATH
OF
PUBLIC
DISCOURSE

---

*Vandana Shiva, *Ecology and the Politics of Survival: Conflicts over Natural Resources in India* (Newsberry Park, Calif.: Sage Publications, 1991), p. 156.

†Ivan Illich, "Hair and the History of the City," *The Dallas Institute of Humanity and Culture* (Dallas, 1985), p. 23.

Once a concept like the commons enters the hearts and minds of the peasants, however, only one way exists to halt its use—only one way to call the people back—and that is to shut down the commons completely.

Indeed, that happened. The idea of the commons proved a bit too deeply embedded in the popular imagination, too many people found comfort there. So much so that landlords, driven by the desire to make more and more money and to silence the underclass, began to enclose the commons and to rent them out for substantial amounts. As peasants found themselves shut out of the common ground—the source of their livelihood, both physical and emotional, the place where they ground grain and told stories—they rebelled:

This process would benefit not only the landlords but also those who could afford to lease the "new" land. But it would be at the expense of the landless peasant, and the medium and smaller peasants, who would be impoverished by the loss of some of their pasture and common rights on which the visibility of their little farms so often depended. Also losing out would be the cottagers, labourers, and industrial workers who would be deprived of the resources that kept them from being entirely dependent on wages or poor relief. So there developed a head-on clash between the lords of the manor and the main body of the peasantry in many parts of the country over their respective rights and whether the landlords and big farmers or the mass of the peasantry were to control and develop those lands. This was the central agrarian issue of the 1630s and 1640s and of the English Revolution.

The enclosure movement was the watershed which transformed people's relationship both to nature and one another. It replaced the customary rights of people to use the remaining commons by laws of private property. The Latin root of the word "private," understandably enough, means "to deprive."*

The ensuing battle between peasants and landowners resembles in rough outline the confrontations between students and administrators over Sproul Plaza during the early days of the free speech movement, involv-

*Shiva, *Ecology and the Politics of Survival*, p. 157. Raymond Williams points out that, in the civil war over the commons, members of the Parliamentary army refused to be called "common soldiers" and insisted on "private soldiers." In attempting to establish a commonwealth, these soldiers "asserted, in the true spirit of their revolution, that they were their own men." Williams concludes that "there is a great deal of social history in the transfer across the range of ordinary description from *common* to *private*" (Raymond Williams, *Keywords: A Vocabulary of Culture and Society* [New York: Oxford University Press, 1976], p. 71).

ing as it did the issues of who should exercise control over the commons and set rules for its use. This peasant revolt marked the beginning of what historians call the English Revolution. Similarly, in many ways, the revolt over the Berkeley commons propelled America's youth into a new political activism that would transform American society over the next decade. One must take into account, obviously, the expanding war in Vietnam and the ripening civil rights movement as percussive forces in the radicalism of the sixties, but powerful local events had fed discontent on the Berkeley campus, precipitating a reaction of surprising proportions. While students wanted to talk about commons, university officials prepared to talk about public and private spaces.

One such cystallizing event took place in May 1960 when a group of students attempted to attend the House Un-American Activities Committee hearings at City Hall, in San Francisco. Students, denied admission to the hearing room—it filled very early with people who had been issued special passes (all members of conservative groups, the students believed)—crowded together on the steps of City Hall, singing and chanting, and refusing to budge. The police turned fire hoses on them, washing the assembled crowd down the steps, where they bounced and banged their way onto a landing. Pulling themselves together as best they could, they once again broke into song: "We Shall Overcome" and "We Shall Not Be Moved." In the confusion, students hit police; police beat some students, and they arrested a great many more.

The altercation radicalized both the students and nonstudents who had participated in the demonstration. The local underground press, along with the campus newspaper, grouped the San Francisco police— referred to as "cops" by the embryonic New Left—with the southern bulls who had blasted black students with fire hoses. Peace officers could no longer be trusted. The involved students and alumni coalesced into a tight and loyal cadre for future campus demonstrations. Many alumni, newly committed to civil rights actions, remained near campus, taking up residence in apartments on Telegraph Avenue. They added their own voices

170

THE
PRIVATE
DEATH
OF
PUBLIC
DISCOURSE

and maturity to organizing efforts on campus. They also had the free time to do the organizing.

Over the next three years, from 1960 to 1963, those who had participated in the HUAC demonstrations formed several civil rights organizations on campus. Their numbers initially remained small, but the fact that they had seen action together turned them into a committed group. Things remained fairly stable until 1963, when national and local events galvanized student attention at Berkeley:

In April 1963, the city of Berkeley narrowly defeated a fair-housing ordinance after an emotional campaign in which a university professor ran for mayor on a fair-housing platform. In May, demonstrating Negroes in Birmingham, Alabama, were met with attacks by police dogs and hundreds of children (as well as adults) were arrested. James Baldwin, the Negro writer, had an audience of 9000 students for his talk on campus shortly after the Birmingham demonstrations began. In June, Medgar Evers, NAACP leader in Mississippi, was murdered as he was entering his home. All through the summer demonstrations swept the cities of the South, some remaining nonviolent and others becoming riotous. In August the various civil rights organizations jointly conducted a march on Washington, in which about two hundred and fifty thousand persons participated to urge the passage of a civil rights bill. Then, just after students had returned to campus—and the day before classes were scheduled to begin—the nation was stunned by the bombing of a church in Birmingham, in which four children were killed. The following day, James Farmer, the national head of CORE, appeared on the Berkeley campus to give a scheduled series of addresses.

A few weeks later [on September 16, 1963,] Malcolm X, then chief spokesman for the Black Nationalists spoke to a crowd of about 8000 students on the Berkeley campus. His speech gave effective expression to his sense of rage and his judgement that whites were complacent about racial discrimination.*

Huge numbers of students all embraced the same ideal: They charged themselves with expunging racism from the American constitution. Their goal could only be achieved, they believed, through direct speech and direct action. Without knowing it, they were drawing strength from what Aristotle called the *bíos politikos*, the "political animal." In the

---

*Heirich, *The Spiral of Conflict*, p. 85.

ancient world, two concepts inform the ideal human community: speech (*lexis*) and action (*praxis*). Together, these two precepts constitute the world of human affairs. Words, those "winged words," as Homer calls them, may indeed fly away and disappear as soon as people utter them, but sometimes, like arrows rather than birds, they hit their marks with stinging accuracy. At those moments, speaking *means* action.

By the early sixties, certain words seemed to have been used up, language seemed weary and tired. After all, Beat poets like Allen Ginsberg, Michael McClure, and Gregory Corso had tried to invigorate language with a bit of shock therapy. Students in the free speech movement aimed at reinvigorating language, in its ancient ideal, for political reform, to effect change. In orality, people view every word as a deed. Action takes shape in vows and promises and sworn oaths, sometimes sealed by a handshake or a kiss. The world changes dramatically when a deed turns into a string of words transcribed onto a piece of paper. My word suddenly means little or nothing. I am asked to put my money where my mouth is. More and more, words turn into deeds, most often in fits of anger, in threats that people back up, like action heroes, with fists, grimaces, and guns. Drive-by shoutings quickly escalate into drive-by shootings.

Even though literacy has less and less of a hold on us, words today carry little meaning unless people commit them to a document—contracts, deeds, guarantees, warranties, licenses, and so on. Lawyers interpret legally binding instruments, sue for appropriate damages or actions. *Litigious* best describes the bulk of our transactions. What did you say? Write it down, date it, sign it, notarize it. Speech gets lost in such a legal maze. Discourse falters. In *The Human Condition*, Hannah Arendt comments on the Aristotelian idea of politics as the core of our condition. In the Ancient world, she observes,

thought was secondary to speech, but speech and action were considered to be coeval and coequal, of the same rank and the same kind; and this originally meant not only that most political action, in so far as it remains outside the sphere of violence, is indeed transacted in words, but more fundamentally that finding the right words at the right moment, quite apart from the information or communication they may convey, is action. Only sheer violence is mute, and for

172

THE
PRIVATE
DEATH
OF
PUBLIC
DISCOURSE

this reason violence alone can never be great. Even when, relatively late in antiquity, the arts of war and speech (*rhetoric*) emerged as the two principal political subjects of education, the development was still inspired by this older pre-polis experience and tradition and remained subject to it.*

And so the students launched themselves by speaking. We could have no country—no country we could proudly claim—students argued, unless we all addressed that monster called racism that kept tearing away at the social fabric. Even the war in Vietnam could be read as a race war, with white power asserting its might over the enfeebled Asians. Perhaps that relationship of power lay at the heart of every problem, from international politics to campus politics: Those in control, those with authority, need to control those without power. In any event, politically committed students at Berkeley spoke out against racism wherever they saw it.

In the fall of 1963, a group of students picketed a drive-in restaurant in San Francisco for discriminating in hiring practices against blacks. On November 22, students listened horrified to the news of President Kennedy's assassination. At Christmas that year, with Kennedy's memory very much in mind, students picketed Berkeley merchants who refused to sign a nondiscriminatory hiring agreement. In February 1964, the campus chapter of CORE joined a Bay-wide "shop-in" against a restaurant chain. On March 2, the chain capitulated. Inspired by the victory, a hundred people ignored a restraining order against picketing San Francisco's Sheraton-Palace Hotel, which had refused to hire minority workers. The police arrested Dick Gregory, some local NAACP officials, and a number of students. Thousands of students got arrested over the following weeks in direct actions against a row of fancy car dealerships on Van Ness Avenue, in San Francisco, and following that at various locations of the Bank of America. Students who came onto campus the fall of 1964 moved into a politically charged, morally invigorated atmosphere. Many of their fellows had already engaged in acts of civil disobedience and were passionately committed to changing attitudes toward race in this country—indeed, to changing

173

"THE
SPACE
OF
APPEAR-
ANCE"

*Hannah Arendt, *The Human Condition* (Chicago: University of Chicago Press, 1958), pp. 25–26.

existing power relationships in the country. First, however, they would have to radically alter power relationships on campus.

Many of the most political Berkeley students felt that the administration continually deprived them of their basic rights, a perception formed early on because of issues of borders and common ground of ideas of inside and outside. Their demand for fairness could be reformulated as a demand for property rights, and it came about through the architectural shift I outlined earlier in this chapter—through the creation of new space (the destruction of old space) around Sproul Plaza. Traditionally, the university required outside speakers who advocated political positions to speak off campus, just outside Sather Gate, with students (the audience) listening, for the most part, from inside the gate on campus property.

But in 1958, the university had moved its boundaries thirty-six feet north, almost a block beyond Sather Gate, to accommodate the new student union. The resulting intersection that marked the entrance to campus moved to the edge of Bancroft Way and Telegraph Avenue. Political activists, who now gathered to speak at the relocated gate, technically violated university rules against proselytizing by outsiders, for they suddenly stood on campus property.

What came to be called the free speech movement started innocently enough, in the spring of 1964, when Alex Sheriffs, vice chancellor for student affairs, received several complaints about excessive noise (bongo playing, mostly) in the student union plaza. Sheriffs discovered that "outside people," a term that stood for nonstudents and one that Berkeley students disliked, had set up tables on a twenty-six-foot-wide strip of brick pavement that looked like a City of Berkeley sidewalk but in fact belonged to the university. Indeed, if anyone had looked down, they would have noticed a key, small plaque in the sidewalk that read: "Property of the Regents, University of California. Permission to enter or pass over is revocable at any time."

While the investigation into the matter proceeded, the Republican National Party announced its plan to hold its nominating convention in

174

THE
PRIVATE
DEATH
OF
PUBLIC
DISCOURSE

San Francisco, and students immediately began distributing anti-Goldwater and pro-Scranton literature at Sproul Plaza. Again, university officials discovered that political activists had set up tables about twenty feet out from the entrance to Sather Gate. In response, the university banned all political activity, including distribution of leaflets, on university property—that is, behind the suddenly significant warning in the sidewalk. Brian Turner, one of the students who had demonstrated in San Francisco and the roommate of Mario Savio, who was to play a key role in later protests, saw the action as a direct attack on civil rights activity, since the only groups engaged in any political activity were for the most part civil rights organizations.

While the administration may have shut down the commons on campus, they could not excise it from the imaginations of the students. Students protested, picketed, sang, and presented their demands to the dean of student affairs, Kathleen Towle, but—and this surprised every school official—they also continued to set up tables to distribute political leaflets and bumper stickers in the restricted zone, in defiance of the ruling.* They wanted the commons back, and they would not accept anything less. On Monday, September 21, 1964, the date that the new prohibition would go into effect, two hundred students picketed the office of the president, Clark Kerr. About one hundred held a vigil later that night.† A first-year woman, who had left her dormitory to take part in the protest, characterizes those early days. She sounds neither hotheaded nor radical, but rather sincere and concerned. She speaks from the context, it seems, of civil rights action: "Friends told me there would be a picketing. As a civil libertarian I wanted to participate. The administration was shutting down on rights advocacy. A non-elite which allows an elite to take away rights without opposition will continue to lose rights. I felt the situation demanded immediate protest, and a picket had been organized."*

The battle was not just about a place to gather, but about the right to speak at all, and where students chose to voice their opinions. Support grew. Even the *Daily Californian*, in a surprise move, changed its position and supported the student demands. Students wanted their own voice; they called Clark Kerr's ban on political literature unconstitutional. A handout for a Wednesday night vigil, September 23, on the steps of Sproul Hall, told students "to act before the administration succeeded in its efforts to silence you. At this moment Cal students are being denied their inalienable rights to persuade and to call for action corresponding to their social mood and political principles. . . . Come to the vigil and support Freedom of Speech NOW!"

It was then that a group called the United Front, an amalgam of eighteen different political organizations on campus, from CORE and Progressive Labor to the Young Republicans and Students for Goldwater, decided to apply more pressure on the administration by picketing the school convocation, scheduled for Monday, September 28, in the student union plaza, with Chancellor Strong as the principal speaker. Before the convocation started,

the United Front conducted an unauthorized rally from "the Rally Tree," which had been the traditional "Hyde Park area" until 1961, when it was declared off limits because the noise from speeches interfered with classes in adjacent buildings. The Rally Tree is directly on the path of students leaving their social science and humanities classes either to attend the convocation, to go to the Student Union, or to leave the campus. The most eloquent speaker at the rally turned out to be a junior in philosophy, a hitherto unknown student named Mario Savio. Afterward a sizable picket line formed. Estimates have put the number of demonstrating students as high as a thousand, though this may be an exaggeration. The picketers moved down the stairs from the Sproul Hall Plaza into the Student Union Plaza, where the convocation was being held, and circled in a serpentine pattern through the aisles that had been set up.†

176

THE
PRIVATE
DEATH
OF
PUBLIC
DISCOURSE

---

*Heirich, *The Spiral of Conflict*, p. 112.

†Ibid., p. 116. Savio, a young man with a slight stammer, had been arrested at the Sheraton-Plaza demonstrations; he had as a cell mate Jack Weinberg, a Berkeley student who had dropped out in the spring of 1964 to work full time for CORE. Out of his friendship with Weinberg, Savio decided to go south for the summer of 1963 to work with SNCC. On his return, he became chairman-elect of University Friends of SNCC. By dint of

Over the next couple of days, Tuesday and Wednesday, September 29 and 30, students and some nonstudents once again set up their tables both at the intersection of Bancroft and Telegraph and at Sather Gate. They refused to get permits, for the permits required a promise of no solicitation of money or members or any advocacy of off-campus activity other than voting.

The question could not be stated flatly: Could off-campus people use school as public property? Could these two groups—students and nonstudents—in the struggle for civil rights, really be categorized as discrete entities? Brian Turner described the situation this way: "The campus—in our view—was public property. We knew that we could collect money, say, on the steps of the post office, so we wanted to not just have the privilege . . . to collect at a little corner on Telegraph and Bancroft. We wanted to establish the right to collect money on any piece of public property, whether it was at Sather Gate, or under the Campanile, or whatever."† The dean of men, Arleigh Williams, accompanied by campus police, walked among the students and announced that anyone sitting at a table was engaged in illegal activity, and he began taking names. Williams singled out eight students for disciplinary action, and President Kerr, without ever knowing if he had authority to do so, ordered them "indefinitely suspended."

At this point, as events began to escalate, the movement began to take on more shape. Very little deliberate planning went into the actions against the administration. Rather, activity began to coalesce around a key event, and around one or two, maybe three or four personalities—hardworking figures who acted as couriers, carrying news back and forth between students and administrators, negotiating behind closed and open doors, and willing to take risks—Mario Savio, his roommate Brian Turner, Art and Jackie Goldberg, and Jack Weinberg.

I quote here at some length from Jack Weinberg's account of what

his office, he automatically became a member of the United Front. He had not been a leader on campus, was not outspoken or outgoing. The occasion must have inspired him somehow to speak forcefully and directly about civil rights issues to the assembled group, because he was certainly not used to performing in public.
    † Ibid., p. 120.

happened that Wednesday as Williams and the campus police began citing people for illegal activity, because Weinberg documents so nicely the overflowing spontaneity of talk that marked the day's events, and he places his own impulse to speak neatly within the context of another speech, one he had heard the night before in Stiles Hall by Hal Draper, a socialist who worked in the library and who edited the journal *New Politics*. Draper's talk, titled "Clark Kerr's View of the University as Factory," offered a critique of Kerr's book *The Uses of the University*. Draper's talk had clarified the issues for Weinberg. He had mulled the ideas over in his mind overnight and was inspired to make his own utterance the following day:

When I saw the first citations being made to students at the tables—it was at Sather Gate—I got up on that wall (by the gate), and I started pointing out what was happening. . . . I was feeling very self-conscious in doing it, because [I was not enrolled that semester]. . . . I think someone else took my place. While this was going on, Mario took a chair from the table, got up on the chair, and began speaking in front of the table. . . . This was when the deans had first come, while they were citing people. . . . All I remember is—the deans are there, and what they were doing, and I tried to gather a crowd—I guess my aims were general agitation. It was partly spontaneous, but partly a conscious act to try to get something going. To get a group together. I was mad about what was happening. . . . Mario spoke for a while pointing out what was happening. This was the first speech of the Free Speech Movement. When Mario got down, I was the second person that spoke. . . . I remember my speech at the time—two things I recall; the night before Hal Draper had given a talk at Stiles Hall. . . . I was at this talk, and Mario was also there for at least part of his talk—at the time I felt I was greatly influenced by this speech. I was essentially trying to fit some of what was happening into the theoretical framework—explaining it in terms of this framework that had been exposited the night before. At the time I felt I was very heavily dependent on the speech.

. . . I remember the first time I ever spoke publicly—about a month before that—I had written everything up and read it. Now I was saying things I had never thought through carefully before . . . and there was this huge group around me, and I really felt I was communicating directly to everybody.

This was around noon, I think. People were coming through Sather Gate. I really expected people to stop and hear what I said.*

178

THE
PRIVATE
DEATH
OF
PUBLIC
DISCOURSE

---

*Ibid., p. 123.

The sit-in at the tables continued for some time, and administrators viewed the situation as a real crisis of authority—they could not make those people move. On the other side, students saw it as a crisis of legitimacy—the campus regulations violated constitutional rights. Weinberg had given his speech hours before, at noon. At midnight, Chancellor Strong proclaimed, rather surprisingly, that "the issue now has been carried far beyond the bounds of discussion by a small minority of students." Strong offered a compromise: Any nonstudent who wanted to speak on campus would have to file for a permit at least seventy-two hours before addressing any forum. The students turned a deaf ear. They wanted to hear from their own, and so some of them began shouting, "Let Savio speak!"

Mario Savio, standing in the back of the group, came up to the front and, seemingly unprepared, spoke for quite a long time—an extended, rambling speech, which finally came to rest on the issue of freedom of speech:

We can look at the university as a kind of little city . . . and then we could ask ourselves is there any part of this so-called open-forum policy which contradicts the ways in which we do things in little cities. O. K.? I say there certainly is.

. . . Let's say that the mayor of Berkeley announced that citizens of Berkeley could speak on any issue they wanted from the steps of the fire building. . . . But let's say that they placed the following restriction upon nonresidents from Berkeley, that they could not do so unless they obtained permission from the City of Berkeley and did so 72 hours before they wanted to speak. You know there'd be a hue and cry going up: "Incredible violation of the First Amendment! Unbelievable violation of the 14th! . . ."

Well, now, look at the university here not as the private property of Edward Carter [Chairman of the Board of Regents]. . . . Let's say, instead, that we look upon it as a little city. Well, then, how come I—before I was expended— . . . all right, before I was expelled—suspended—I could get on the steps of Sproul Hall and say anything I wanted as long as I didn't start giving arms to people. You know, I could say anything I wanted without notifying anybody. But a nonstudent would have to obtain permission from the university and do that 72 hours before he wanted to speak, and the university might just not like what he had to say and might well deny the permission.

Now, consider the analogy with the city. Consider how gross—how gross a violation of the spirit of the First and Fourteenth Amendments that is! Here's the legal principle. I think it's more a moral principle.

We hold that there ought to be no arbitrary restrictions upon the right of freedom of speech. Now what does an arbitrary restriction mean? An arbitrary restriction is one based upon an arbitrary distinction. For example, between students and nonstudents.

Now, note . . . sometimes the distinction is very material: if, for example, you consider classrooms . . . perfectly reasonable, material distinction. . . . But now the issue is freedom of speech. We have people out in Sproul Hall. There's not a class going on there. . . . What therefore is the material basis for the distinction in this instance between students and nonstudents?

. . . Why 72 hours for nonstudents and no time for students? Let's say, for example, and this touches me very deeply, let's say that in McComb, Mississippi, some children are killed in the bombing of a church. . . . Let's say that we have someone who's come up from Mississippi . . . and he wanted to speak here and he had to wait 72 hours in order to speak. And everybody will have completely forgotten about those little children because, you know, when you're black and in Mississippi, nobody gives a damn. . . . 72 hours later and . . . the whole issue would have been dead.

180

THE

PRIVATE

DEATH

OF

PUBLIC

DISCOURSE

Or let's say that some organization here . . . objects to some action of the administration in Vietnam . . . and has to wait 72 hours to object. By that time it's all over. You know, we could all be dead.*

At 2:00 A.M., after deciding that only a mass of people at the tables could prevent the university from picking off a few and suspending them, the sit-in disbanded. Each of them, they all agreed, had to be willing to take a stand.

The next day, Thursday, October 1, very early in the morning, people began setting up tables in front of Sproul Hall. By eleven o'clock, Dean Murphy, accompanied by a Lieutenant Chandler from the university police, approached Jack Weinberg at the CORE table and directed him to leave. When he refused, Chandler told him he was under arrest for violating section 602.L of the penal code—trespassing. (Since Weinberg refused to give his name, Chandler said he could only assume he was a nonstudent trespassing on private property.) As Chandler tried to remove Weinberg, the assembled group, in what can only be called a spontaneous act of solidarity, sat down and locked arms, blocking the way. Two police officers from the Berkeley Police Department came to Chandler's aid and managed to push and shove Weinberg through the crowd to a waiting car.

---

*Ibid., pp. 134–35.

And here the free speech movement really comes to its point—both visually (graphically and architecturally) and politically. All the issues, all the principal parties, for and against, organize themselves and settle, like metal filings, around an icon of authority—the Berkeley Police car. Those students who advocated free speech went a few steps further: They co-opted the car, neutralizing all of its power by using it as a platform—a podium—from which they could now deliver speeches.

Over the next several hours, left-wing students spoke in favor of the demonstration, while most fraternity members—"Freddies"—hectored them to give up the car. For the student leaders, possession was not the issue. With Weinberg inside, the car would no longer function as a police vehicle. Students had transformed it, with their words, into something else. They no longer considered the car private property; it had become a public object. Their actions had surprised even them, bringing them up against the awesome power of speech fused with action.

Initially, some thirty people sat down—again, quite spontaneously, as participants admitted afterward—half in front of the car and half behind it. They began singing "We're fighting for freedom; we shall not be moved." In time to the chant, others began walking over to the car and they, too, began sitting down, joining in the singing. Quickly, very quickly, those sitting on the ground grew to fifty or seventy-five.

Someone yelled for Savio to speak. At this point, Savio still saw that immobilized piece of metal as a police car, and so as not to dent the hood he very slowly took off his shoes, and very carefully climbed up on top of the car. It had thus become a speaker's podium with Jack Weinberg ensconced inside. Savio had no choice, it seems, but to make his statement, for the students' actions had quite clearly forced the issue: They would not release the police car until the administration dropped its charges against Weinberg and released him. Then the car could become a car again. Savio went on to enumerate the group's other demands:

ONE: They must immediately, that is, the Chancellor—Chancellor Strong, seeing as he's the one who did it—must immediately say that no students have been suspended from the university.

TWO: Chancellor Strong—Chancellor Strong must agree to meet with representatives of the off-campus political organizations to discuss with them reasonable regulations governing freedom of speech on the campus, which means no arbitrary restrictions of any kind on freedom of speech on the campus! He must agree to such a meeting.*

The sit-in continued all day Thursday with enough momentum to take it through the night. On Friday morning, October 2, the university, eager to end the demonstration before Saturday, Parents' Day, called out the California Highway Patrol, as well as police from Oakland, Alameda County, and the City of Berkeley. Some five hundred officers, including more than a hundred motorcycle officers, took up positions on campus. The scene became tense. The standoff continued for about two hours before students and Clark Kerr finally reached an agreement, at 5:00 P.M. Friday. A group of faculty members and students negotiated a list of compromises, and two hours later, student leaders and Clark Kerr signed the agreement. For the time being, both students and nonstudents could continue their political actions at Sproul Plaza. While that ended the first phase, the protests would go on for many more months.

182

THE
PRIVATE
DEATH
OF
PUBLIC
DISCOURSE

The free speech movement really turned into a struggle over space. The capturing of the commons meant political freedom, a necessary and symbolic place from which to talk, for anyone who wanted to say something on any topic whatsoever. Every action, every speech and event, became a part of the history of this commons. Each person who committed an act of civil disobedience there (in the name of securing *voice*) wove another story, added another layer to that history. Around that geographical core a body politic took shape, one with which the authorities had to reckon. But it could only happen because people gathered, because those students and nonstudents came together and began to organize and articulate an argument. They rallied together and soon found themselves, to the surprise of

---

*Ibid., p. 35. Around four o'clock in the afternoon, a woman finally climbed on top of the car to speak. She identified herself as Bettina Aptheker, and remained on top of the car throughout most of the demonstration that entire day.

many, a fairly powerful political movement: *Movement* meant they had direction and a goal, a program and a platform; it meant they were heading somewhere. In fact, the free speech movement stumbled along, changing direction as each day progressed.

Whatever socializing took place at the plaza got subsumed in larger political concerns. Under the thin veneer of the social, politics, like a hidden engine, began to drive every action and event. For instance, on the first day of the demonstration around the police car, when someone shouted, "Where's Mario?"—a line that sounds very much like one friend calling to another to come out and play—I doubt whether that person knew "Mario" at all, the social now indistinguishable from the political. When Savio responded, and climbed onto the police car, he knew exactly what the crowd needed and wanted. He, too, had turned wholly political. He found himself in command of a newly formed space, created by myriad entangled relationships—car and law, public and private, inside and outside, Weinberg and friends, those against and those for, university and students, students and administration, and above everything else, students and power—power that they had suddenly hauled up from deep inside themselves and made audible.

Space is crucial. Without space, people have a difficult if not impossible time creating politics with each other, working out relationships of power for some common goal, for some common good. Without space, people retreat into an isolated sphere, where, without contact with others, they can imagine the worst about their neighbors. Politics devolves into voting once a year for one of the two major political parties; voices grow loud, so they can be heard from places of isolation and hiding. In practice, the social cannot be separated from the political. Removed from contact with fellow human beings—removed from a social base—people exert power in the most distorted, perverted ways, and this we call tyranny.

The ancient Greeks, arguably the most political people in history, did not even have a word for the social. For the Greeks, a desire for sociability did not separate human beings from animals, for animals, too, must band together for biological needs. For the Greeks, then, there was the world of home and family (the private) and the political (the communal). The Romans, however, did recognize a state called the social. And so they translated Aristotle's *zoon politikon* as *animal socialis*; hence Thomas Aquinas: *Homo est naturaliter politicus, id est, socialis* (Man is by nature political, that is, social). Thus social/political space can only arise out of a dynamic, from the interaction of live people. No computer program can virtualize power.

We human beings seem to make our presence known, the way a shadow attests to the substance of an object, in an articulated space around us. In Berkeley, hundreds, even thousands, of collective voices came together in the free speech movement, a name that invokes both word and act (speech and movement) and highlights the kind of commons needed, the sort of communal space required, for the founding of social cohesiveness. The people who made up the free speech movement wanted something and were not afraid to ask for—even demand—it.

184

THE
PRIVATE
DEATH
OF
PUBLIC
DISCOURSE

However we wish to define victory or success, whether we justify or condemn those campus activities, Berkeley students came to feel power in just the way that Hannah Arendt has so eloquently defined it, as something actualized "only where word and deed have not parted company, where words are not empty and deeds not brutal, where words are not used to veil intentions but to disclose realities, and deeds are not used to violate and destroy but to establish relations and create new realities."* I repeat one of Arendt's key points here: Of all the activities "necessary and present in human communities," Aristotle only claims two as part of the *bios politikos*—practice and speech—around which the realm of human affairs consolidates. Berkeley students—the children of Spock—spent their days talking with passion and without brutality, and acting on their talk. They demanded a response. We cannot ask for much more.

Arendt likes to talk about something she calls "the space of appearance"; and I take her term to mean the forging of a Platonic ideal, as when we say the *arena*, or the *realm*, or the *sphere* of politics, suggesting when we

---

*Arendt, *The Human Condition*, p. 72.

utter those phrases a locality for political activity. Arendt envisions all discourse taking place in a commons—metaphoric or real, large or small—which people create with each other only in face-to-face contact. It is a commons that only power can bring into being. Not a power of domination or suppression (for that she reserves the term *force*), not something we should shun or fear, but a power that invigorates and braces—a potentiality that comes alive only where people act together and that vanishes altogether when they leave. Power, like action, Arendt asserts, is boundless. It simply requires human interaction to keep it alive, and so, unlike strength (situated in isolation in a single human being), power thrives on plurality. Thus, when we isolate ourselves, and here we come to the heart of the contemporary problem, we fall into impotence.

I quote here again from Arendt, this time at some length. I find her observations remarkable for the way they reveal so many of the issues that underlay the political manuevering in Berkeley, as well as the consequences when politics dissipates and falls out of the range of possible human undertakings. Buried in her analysis lies the idea of goodwill arising out of play and the invisible web of relations, culminating in a very real "artifice." We give shape to the world by talking about and in it, in stories that we string together with others in a community of meaning. Her conclusion, about the disappearance of space that only power can promote and maintain—a conclusion really about suffocation and the loss of voice, a straitened condition akin to anger—brings us to our present dilemma:

Power preserves the public realm and the space of appearance, and as such it is also the lifeblood of the human artifice, which, unless it is the scene of action and speech, of the web of human affairs and relationships and the stories engendered by them, lacks its ultimate *raison d'être*. Without being talked about by men and without housing them, the world would not be a human artifice but a heap of unrelated things to which each isolated individual was at liberty to add one more object; without the human artifice to house them, human affairs would be as floating, as futile and vain, as the wanderings of the nomad tribes. The melancholy wisdom of *Ecclesiastes* — "Vanity of vanities; all is vanity. . . . There is no new thing under the sun. . . . there is no remembrance of former things; neither shall there be any remembrance of things that are to come with those that shall come after"—does not necessarily arise from specifically religious experience; but it is certainly unavoidable wherever and whenever trust in the world as a place fit for human appearance, for action and speech, is gone. Without action to bring into the play of the world the new beginning of which each man is capable by virtue of being born, "there is no new thing under the sun"; without speech to materialize and memorialize, however tentatively, the "new things" that appear and shine forth, "there is no remembrance"; without the enduring permanence of a human artifact, there cannot "be any remembrance of things that are to come with those that shall come after." And without power, the space of appearance brought forth through action and speech in public will fade away as rapidly as the living deed and the living word.*

The space of appearance begins—that is, we begin to make ourselves felt—in a projected space that speaks itself into being just in front of our faces, as W. H. Auden so delightfully puts it:

Some thirty inches from my nose
The frontier of my Person goes
And all the untilled air between
Is untilled pagus or demesne.

Stranger, unless with bedroom eyes
I beckon you to fraternize
Beware of rudely crossing it
I have no gun, but I can spit.†

186

THE
PRIVATE
DEATH
OF
PUBLIC
DISCOURSE

In social discourse, one builds out of words a sphere of influence around oneself, what in the past has sometimes been called "personal space" or "social distance."‡ With the collapse of the commons, it is now that space, personal space, that seems to concern people so much. The words that come out of our mouths we expect to make a mark—we expect to matter and, probably unconsciously, to create a small and manageable commons. The personal commons may begin, as Auden indicates, just "thirty inches from my nose."

---

*Ibid., p. 204.

†W. H. Auden, postscript from "Prologue: The Birth of Architecture," *W. H. Auden: Collected Poems* (New York: Random House, 1965).

‡See Robert Sommer, *Personal Space: The Behavioral Basis of Design* (Englewood Cliffs, N.J.: Prentice-Hall, 1969). Sommer defines personal space this way: "An area with invisible boundaries surrounding a person's body into which intruders may not come. . . . Personal space is not necessarily spherical in shape, nor does it extend equally in all directions" (p. 26). In this regard, see also Kurt Lewin's early work on what he called "life space," in his *A Dynamic Theory of Personality* (New York: McGraw-Hill, 1935).

Evidently, enough people want to deny even that intimate commons, for the courts now define and guarantee a minimal amount of personal space. The effective distance may extend farther than the reach of my voice, but the courts will now determine what it means to get "into my face." The issue here is an odd one: At what distance does social discourse begin to turn meaningful? The problem has surfaced in a protracted battle over one of the most basic human rights, reproduction, and crosses over into definitions and boundaries separating the private from the public.

In 1994, the Supreme Court upheld a thirty-six-foot buffer zone around an abortion clinic in Melbourne, Florida.* The Buffalo, New York, Federal District Court responded to violent protests outside local clinics by issuing an injunction in 1992 that created a floating, fifteen-foot space— Auden's "frontier"—around people and automobiles entering and leaving any clinic. Any antiabortion protestor (a "sidewalk counselor") could approach a prospective client to dissuade her, but had to withdraw to the fifteen-foot boundary as soon as she indicated a desire to end the encounter. In 1995, a federal appellate court (the Second Circuit Court of Appeals) in New York upheld the order, arguing that the floating area was "far more solicitous of the demonstrators' interest than the much wider zone approved by the Supreme Court in the Melbourne, Florida, case." The New York injunction also allows demonstrators to approach patients uninvited and to keep talking until patients walk away or tell them to stop.

Jay Allan Sekulow, chief counsel of the American Center for Law and Justice, founded by Pat Robertson, challenged the injunction in October 1996 in the Supreme Court. Sekulow argued that the fifteen-foot moving zone, called the "floating bubble," constituted a suppression of speech, because the zone travels with the person "without geographic limitation." Sekulow believed the commons should stay on the ground, and once outside that commons, any woman became fair game. He noted that no bor-

---

*Chief Justice William Rehnquist wrote the decision. Acknowledging the free-speech rights of the demonstrators, Rehnquist found that the buffer zone "burdens no more speech than necessary to accomplish the governmental interest at stake," thus ensuring public safety and protecting unimpeded access to the clinic.

ders could be observed unless they were, first, firmly established and, second, remained permanently in place. For him, no negotiation of power could be undertaken without a fixed boundary.

A good part of the argument by the justices centered on space and speech—and they seemed to recognize that free speech must have its own space before it can take on meaning—the same issues students faced in the free speech movement, but now updated. By arguing for the elimination of the moving frontier, Sekulow said in effect that the notion of a political exchange—and thus an exchange of power—between two people must give way to display of force, perhaps even violence. The desire to get "in a woman's face" reflects a desire, it appears, to be more than heard. Witness the following exchange between Justice Stephen Breyer and Sekulow:

188

THE
PRIVATE
DEATH
OF
PUBLIC
DISCOURSE

Looking down at Sekulow, Breyer queried, "We're fifteen feet apart now. Here we are. We're having a conversation. Give me a word, expression or idea that you can only communicate when I'm closer to you than I am at this moment."

Sekulow responded: "A person who wants to communicate with a woman who is about to engage in an abortion procedure wants to do it one on one. It is not possible to carry on an intimate conversation from fifteen feet away."

Then Justice John Paul Stevens asked if five feet would work. Sekulow said no. Stevens then asked about two feet. Perhaps, said Sekulow. Justice Antonin Scalia asked Sekulow if he would accept an injunction that barred shouting. Sekulow said no, "that's robust speech in a public forum. Abortion clinics do not become enclaves protected from the First Amendment."

Justice David Souter seemed to favor the fixed thirty-six-foot buffer zone that Florida had enacted. With a fixed zone, he said, "everyone will know where the line is, and the First Amendment won't suffer as a result."*

---

*Linda Greenhouse, "Court Hears Challenge to Anti-Abortion Curb," *New York Times*, October 17, 1996, sec. A, p. 6.

The *New York Times*, endorsing the fifteen-foot buffer (which the Supreme Court eventually upheld), ended an editorial on the case by focusing on something it called "individual privacy," which I take to be an inviolate distance like an invisible shield—an aura of protection—necessary in the transaction of free speech, or social discourse. The Court took "in your face" seriously: "As the Court has previously recognized, the First Amendment gives protestors a right to be seen and heard. But it is not a license to instill fear and violate individual privacy with aggressive face-to-face badgering."*

Since e-mail has eliminated much of the need for face-to-face contact, perhaps people must now reconfigure social distance, in a mad desire to get back into our neighbor's face, not necessarily to badger but just to be heard. For Auden, thirty inches made the difference—inside that range and you were too damned close, invaded his space, his frontier. Auden doesn't seem to care, call it *pagus* (open country, a commons of sorts) or *demesne* (private property), the first thirty inches belong to him. Inside that range, you intraface. Move inside that space, he tells you, and you can be assured of getting the speaker's attention. He'll turn mean and nasty, and spit in your eye.

And if he had a gun, he might shoot you. . . .

---

*Editorial, *New York Times*, October 20, 1996.

6

Americans enjoy a unique history. No other country has believed so strongly in its ability—or, more accurately, in its right—to expand indiscriminately, sweeping up everything in its path, while in the process sweeping aside, with apparent disregard for limits, its own domestic borders. Americans claim and reclaim space: Revolutionary freedom demands nothing less. We live, after all, in a country that, unlike any other, beckons all the world's immigrants to its shores. Our national statue, the goddess Liberty, planted so solidly on Liberty Island, welcomes with her beacon of light "your tired, your poor, your huddled masses yearning to breathe free," making the same promise to all the world's citizens.* Her light illuminates every square inch of American soil: Look, she says, this is no illusion. We can accommodate you. Our capacity is endless.†

History records, of course, how our obsessive drive toward greatness required governmental action to relocate Native Americans, enslave African Americans, and intern Japanese Americans. At times, the constitutional liberties of some groups simply had to be sacrificed for the freedom of the frontier, to expansion on the ground. Perhaps above everything else—above almost every other ideal—we Americans value space. We defend as our national heri-

---

*Emma Lazarus wrote these lines—a sonnet, really—in 1887.

†The Liberty Party came into being in 1840 to oppose the spread and to restrict the political power of slavery; the Free-Soil and Republican Parties descended from the Liberty Party.

tage the institution of private property and at times protest the privatization of public land.

Americans not only believe in expansion, they demand it. William Gass, for example, in an essay entitled "Gertrude Stein and the Geography of the Sentence," asserts that "democracies have never had a history; that they cannot run in place; they must expand; they must have space."* We have over the decades grown used to everything in America expanding—the Dow-Jones averages, productivity, horsepower ratings, the Gross Domestic Product, hourly earnings, business openings and housing starts, computer bytes, consciousness levels, campaign expenses, firepower, refrigerators, malls, movie budgets, and of course the population itself, not just in sheer numbers, but in weight and height, as well. We think big. We act big.† At the close of World War II, America dropped the Big One; in California, people nervously keep track of Richter scale readings, waiting for the Big One. The Grand Slam, the Super Bowl, the World Series, the Triple Crown, Macy's Thanksgiving Day Parade—all Big Ones.

In the nineteenth century, America expanded the definition of an old word, *inflation*, to describe a new economic condition: growth at too fast a rate, an economy pumped up with hot air. Without growth—"real growth," adjusted for inflation—America knows no progress. Capitalism requires a continually expanding economy, just as democracy demands a continually expanding system of rights, a constant struggle against imagined or actual acts of oppression. Unless every last man, woman, and child enjoys full freedom, and not just the seeming protection of inflated rhetoric, democracy fails as an institution. In this context, a concept like "downsizing" seems un-American, a shocking, regressive move, yanking the country back to a mean and niggardly state. But oddly enough, even downsizing is justified in terms of growth: Only by cutting out mass inefficiencies, the argument goes, can corporations hope to grow larger.

---

*William Gass, *The World within the Word* (Boston: David Godine, Publisher, 1979), p. 72.
†In 1996, according to government figures, Americans invested a record $222 billion in mutual funds, almost $100 billion above the previous record set in 1993.

The dedication to expansion, to the consumption of space, requires a steadfast revolt against the status quo. Whatever exists must be systematically destroyed, exploited, or consumed in the never-ending move toward something larger. Innovation and invention keep the wheels of industry turning, just as political demonstrations—pressure—keep liberation moving. The civil rights movement, the free speech movement, and the various liberation movements around feminism, black power, gay rights, and ethnicity all follow a pattern of expansion, as power begins to take hold inside individuals and fills them out. People who become empowered feel bigger, more expansive. They grow.

Like the Big Bang theory of the creation of the universe, whereby life explodes in a continually expanding space—a balloon that swells and swells and never breaks—liberation (creativity, if you will) keeps on expanding, too. It continually asserts itself. Like the universe itself, the world of ideas must grow and grow; one interesting idea engenders several others. But creativity or liberation must have space (interior space) to house it and external space (a commons) in which to unfold itself.

Revolution and expansion have greatly affected language itself—spoken language, discourse. American talk takes up an enormous amount of space. It has to, for American English is a spoken revolt against British English. It grabs what it needs; it amalgamates and colloquializes—makes up words, loves slang and street lingo, would rather utter a two-bit word than a two-dollar phrase. American talk loves the rough and tumble, refuses to have much truck with the highbrow and the highfalutin, and just cannot abide a strict adherence to manners and rules.

Midwestern farmers, mobsters, the mad and the maligned; Jews, Italians, Greeks, Poles, Slavs, blacks, Asians, and Hispanics—no two of them sound alike, but they all sound the language of America. How ironic to think that, with a language in perpetual motion, one would have to come closer than thirty-six feet, or even fifteen feet, to make a point. In a series of lectures on language, Gertrude Stein pointed to the difference between speaking on an island, bounded by water and speaking on a body

192

THE
PRIVATE
DEATH
OF
PUBLIC
DISCOURSE

of land that seems to go on with no end. The rhythms we speak make us.*
In his remarkable essay "What America Would Be Like without Blacks,"
Ralph Ellison points to the magisterial role American English played in
forming the American character:

The American nation is in a sense the product of the American language, a colloquial speech that began emerging long before the British colonials and Africans
were transformed into Americans. It is a language that evolved from the king's
English but, basing itself upon the realities of the American land and colonial
institutions — or lack of institutions, began quite early as a vernacular revolt
against the signs, symbols, manners, and authority of the mother country. It is a
language that began by merging the sounds of many tongues, brought together
in the struggle of diverse regions. And whether it is admitted or not, much of the
sound of that language is derived from the timbre of the African voice and the listening habits of the African ear. There is a dez and do'z of slave speech sounding
beneath our most polished Harvard accents, and if there is such a thing as a Yale
accent, there is a Negro wail in it — doubtlessly introduced there by Old Yalie John
C. Calhoun, who probably got it from his mammy.

Whitman viewed the spoken idiom of Negro Americans as a source for a native
grand opera. Its flexibility, its musicality, its rhythms, freewheeling diction, and
metaphors, as projected in Negro American folklore, were absorbed by the cre-
ators of our great nineteenth-century literature even when the majority of blacks
were still enslaved. Mark Twain celebrated it in the prose of *Huckleberry Finn*:
without the presence of blacks, the book could not have been written. No Huck
and no Jim, no American novel as we know it. For not only is the black man a co-
creator of the language that Mark Twain raised to the level of literary eloquence,
but Jim's condition as American and Huck's commitment to freedom are at the
moral center of the novel.†

Ellison would not, I suspect, subscribe to what has recently been
called Ebonics, black English as a separate language. Every nationality contributes to the swirl of American English. Just as the black dialect has
affected the speech of white Americans, as Ellison argues, so the opposite
has also occurred. Language, American language in particular, has always
been porous, dialect passing into dialect. The great strength of the black

---

*Gertrude Stein, *Narration: Four Lectures* (Chicago: University of Chicago Press, 1937), p. 6.
   †Ralph Ellison, "What America Would Be Like without Blacks," first published in *Time*, April 6, 1970,
and collected in *Going to the Territory* (New York: Vintage Books, 1987), pp. 108–9.

dialect, Twain noticed, was that no one, no institution, no rule or pro-
scription, no signs hanging over drinking fountains or on buses, could
enslave it.

"Jim's condition as an American and Huck's commitment to freedom": The two cannot be separated. Jim gives birth to Huck on that raft.
Recall, at the beginning of the book, Huck has led everyone to think that he
has been murdered. He assumes aliases the entire way down the Mississippi: he is a girl at one point, a sick boy, and even Tom Sawyer. At the end,
Huck speaks Jim's language, "the spoken idiom of American Negroes"—language in motion. So much does he resemble Jim that one Twain scholar,
Shelley Fisher Fishkin, wrote a book entitled *Was Huck Black?*, which
shocked some scholars with its brash question. Fishkin recalls telling David
Bradley, the author of *The Chaneysville Incident*, about the revelation that
startled even her: "This may sound crazy, but I think I've figured it out—
and can prove it—that black speakers and oral traditions have played an
absolutely central role in the genesis of *Huckleberry Finn*. Twain couldn't
have *written* the book without them. And hey, if Hemingway is right about
all modern American literature coming from *Huck Finn*, then all modern
American literature comes from those black voices as well. And as Ralph
Ellison said when I interviewed him last summer, it all comes full circle
because *Huck Finn* helps spark so much work by black writers in the 20th
century."*

The Mississippi seems endless, and so does the great American
land mass. Twain sent Huck down the length of that river and had him
speak, like its mighty current, every mile of the way. Twain seems to say, I
give you discourse, a correspondence between man and boy, land and river,
theory and practice, slave and free, black and white, *lexis* and *praxis*. I give
you talk, and more talk, words spoken with God's power. Huck says *slave*,
referring not to an abstract concept or category, but to a person. He means
Jim. "The spoken idiom of American Negroes," Ellison says, and brings us
to the root of all literature—the spoken word. We take Huck as the author

194

THE
PRIVATE
DEATH
OF
PUBLIC
DISCOURSE

---

*Shelley Fisher Fishkin, "Huck's Black Voice," *Wilson Quarterly* 20 (Autumn 1996): 84.

of *Huck Finn*, but we know, really; that only Mark Twain deserves that title. We have no such confusion with Jim: He lives in orality only; he makes no claims as a novelist. In his essay for the introduction to *The Norton Anthology of African American Literature*, Henry Louis Gates, Jr., addresses what he describes as Jim's "oral expressive culture," which eventuates, for those who want to be authors, in the full expression of the self, in literacy:

Historically, anonymous vernacular literature almost certainly preceded the tradition of written letters among African-Americans, and indeed all the world's great literatures have developed from an oral base. But in the instance of the African-American literary tradition, the oral, or the vernacular, is never very far from the written. Oral expressive culture—rap poetry, for example, and the customs of "signifying" and playing the "dozens"—still surrounds the written tradition almost like a Mobius strip, in a way reminiscent of the traditional antiphonal "call-and-response" structures peculiar to African and African-American culture. (A visit today to a beauty parlor or barbershop in a black neighborhood easily verifies that this oral, dialectical tradition is alive and well.) Not only has the vernacular tradition served as the foundation of the written tradition, but it continues to nurture it, comment upon it, criticize it.*

While Huck floated down the river, Whitman adopted a different strategy. To describe not just the endlessness of America but the curious way the language equalizes and democratizes—his version of the spoken word—he stayed put. He needed but a bit of help from grammar, so that he could level, make equal, ideas and things and places by stringing together a series of sentences connecting one thing to another with a device from orality—an *and*. Under the influence of his pen, disparate things lay down as equals. The grammar of *and* permeates the Bible, particularly the Old Testament, where one sentence begets another, one generation begets another— page after page held together by that simple connective. Generations have read the Bible from start to finish, like an ancient prayer wheel, and then start over again: *And* then there was light.

Whitman borrowed biblical grammar for his poem of begetting, *Leaves of Grass*. Following Whitman, Gertrude Stein adopted the same lin-

---

*Henry Louis Gates, Jr., and Nellie Y. McKay, eds. *The Norton Anthology of African American Literature* (New York: W. W. Norton, 1997), p. 9.

guistic strategy, and after her, Hemingway. Although Gertrude Stein probably had little or no knowledge of Frederick Jackson Turner, she still could sound like him: "In the United States there is more space where nobody is than where anybody is." Taking off from this line, William Gass observes that "there is no question that she, like Turner, thought human behavior was in great part a function of the amount of free land available. On the frontier, Turner believed, civilization was regularly being reborn. When westward the course of empire no longer took its way, Americans moved 'in' and went east to Paris in order to go west within the mind—a land like their own without time. And Gertrude Stein believed Americans were readier than Europeans, consequently, to be the new cultural pioneers. The mind . . . The human mind went on like the prairie, on and on without limit."*

196

THE
PRIVATE
DEATH
OF
PUBLIC
DISCOURSE

And works especially well for Americans, the perfect word for capturing the democratic impulse. The poet Randall Jarrell sees Whitman as a kind of grammatical abolitionist and uncovers the secret of the poet's strategy in that one simple word:

Whitman is more coordinate and parallel than anybody, is *the* poet of parallel present participles, of twenty verbs joined by a single subject: all this helps to give his work its feeling of raw hypnotic reality, of being that world which also streams over us joined only by *ands*, until we supply the subordinating conjunctions; and since as children we see the *ands* and not the *becauses*, this method helps to give Whitman some of the freshness of childhood. How inexhaustibly interesting the world is to Whitman! . . . The *thereness* and *suchness* of the world are incarnate in Whitman as they are in few other writers.†

Walt Whitman, so American and, as Gertrude Stein says, "so measureless." What Whitman accomplished in poetry, Twain accomplished in prose, creating in Huck the huckster the literary embodiment of liberation. Indeed, *Huckleberry Finn*, in seeking to unseat its European models, asserts its presence as the literary counterpart to the Declaration of Independence,

---

*Gass, *The World within the Word*, p. 70.

†Randall Jarrell, "Some Lines from Whitman," in *Poetry and the Age* (New York: Random House, 1953), p. 118.

so much unlike those earlier novels of manners and decorum, larded with dialogue about class and money. No gentility here, not from a man who fills his novel with feuds and fraud, gambling and drunks—a glimpse of the rough life without the varnish of civility—and with a smart-alec as hero, to boot, a wisecracking adolescent ready to take on all comers. Both Whitman and Twain know the raw power of orality. Whitman, playing Adam, names the parts of the world and they come to be: "I and mine do not convince by arguments, similes, rhymes, / We convince by our presence." Whitman sings the body electric. Twain's novel records talk. *Huckleberry Finn* speaks. And it speaks in an idiom designed to shock the sensibilities of the genteel.

Three important themes emerge in Mark Twain's work that foreshadow the explosion of liberation movements in the sixties. The first of these points to the collapse of what had been for so many years in America two discrete spaces—black and white. As we have seen, Ralph Ellison made a crucial observation, an observation that contemporary critics glossed over because it sounded so shocking, that without blacks this country would not have had many of its major writers. Indeed, he broadened his argument to include jokes, tall tales, sports, and by extension, music. Not one of the New Critics would have concurred, obviously, with Ellison:

Had there been no blacks, certain creative tensions arising from the cross-purposes of whites and blacks would also not have existed. Not only would there have been no Faulkner; there would have been no Stephen Crane, who found certain basic themes of his writing in the Civil War. Thus, also there would have been no Hemingway, who took Crane as a source and guide. Without the presence of Negro American style, our jokes, our tall tales, even our sports would be lacking in the sudden turns, the shocks, the swift changes of pace (all jazz shaped) that serve to remind us that the world is ever unexplored, and that while a complete mastery of life is mere illusion, the real secret of the game is to make life swing. It is its ability to articulate this tragic-comic attitude toward life that explains much of the mysterious power and attractiveness of that quality of Negro American style known as "soul." An expression of American diversity within unity, of blackness with whiteness, soul announces the presence of a creative struggle against the realities of existence.*

---

*Ellison, "What America Would Be Like without Blacks," pp. 109–10.

Twain would not have been shocked by Ellison. He recognized the ironies in talking about such fuzzy, abstract categories as "free" and "slave" and acknowledged how important blacks had been in shaping white consciousness in this country. He offered a literary strategy that reeked of more than political irony, something we might call political blasphemy: Freedom for Huck—no, power itself, and liberation—comes through negotiations of experience, emotion, and morality *only* with the slave Jim. It may sound like a kind of cuteness to talk about liberation for a white adolescent in America, until we realize that Huck cannot count himself as free so long as he carries in his heart—believes in—the idea of slavery. Setting Jim free, he sets himself free as well. To possess always entails some degree of being possessed.

This leads us to our second theme, one that may not make itself immediately apparent to Twain's readers. On that small piece of wood —that floating raft of consciousness—Huck learns that he can give voice to whatever he thinks. He learns his lessons in loosely connected sentences, in uncensored palaver, liberated from convention and expectation. (Maybe only a slave can understand the difficulties of freedom.) Over time, Huck and Jim come to speak virtually the same sentences. They live in each other's face; they share a floating commons. Free speech comes, it seems, not from highly polished, revised, and literate sentences, but from someone, say, like Mario Savio, seizing the microphone and spontaneously addressing an audience—speaking from the heart.

On land, Huck finds something entirely different. He cannot argue with Pap; he cannot sass the Widow Douglas; he cannot make his point with Judge Thatcher. Huck's a kid; no one takes him seriously. And so he simply takes the most expedient route: Huck lies to get out of jams. True, he also lies to Jim, but Jim shames him into speaking the truth, no matter the cost, and always in plainspeak.

In what may pass as the most morally charged passage in *Huckleberry Finn*, Jim makes it clear that one does not lie to a friend. This occurs when the two get separated from the floating commons one night in the fog—Huck adrift in a canoe, Jim on the raft. A storm churns the Missis-

198

THE
PRIVATE
DEATH
OF
PUBLIC
DISCOURSE

sippi into a raging current, disorienting them both. As the fog clears, Huck spots the raft with Jim asleep on it.

When Jim awakens, absolutely delighted to see his pal, who he thought had died in the storm, he tells Huck how he cried himself to sleep in terror over Huck's plight. Huck tells him he must have been dreaming: He has been on the raft the whole time. There has been no storm. For a moment, Jim buys Huck's story (he takes him at his word, as he does everyone—until Huck points out all the leaves and debris that the storm has blown onto the raft. Jim feels humiliated. He tells Huck, in Ellison's "Negro idiom"—in the powerful way that orality holds attention fast—Jim tells his young friend what power he can wield with just his voice:

When I got all wore out wid work, en wid de callin' for you, en went to sleep, my heart wuz mos' broke bekase yuo wuz los', en I didn' k'yer no mo' what become er me and de raf'. En when I wake up en fine you back again, all safe and soun', de tears come en I could a got down on my knees en kiss yo foot I's so thankful. En all you wuz thinkin' 'bout wuz how you could make a fool uv ole Jim wid a lie. Dat truck dah is *trash*, en trash is what people is dat puts dirt on de head er dey fren's en makes 'em ashamed.*

Huck must now apologize. He wants his old relationship with Jim back. What can he do? He has, under the cover of fog, opted for meanness, in both senses of size and emotion: "It made me feel so mean I could almost kissed *his* foot to get him to take it back." Some time passes, but Huck does just that: "It was fifteen minutes before I could work myself up to go and humble myself to a nigger—but I done it, and I warn't ever sorry for it afterwards, neither. I didn't do him no more mean tricks, and I wouldn't done that one if I'd a knowed it would make him feel that way."

Huck plays a trick and it backfires. Mark Twain always plays the trickster, so why shouldn't his major creation, young Huck? The third point in this discussion touches on that sense of play, which also informed the political demonstrations of the early sixties. And here I draw on a notion from the existentialism popular in the sixties—the idea of the absurd. I

---

*Mark Twain, *The Adventures of Huckleberry Finn* (New York: Penguin Books, 1985), pp. 24–25.

recall an image from that famous summer of 1968, when Parisian students went out on strike and did battle with the gendarmes. In the middle of the melee, with students hurling cobblestones at the police and the police lobbing tear-gas canisters back at the students, a young man calmly showed up, pedaling a small upright piano, tricycle style, banging out Scott Joplin rags, seemingly oblivious to the chaos erupting around him. That student punctured what both Sartre and Camus, the leading names in existentialism, referred to as *esprit de serieux*, a commanding sense of gravity that informs most people's actions, and that periodically must be shattered by some joke or trick so that they can see how silly and unimportant most events really are. We merely assign to them high seriousness and significance; they have little or no inherent status.

200

THE
PRIVATE
DEATH
OF
PUBLIC
DISCOURSE

In this Paris example, the juxtaposition of tricycle and lively music with gas masks and cobblestones—these absurd gestures—reduced the high seriousness of political confrontation to a playground game, to no more than a joke. Action stopped, and in an interlude that liberated the players from their roles, both sides stared at each other and burst into laughter. Very quickly after that incident, students began negotiating their demands with university and city officials. The serious issues had not vanished, but laughter suddenly allowed both sides to see the conflict stripped of all its high drama and hysteria. That young musician made them aware, in a single moment, that they could actually stop fighting and do something totally different, namely, talk and negotiate. Laughter, not fighting, provided them with common ground.

That incident might makes us reconsider Huck's practical joke: Did it really backfire and fail? Had he not felt humiliated by his own actions, he would not have learned the lesson about friendship—at least not so quickly, so immediately. He did it, and he felt responsible. He also would not have understood quite so dramatically, quite so deeply and thoroughly, the way slavery demeans. In pulling off his prank, Huck treated Jim as an object, a plaything, a convenience—much the way slavery itself treated him.

Huck's trick renders him speechless; it forces him to action. The word *absurd* derives from the Latin *surdus*, "deaf or mute," and that in turn derives from the Greek *alogos*, "speechless or irrational." Huck has reached the proper state. Indeed, it's when we don't immediately talk back, respond, argue, but instead dive into a speechless state—here, the absurd—to ponder and think, that discourse really begins. People move into that state more often during joke-telling than during discussion. The social cues are different; we listen differently.

Lenny Bruce brought that spirit of the absurd to campus politics. In a moment of amazing historical timing, the police arrested Lenny Bruce for the first time, on obscenity charges, in 1964, in Berkeley. Comedy and laughter—particularly the laughter of free speech, the giddy exhilaration of having been heard, of seeing one's words turn into actions—had invaded the academy.* The irony here runs deep—that when others finally take us seriously, it makes us euphoric. Anyone who has ever fired off some well-wrought sentences and moved the other person to silence—to that absurd state—knows the performer's thrill. Bruce started out performing routines with a black jazz musician, Eric Miller, and early on did shticks around a 1958 film, *The Defiant Ones*, about a black man (Sidney Poitier) chained to a white man (Tony Curtis), both of whom have escaped from a roadside work gang:

There on the stage, in living flesh, Bruce came out chained to Eric Miller. *The Defiant Ones* came to life before a startled audience, except the dialogue had changed; the issues had radically altered; the affect took a different slant. Bruce had carnivalized race, turned the issues upside down, brought his own meaning to bigotry. And again, he moved the ideas beyond a mere act. . . .

. . . In the film, Curtis plays a bigot, and he has to confront his own prejudices to ensure his survival while shackled to his fellow prisoner. *The Defiant Ones* captured the attention of American movie-goers. . . . It won Oscars for Best Cinematography and Screenplay. Who could mess with such a gem? But Bruce rewrote the movie. Here's the movie we should have gotten, his routine announced, and here's the theme up front: These two guys hate each other, kind of hate each other, maybe because they've been told to—and these two guys love each other, really love each other, though they can't tell each other.

---

*Bruce's stand-up routines came in the midst of southern sit-down demonstrations. Bruce quite literally *stood up* for what he believed, while students sat down for many of those same beliefs and convictions.

Lenny Bruce knew that, if civil rights were to be taken seriously, blacks and whites would have to discuss their deepest, most stereotypical prejudices frankly and openly, with an acknowledgment not only of huge issues but also of silly prejudices on both sides. . . .

. . . By the end of the routine . . . it was clear, absolutely clear, that Lenny Bruce and Eric Miller were friends—close friends—that they truly enjoyed each other. The old *bête noire* raised its head again—those two guys took great pleasure in making everyone laugh.*

Audiences howled, but they also thought and reconsidered their own beliefs and attitudes as Bruce exposed to them the absurdities of segregation and racism. In 1959, he told audiences that Little Rock had solved the segregation problem: "They've done it through legislation. If the colored people can pass the literacy test they get to vote. And it's very fair. [With a heavy southern accent]: 'Well, let's see now, line up all the colored people here; and if they pass the test they get to vote here. It's very easy, you just sign your name. Here's the ball point pen, the piece of wax paper . . . '"

Beginning in the late fifties, and running all through the sixties and well into the seventies, students got to hear not just Bruce, but Mort Sahl, Shelly Berman, Dick Gregory, and later, the wonderfully zany, disjointed monologues of Richard Pryor. They all brought their outspoken, irreverant, brand of comedy, in a great swirl of language and laughter and politics, onto college campuses.

Bruce really freed comedy from its rather tired routines handed down from vaudeville and the Catskill circuit. He crossed color lines. His routines were mini-demonstrations in favor of liberation and the broadening of perceptions. In the mid sixties, many students got their political training first by listening to the likes of Lenny Bruce, who taught them to look behind the scenes, behind the government's official rhetoric, for the truth. Without him, the antiwar movement would not have found its power and direction so fast.

Laughter and comedy serve as the natural leavening agents for

202

THE
PRIVATE
DEATH
OF
PUBLIC
DISCOURSE

---

*Barry Sanders, *Sudden Glory: Laughter as Subversive History* (Boston: Beacon Press, 1995), p. 261.

anger; the combination may actually give the firm edge to what we call *wit*. Jerry Rubin and Abby Hoffman, along with Ken Kesey's band of Merry Pranksters, carried that spirit of playful abandon into a political theater that they played out on the streets. The Yippies! represented the culmination of a drive toward carnival in politics, in which the traditional values and roles turned upside down. They found easy targets in racism and segregation. Toward the end of his career, the police hounded Lenny Bruce, arresting him for foul language every time he took the stage. He began to talk only about the judicial system and justice and about the limits of First Amendment rights. He called for—he pleaded for—free speech. He tried to bring to light the absurdities of imprisonment, and the violent reaction people have to certain words. He argued his own case on stage, as if the nightclub were a courtroom, merging the drinking bar with the legal bar. The monologues still drew laughs, but the people laughed with more reserve, as Bruce began dealing them highly serious stuff—no more routines, only soliloquies; no more abstract, theoretical talk about cops, only the law. Like a black church service, Bruce was signifying and testifying.

The bridge to our contemporary problems lies, in part, in the way we treat comedy and play and joking. Today, anger and meanness do their nasty work without the restraint of humor. Comedians no longer play college campuses. Former presidents, politicians, and rock stars have taken their place as popular speakers. Dick Morris gets more money than Dick Gregory. We leave the matter of laughing wholly to a cadre of professionals who perform far away from the action, on stages in nightclubs, in sitcoms on TV, or on specials on HBO, or the comedy channel.* Political correctness has gagged too many gags. Laughter has somehow been disembedded from daily life, removed from the quotidian. We don't seem to have enough air to laugh ourselves, and so we hire surrogates. Laughter and joking may

---

*In 1960, *The Button-Down Mind of Bob Newhart* reached number one on *Billboard* magazine's charts, the first comedy album to do so. The album remained number one for fourteen weeks—a record never broken. Decades before Allan Bloom recommended the shutting down of the American mind for cultural survival, Newhart opened the sixties with the buttoned-down, Ivy League possibilities of his own mind. In recent years, Jeff Foxworthy and Adam Sandler have had comedy albums that sold extraordinarily well, but they first established themselves as stars on TV.

be the nemesis of anger and meanness. Laughter and joking—the absurd—integrated themselves into the political life of the sixties. And, indeed, much of the political talk in those days centered on *integration*, the hope that the races would live and work together as equals, and that the old barriers to social intercourse, even marriage, between whites and blacks would fall away. Race would become a meaningless term. Today political talk turns to separatism and nationalism.

For the most part, a good many people seem unwilling to accept the legacy of liberation from the sixties, and I mean here in particular the impetus that came directly from blacks in the South and that moved northward to whiter, more elite campuses. Before I pursue that idea, I want to reach back to the beginning of our discussion to look at New Criticism and its collapse in the 1960s. Writing over the blueprint of nineteenth-century liberation drawn so generously by Twain and Whitman, New Criticism placed a tight hold on the idea of expansion, especially with its neglect of black life, a hold so tight that it choked off the possibility of anyone's taking in a full breath of air. The New Critics had shrunk literature to make it fit on the page. Only the penetration of some truly subversive ideas into their well-inoculated literature could make the New Critics loosen their death-like grip. I want to look now at how and why they opened their fists.

In the early sixties, the disturbances that rattled lunch counters and shook barricades took place at the same time on the pages of textbooks, destroying their margins. The great avatar of the New Critics, the anti-internationalist T. S. Eliot, who had insisted that poets and critics adhere to a strict English tradition, began to lose his pedagogic hold on English departments across the country. Eliot maintained that America merely mirrored England, that no distinctions could be made, really, between the two countries.

For forty years, the poet Michael Benedikt points out, the branch of the New Critics that called itself the Fugitives promoted a literary insularity with intense fervor:

204

THE
PRIVATE
DEATH
OF
PUBLIC
DISCOURSE

Eliot's critical assumptions lasted as axioms, particularly among the leading group of the so-called New Critics in the US—one wing of which called themselves, significantly, the Fugitives. They were fleeing cosmopolitan forces; prescriptive and rigid, self-professedly neoclassical in direction, and generally recommending traditional or British literary links, their critical perspectives filled the best-known literary and scholarly quarterlies until late in the 1950s. By that decade, Randall Jarrell, a poet-critic who was more adventurous than many of his critical contemporaries, could rightfully, if uneasily, refer to his entire period as "The Age of Criticism."

In effect, American poetry was in a kind of psychic slavery to overweening English influences (particularly English "restraint"), from which it should have been free, at least in theory, for roughly two hundred years—and certainly since the time of Whitman.*

What had happened? Whitman had asked his readers to take in a gale of breath, as huge as the length and breadth of the entire United States. People were frightened, however, to exhale. At least it took them almost eighty years to relax enough to exhale. Or perhaps it took them almost eighty years to relax enough to risk it. The stimulus for change came primarily from a group of nineteenth-century French poets who had tried to insinuate into prose the rhythm and compression of the poetic line. Reading poets like Baudelaire, Rimbaud, Valéry, Mallarmé, André Breton, and Max Jacob radically altered literary sensibilities in this country in the early sixties. These poets had broken the formal boundaries between prose and poetry and asserted, as Benedikt says, "psychic energy as the chief value" of everything they ever thought or wrote. They had pursued the odd, the strangely humorous, the surreal.

In the hands of those French poets, decorum had died. This had opened the possibility, as it also had with Wordsworth and Coleridge, of using "everyday speech"—an orality that moved more in flow with the unconscious mind. Voice, and more voice, voice unmediated by revision, runs closer to the core of one's inner being. Paul Valéry believed in the close

---

*Michael Benedikt, *The Prose Poem: An International Anthology* (New York: Dell Publishing, 1976), p. 40. The original idea for the book, Benedikt says, Jarrell formulated in 1964, but the form had fallen short by a few years of driving the New Critics out of business.

connection between poetry and song. As he says in the prose poem "Litera-ture," "a poem must be a holiday of Mind. It can be nothing else." Thus he allows meaning to come in a tumble of words:

In the poet:
The ear speaks,
The mouth listens;
It is intelligence, vigilence, that gives birth to dream;
It is sleep that sees clearly;
It is the image and the phantom that look;
It is the lack and the blank that create.

Lyric poetry is the kind of poetry that thinks of the *voice in action*—the voice as direct issue of, or provoked by,—things that one sees or that one feels as *present*.

For a long, long time the *human voice* was the foundation and condition of *litera-ture*. The presence of the voice explains the earliest literature from which classi-cal literature derived its form and its admirable *temperament*. The whole human body present *beneath the voice*, as a support and necessary balance for the idea. . . .

Then came the day when people knew how to read with their eyes, without spell-ing out the words, without hearing, and literature was thereby entirely altered.

Evolution from the articulated to the glanced-at—from the flowing and progres-sive to the instantaneous—from that which is demanded by an audience to that which is demanded and snatched by a quick and avid eye running over the page.*

In statements here and there published by this band of poets, one can catch the power, the playful abandon to the emotional charge of the psyche. Max Jacob, for instance, talks about trying "to seize, from within myself, in any way I could, the *imperatives of the unconscious*: words given liberty, risky associations of ideas, dreams both day and night, hallucina-tions, etc."† Lyrical and narrative telling criss-crossed in the same para-graph; dreams and realities fused. Readers could scarcely tell outside reality from inside hallucinations. Furthermore, they did not seem to care.

206

THE
PRIVATE
DEATH
OF
PUBLIC
DISCOURSE

---

*Paul Valéry, *Selected Writings* (New York: New Directions Publishing, 1950), pp. 149–50.
†From the preface to Jacob's *The Dice Cup*, quoted in Benedikt, *The Prose Poem*, p. 44 (emphasis mine). Other citations here from the prose poets can also be found in Benedikt.

The prose poets believed in shattering all categories, in creating a new, immense space for poetry that could hold the immensity of a grand internal journey; no longer restricted by formal line breaks, their poems took longer, deeper breaths. Such journeys have perhaps best been described by Charles Baudelaire in his prose poem "Invitation to the Voyage," an exploration that secularizes Teresa of Avila's metaphor of the interior castle: "The whole range of earthly treasure abounds here, as in the house of some industrious individual, a worker to whom the whole world has come into debt. A remarkable country, and quite superior to all others." These poets, like Huck, would rather stay lost in a fog on the raging Mississippi than take up a becalmed and clear life on the shore. Antonio Machado, a Spanish prose poet, describes the poetic process this way:

Mankind owns four things
that are no good on the sea.
Anchor, rudder, oars,
and the fear of going down.

As I indicated earlier, the New Critics installed themselves as figures of authority: They set the parameters of discussion; they exercised control; they established order. The great father figures, Cleanth Brooks, I. A. Richards, Robert Penn Warren, William Empson, R. P. Blackmur, F. R. Leavis, John Crowe Ransom, and Allen Tate, dominated the textbooks and the classrooms. The psychic energy of French surrealism overturned the pantheon of those founding fathers and loosened their mighty grip on the teaching of literature in the classroom. It put an end to the age of criticism. What an idea!—the liberation of literature itself. The genie had been let out of the bottle. And of course this spirit spilled over from literature into virtually every aspect of life.

The transformation of the classroom was wholesale—in the actual teaching of literature, in the manner of its composition, and most dramatically, in the choice of literary texts—a great sea change that mirrored activities on campuses across the country. The canon began to expand here. The poem no longer lay on the page as an inert object. The best way to know a poem was to hear it recited out loud: Let Ginsberg howl.

In the introduction to *Empty Mirror*, a collection of Ginsberg's poems written before "Howl" but published afterward, William Carlos Williams places the poet within the new wave. Williams's introduction, written at Ginsberg's request, is dated 1952:

A new sort of line, omitting memories of trees and watercourses and clouds and pleasant glades—as empty of them as Dante Alighieri's *Inferno* is empty of them—exists today. It is measured by the passage of time without accent, monotonous, useless—unless you are drawn as Dante was to see the truth, undressed, and to sway to a beat that is far removed from the beat of dancing feet but rather finds in the shuffling of human begins in all the stages of their day, the trip to the bath-room, to the stairs of the subway, the steps of the office or factory routine the musical measure of their passions.

. . . In the mystical beat of newspapers that no one recognizes, their life is given back to them in plain terms. Not one recognizes Dante there fully deployed. It is not recondite but plain.

. . . The writing cannot be made to be "a kind of prose," not prose with a dirty wash of a stale poem over it. It must not set out, as poets are taught or have a tendency to do, to deceive, to sneak over a poetic way of laying down phrases. It must be prose but prose among whose words the terror of their truth has been discovered.*

About his own collection, Ginsberg wrote to Neal Cassady that "in a new poem I am beginning to explore some of the uncharted verbal rhetorical invented seas that Jack (& yrself) sail in. . . . After 'Empty Mirror,' which for me stript yakking down to modern bones, I would like to build up a modern contemporary yak-poem, using the kind of weaving original rhythms that Jack does in his prose, and the lush imagery."†

Robert Bly, in his essay "Catching Dragon Smoke," talked about the great poets in new terms, measuring their greatness by just how much space they could leap in a single bound. The truly great ones, Bly asserted, make bold and wild associational leaps—over logic, over reason, over expec-

---

*William Carlos Williams, introduction to *Empty Mirror*, by Allen Ginsberg (New York: Corinth Books, 1961), pp. 5–6.
†Quoted in Barry Miles, *Ginsberg: A Biography* (New York: Simon and Schuster, 1984), p. 154.

tations. They drop, head first, into the unconscious. They rejoice in what they find. Borders mean nothing—leap over them. Let the psyche expand—a hearty exhalation these French expected from *everyone*:

In many ancient works of art we notice a long floating leap at the center of the work. That leap can be described as a leap from the conscious to the unconscious and back again, a leap from the known part of the mind to the unknown part and back to the known. . . . In all art derived from Great Mother mysteries, the leap to the unknown part of the mind lies in the very center of the work. The strength of "classical art" has much more to do with this leap than with the order that the poets developed to contain and, partially, to disguise it.*

A great many aesthetic movements in the twentieth century— Arts and Crafts, Bauhaus, Vienna Secession, Wiener Werkstatte, dada— defined themselves politically and followed political agendas.† They saw themselves, that is, as changing the status quo. And generally that political stance declared in one way or another its liberation of the individual—psychically, emotionally, and aesthetically. The New Critics, too, wanted their theories to serve as political statements. But the assumptions of the New Critics could never have resulted in disobedience, civil or uncivil. Indeed, by their insistence on borders and the self-containment of power, the New Critics encouraged just the opposite: a strict adherence to rule; an application of key principles to the text; an acceptance of select authorities, not just as models of excellence, but as the only models of excellence. The prose-poem came like a great wave from every conceivable country— Spain, Italy, Russia, Germany, from Middle European countries, from Scandanavia, Portugal, and Japan. Students now felt free to read from all over the globe.

The answer to the question of what *free* means in the phrase "free speech movement" takes on broader significance in the context of these changes taking place *inside* the classroom. Free speech means that one need

---

*Robert Bly, "Looking for Dragon Smoke," in *Leaping Poetry: An Idea with Poems and Translations* (Boston: Beacon Press, 1975), p. 1.

†Marcel Duchamp started a dada journal titled the *Freeman*. Duchamp and the dadaists wanted freedom every bit as badly as the militia group known as the Freemen.

not feel inhibited about speaking on any subject, virtually anywhere; that one need have no inhibitions about language itself (witness the placards some student protestors carried that read F. U. C. K.: Freedom under Clark Kerr). But, more important, *free* points to a psycholinguistic phenomenon whereby people move toward liberation by speaking their minds—a principle that guided the French poets. We talk ourselves into living. And we keep talking ourselves into a larger and larger existence.

Huck "grows up" this way. His departure, however, his lighting out for the territory, Twain wants us to read, finally, as a defeat. For in order for Huck to sustain what he has learned on the river from Jim, in order to turn his journey inward, to abstract it into metaphor, he needs literacy. Who better to say it than Whitman: "interior consciousness, like a hitherto unseen inscription, in magic ink, beams out its wondrous lines to the sense."

210

THE
PRIVATE
DEATH
OF
PUBLIC
DISCOURSE

Huck needs all the instruction that Miss Watson and Aunt Sally can give him. No matter how much Twain touches the rebel in us near the end of the novel, no matter how loudly we root for Huck to get the hell out (wouldn't we all like to retire to some tropical island?), we have to fight against his leaving and say no. As readers, we want to play the impetuous Huck, but Twain makes us side with authority: Twain makes us play Miss Watson, for we know that Huck needs not only to grow up, but to mature. As Huck grows older, he will have to learn to read and write. The business world, that is to say, the white, managerial world, demands literates. If he stays with Aunt Sally, he will have to assume responsibility for his actions, which will involve the most radical shift in his young life. He will have to become literate. That will be the means of establishing his membership in the white world. But Huck can only see it as enslavement to a constricting books-and-Bible, spelling-and-Sunday-school world. Huck loves his freedom, but it is an adolescent freedom, measured by the absence of rules, not by an ability to make choices or to understand complex issues. It equates broad, open spaces with liberation and disregards the vastness of the soul.

Without literacy, Huck has opted for slavery.* Only literacy can provide him with the internal apparatus—all those things we have discussed, but most essentially a self—to carry on the journey toward expansiveness that he has undertaken. The Mississippi stops at a certain point (Huck runs out of fluency), but Huck has to keep going—he knows that. While the Mississippi runs through the great slave-driven heart of America—"[Twain's] great river, for all its fine amplitude, kept rolling along, passing villages filled with fierce monotheistic folk in thrall to slavery, while at river's end there were the slave markets of New Orleans"†—Huck simply does not recognize that he can continue traveling, that he can take the most exciting trip imaginable, by staying in one place.

Huck, in short, does not know how to handle liberation. Likewise, a good many people today have trouble handling the legacy of liberation that has been churning in this country for over three decades. This country, America, *is* liberation. That's why so many immigrants flee their own countries to take up a new life here. But a good many Americans have lighted out for the territory, turned their backs, closed their minds, narrowed their perceptions—all in self-defense. They feel assaulted: Too many gays and lesbians, blacks and Chicanos, women and Asians want, or rather, demand too damned much from them. A new reality, a different, more controllable reality makes much more sense, and so those who feel assaulted take comfort either in the wide open spaces or in the electronic frontier, both places obliterating the need for face-to-face human interaction.

Although it promises total power, electronic communication in particular has killed off the possibility of liberation by destroying the prospects for literacy. Computer designers assign human terms to their

---

*Only with Ted Turner's estimated $2.7 billion fortune could Huck possibly fill out his dream. The *New York Times* tells us that "starting from scratch nine years ago, Mr. Turner has amassed 1.3 million acres of ranch land, roughly enough to fill the state of Delaware, on eight ranches in Montana, New Mexico, and Nebraksa. . . . He is now negotiating the purchase of his first ranch outside the United States, a 9,000-acre spread in Argentina" (Geraldine Fabrikant, "Ted [Don't Fence Me In] Turner," *New York Times*, November 24, 1996, sec. 3, p. 1).

†James Dickey, introduction to *The Adventures of Huckleberry Finn*, by Mark Twain (New York: Harper Collins Editions, 1990), p. 7.

machines with a purpose in mind. Words like *memory, language, interactive, digital*, and *interface* are designed to make up for personal loss. Those terms also acknowledge that we must somehow compensate for that loss. The most frightening situation may be the use of the infinity of cyberspace for the miracle of an internal journey. By robbing us of internal metaphors, technology moves us away from real insight. Technology can only do the obvious: make us marvel at the wonders of technology.

As Americans have become more and more shallow—one could make the case for the thinness of popular culture—they have inevitably turned tougher. How hard it is to be heard under the best of circumstances. How much more difficult, how futile, without a voice. That silence, I do not count as absurd, only tragic. Volume (loudness), as I have said before, cannot make up for volume (space). Once we shrink into shallowness, we tend to see others merely on the surface, as well—only their skin color, for instance—"the color of their skin," reversing Martin Luther King, rather than "the content of their character."

212

THE
PRIVATE
DEATH
OF
PUBLIC
DISCOURSE

But the truth lies at a deeper level and is certainly more complex. The seventeenth century may have begun to articulate personal, *unalienable* rights for everyone (a seventeenth-century word *unalienable*), but the sit-in movement proved that those rights mean nothing if one does not press them, test them, put them into practice—against even the most oppressive forces. Rights cannot exist as a potentiality.*

The civil rights movement, everyone knows, started in the South. But we hardly ever hear the full story. The civil rights movement would not have taken place without the agitation of several defiant and courageous women. Four black freshmen, at North Carolina Agricultural and Technical College, as I have already pointed out, initiated the sit-ins of the sixties. They took their inspiration from the bus boycott started by a forty-two-year-old seamstress and prominent member of the community (secretary of the local chapter of the NAACP) named Rosa Parks. I. F. Stone had writ-

---

* *Inalienable*, which means the same as *unalienable*, appears later in the seventeenth century.

ten in his *Weekly* on October 3, 1955, that "the American Negro needs a Gandhi to lead *him*, and we need the American Negro to lead *us*"—sentiments echoed nearly twenty years later by Ralph Ellison. That Gandhi would appear in a very short time.

In fact, two months after Stone's article appeared, on December 1, 1955, Rosa Parks sat down in the Cleveland Avenue bus for the ride home from her job at the Montgomery Fair Department Store. It turned out to be a ride heard around the world. The debate centered on many of the same issues as the free speech movement in Berkeley, the idea of the commons and the ownership of space. What space did Rosa Parks occupy—black or white? Here is the way Taylor Branch tells the story in his *Parting the Waters*:

All thirty-six seats of the bus she boarded were soon filled, with twenty-two Negroes seated from the rear and fourteen whites from the front. Driver J. P. Blake, seeing a white man standing in the front of the bus, called out for the four passengers on the row just behind the whites to stand up and move to the back. Nothing happened. Blake finally had to get out of the driver's seat to speak more firmly to the four Negroes. "You better make it light on yourselves and let me have those seats," he said. At this, three of the Negroes moved to stand in the back of the bus, but Parks responded that she was not in the white section and didn't think she ought to move. She was in no-man's-land. Blake said that the white section was where he said it was, and he was telling Parks that she was in it. As he saw the law, the whole idea of no-man's-land was to give the driver some discretion to keep the races out of each other's way. He was doing just that. When Parks refused again, he advised her that the same city law that allowed him to regulate no-man's-land also gave him emergency power to enforce the segregation codes. He would arrest Parks himself if he had to. Parks replied that he should do what he had to do; she was not moving. She spoke so softly that Blake would not have been able to hear her above the drone of normal bus noise. But the bus was silent. Blake notified Parks that she was officially under arrest. She should not move until he returned with the regular Montgomery police.*

On December 5, 1955, the Women's Political Council of Montgomery—some three hundred women strong—led by an English teacher from

---

*Taylor Branch, *Parting the Waters: America in the King Years, 1954–63* (New York: Simon and Schuster, 1988), p. 129. On March 2, 1955, the police arrested a black high school student, Claudette Colvin, for refusing to give up her seat to a white woman. In October of that same year, the police arrested another black

Alabama State College, Jo Ann Robinson, who had herself been chastised for riding in the front of the bus in 1949, had been organizing and preparing for a bus boycott, just waiting for the right moment.† Like Mario Savio, she did not particularly like speaking in public, and so the council decided that the group needed a new coordinating committee and a vocal president, someone with charisma. The new group called itself the Montgomery Improvement Association and elected a young local minister as its president, the Reverend Martin Luther King, Jr.

King's first speech as president came just an hour or two after his election; he had no time to prepare. He would have to rely on the power of his own voice. This would be the first time that the great majority of those assembled, estimated conservatively at more than five thousand people—that's how eager blacks were to stage this boycott—had heard Martin Luther King.

In this first speech, with only the barest of notes scribbled on a scrap of paper, King referred to political inoculation, to the penetration of human interiority by external political motives: "If you will protest courageously, and yet with dignity and Christian love, when the history books are written in future generations, the historians will have to pause and say, 'There lived a great people—a black people—who injected new meaning and dignity into the veins of civilization.'"‡ He went on, improvising, working with the crowd, images piling on images, audience and speaker moving each other higher and higher and making King, in the commons of that Holt Street church, a public figure. So dramatic was his "first speech," I want to quote once again from Taylor Branch, who regards King's forty or forty-five minutes in front of the audience with both passion and a clear eye:

214

THE
PRIVATE
DEATH
OF
PUBLIC
DISCOURSE

---

woman, Mary Louise Smith, for refusing to give up her seat for a white woman. The court convicted her and fined her nine dollars. For various reasons, the Women's Political Council found both these cases unsuitable for their political purposes. They wanted the precisely right situation and person.

†Jo Ann Robinson had served on Martin Luther King's political affairs committee at his Dexter Avenue Baptist Church in Montgomery.

‡Martin Luther King, Jr., *Stride toward Freedom: The Montgomery Story* (New York: Harper and Row, 1958), p. 63.

[King] paused slightly longer. "And you know, my friends, there comes a time," he cried, "when people get tired of being trampled over by the iron feet of oppression." A flock of "Yeses" was coming back at him when suddenly the individual responses dissolved into a rising cheer and applause exploded beneath the cheer—all within the space of a second. The startling noise rolled on and on, like a wave that refused to break, and just when it seemed that the roar must finally weaken, a wall of sound came in from the enormous crowd outdoors to push the volume still higher. Thunder seemed to be added to the lower register—the sound of feet stomping on the wooden floor—until the loudness became something that was not so much heard as it was sensed by the vibrations in the lungs. The giant cloud of noise shook the building and refused to go away. One sentence had set it loose somehow, pushing the call-and-response of the Negro church service past the din of a political rally and on to something else that King had never known before.

There was a rabbit of awesome proportions in those bushes. As the noise finally fell back, King's voice rose above it to fire again. "There comes a time, my friends, when people get tired of being thrown across the abyss of humiliation, where they experience the bleakness of nagging despair," he declared. "There comes a time when people get tired of being pushed out of the glittering sunlight of life July, and left standing amidst the piercing chill of an Alpine November. There . . ." King was making a new run, but the crowd drowned him out. No one could tell whether the roar came in response to the nerve he had touched, or simply out of pride in a speaker from whose tongue such rhetoric rolled easily. "We are here—we are here because we are tired now," King repeated.*

Jo Ann Robinson and Rosa Parks, along with the women of the Political Council of Montgomery, handed to the sixties, to those young people confronting the management at Woolworth's, a powerful legacy. Out of it, as I have said, came virtually every political movement familiar to us today that has as its goal the assertion of inalienable rights. During the sixties in particular, blacks made it clear that political liberation would have to be read in the broadest way possible, to include something called "lifestyle." Thus, blacks effected changes in musical styles, clothing, speech, dance, and obviously sports, for an enormous number of young, white students across the country.

"Letting it all hang out"—a cool and loose style, or what Ellison called an ability to swing—freer and looser hair styles, a casual way of

---

*Taylor Branch, *Parting the Waters*, pp. 139–40.

speaking, walking, and writing, came to be a standard for a whole lot of young people in this country, starting in the sixties. In the early years of that decade, young white people craved that elusive quality called "soul." The penetration of the white world did not go unnoticed. Norman Mailer published his famous essay in 1957 about black sexuality titled so provocatively and boldly, "The White Negro: Superficial Reflections on the Hipster." In the watershed year 1964, the literary critic Leslie Fiedler, always good for a shock or two, especially about American youth, wrote the following:

There is scarcely a father of an adolescent in the United States who is not presently becoming aware (though he may feel it as a pain, rather than know it as a fact) that his son is in his whole life-style, his speech, his gait, the clothes he wears, the music he loves, as well as the vices he emulates, closer to the lifestyle of Negroes than he could have foreseen on the day of his son's birth. He may find him, in fact, in posture and in gesture, in intonation and such outward behavior, closer to the great-grandfather of his Negro friends, or at least to what those great-grandfathers have meant to the white imagination, than to their own great-grandfathers.*

216

THE
PRIVATE
DEATH
OF
PUBLIC
DISCOURSE

    Allen Ginsberg claims Lester Young, the jazz tenor saxophonist, for his inspiration for "Howl": "Howl is all 'Lester Leaps In,' and I got that from Kerouac. . . . he made me listen to it."† W. T. Lhamon, Jr., who wrote a book about the pace and style of American life in the fifties, connects Ginsberg and Kerouac at the level of black music: "In fact with the enthusiasms for black music in his novels, Kerouac made a lot of people listen to it. More significant than their enthusiasms, though, were Kerouac's and Ginsberg's reenactments of the blues ethic. Kerouac's improvisations, repetitions, stuttering starts and stops, insistence on coexisting with the world as it is, and love of late-night performance all come directly from the jazz worlds he entered on both coasts and both banks of the Mississippi River."‡

---

* Leslie Fiedler, *Waiting for the End* (New York: Stein and Day, 1964), p. 34.

  † Allen Ginsberg, *Composed on the Tongue*, ed. Donald Allen (Bolinas, Calif.: Grey Fox Press, 1980), p. 81.

  ‡ W. T. Lhamon, Jr., *Deliberate Speed: The Origins of a Cultural Style in the American 1950s* (Washington, D.C.: Smithsonian Institution Press, 1990), p. 70.

If Kerouac did indeed prompt people to listen to black music, most of them must have been white students in northern college campuses for whom Kerouac, particularly the Kerouac of *On the Road*, had reached cult status.

Recent liberation movements seem, to many observers, much too ubiquitous and much too successful. As a result, the country now is pulled in two opposing directions, one expansive and the other restrictive. One set of Americans either participates in, or feels sympathetic to, the struggles of various groups of people for liberation. Others, however, feel threatened, disgusted, or just frightened by such movements, and react by narrowing their own lives—reducing what they will accept, who they will embrace, where they will live, what they will think. This part of the population—a significant part—has had enough. No more immigrants! No more welfare! No more affirmative action! No more prenatal care or free schooling for illegals! The most extreme arm themselves. They move out to isolated parts of the country, join militia movements. Ironically, they too are fervent about liberty and liberation. They want the government off their backs; they want their rights defended; they want their Constitution enforced. Unfortunately, they also tend to shy away from political dialogue and civic participation.

    These two perspectives confound the traditional system of two-party politics in this country. We no longer have legislators speaking across the aisle, but people screaming at each other across a vast chasm. The debate no longer turns on issues of more governmental assistance as opposed to more individual autonomy, but on the question of who this country belongs to and who belongs here, on what constitutes an American, a citizen—even a human being. Most dangerous of all, this division allows only the politicians to choose the issues and to frame the discussions. Under such conditions, the people can only fall silent. Discourse must inevitably die.

    In the system of Democratic and Republican politics, expediency moves debate toward an illusory, palatable middle—a virtual common ground—as Robert Levine, deputy director of the Congressional Budget from 1975 to 1979, so aptly describes:

Led by the politics-as-a-game media, we have defined American politics along a single right-to-left dimension. We know that the new conservatives of the House of Representatives are on the right and the old liberals of the Kennedy-Johnson tradition are on the left. And the votes are in the middle, so that's where President Clinton and ex-senator Bob Dole have gone. The middle of the road may be mathematically equidistant from the right and left, but the symbolic middle toward which both candidates have moved is meaningless for making real national policy.*

As the political process careens toward the symbolic mean, the debate, understandably enough—since no one feels satisfied—grows meaner and meaner. The results frustrate nearly everyone. Levine makes the case: "For most Americans, who just want solutions to the nation's problems, the symbolic middle is useless, because it provides only symbolic solutions. We need real solutions. The correction of our national problems requires neither right nor left, neither moderation nor extremism. The political debate needs a new dimension: reality."†

I agree. America needs a new dimension—more space, the kind of space that can only be generated through free and spirited public discourse. And that in turn requires a reinvigoration of interior life. Whatever enables people to breathe again, whatever permits them to break out of their claustrophobia, can help change the direction of this country. In my view, the first step involves turning away from the screen to undertake a psychic journey that is now, for the most part, bypassed. In other words, people must return to the noisy and chaotic world of talking and listening, and from there, to reading and writing. I am of course talking about a change that must take place at the most fundamental and personal level, a chance to create a sense of greatness that only someone like Walt Whitman could imag-

218

THE
PRIVATE
DEATH
OF
PUBLIC
DISCOURSE

---

*Robert A. Levine, "The Empty Symbolism of American Politics," *Atlantic Monthly*, October 1996, pp. 80–81.

†Ibid, p. 81.

ine, that only a poet, not a politician or a social scientist, could ever hope to describe.

For me, liberation does not mean, and this should be obvious by now, that the country must physically expand. It means something much more difficult but in the long run much more important: That people—everyone—must expand, must conspire together in breathing what the eighteenth-century British statesman and political writer Edmund Burke, in a startling phrase, called the "wild gas of liberty": "When I see the spirit of liberty in action I see a strong principle at work: and this, for a while, is all I can possibly know of it. The wild *gas*, the fixed air is plainly broke loose."* Burke describes here a rush of air, a wild in-breathing of O_2 "broke loose" from tradition and order.

I can only call this reconstruction project—the rebuilding of the country—a liberation through language. How do we retrieve a sense of the self? How do we people the country again with human beings? How do we start breathing once again—not just the fortunate few, but all of us—how does every man, woman, and child breathe with that "wild gas" of liberty? To move beyond meanness, people need to demonstrate their strength, not in shouts and screams beyond a barrier of thirty-six feet or from opposite ends of the congressional floor, but in articulate and vibrant voices—voices that can whisper, or even choose (a key to power) to remain silent.

The spoken word is a tricky concept. When it works best, speech grows out of literacy, or rather, I should say, out of thinking and analyzing, both of which get formed in literacy. In a literate culture, all people, even those who can't read, utter sentences shaped by the written word, for those are the sentences that most of them hear most often. But, as I have argued elsewhere, literacy itself begins, takes root in, orality, in speaking and lis-

---

*Edmund Burke, *Select Works*, ed. Edward J. Payne (London: Clarendon Press, 1897), p. 189 (emphasis mine). An appropriate metaphor for liberty, gas had only been coined a short time before, by a chemist named J. B. von Helmont (1577–1644). First used in 1658, *gas* referred to an occult principle contained in all bodies, one that continually expanded. For Burke, liberation meant inflation in the old sense, without any economic overtones.

tening.* Orality provides the armature—the pitches and intonations, the withholding of information for suspense, the increased tempo toward climax—around which literacy forms. No one would mistake Martin Luther King or Mario Savio, even with all their brilliant rhetorical flourishes, for nonliterates or illiterates. We can hear literacy in their sentences. From orality to literacy to spoken sentences: Thus the wheel turns in its civilizing process as people acquire their voices.

When I say *voice*, I mean, of course, more than timber, pitch, or volume—more even than recognizable inflections. I mean an inclination toward power and persuasion, a rhythm of reason, and a flow—the *course* of dis*course*—of ideas. I mean the voice one hears not with the ear but with the heart and mind. I have spent time in this book on the oral—on black speech, for instance, and the techniques of Twain and Whitman—because reasoned discourse thrives best when it is informed by orality. Otherwise, discourse falters. Speakers shape their ideas and thoughts with rules of syntax and grammar that characterize literacy: They cast the die of literacy in the spontaneity of orality. Orality and literacy dance with each other, back and forth—what Ezra Pound called *logopoeia*, the "play of words"— toward that miracle called articulation.

Mario Savio gave his most famous, his most well remembered speech on December 2, 1964, on the steps in front of Sproul Hall Plaza. The free speech movement had delivered a new ultimatum to the administration, and handed them a deadline of noon for a response. The Board of Regents in a November meeting had initiated disciplinary procedures against CORE, the Young Socialists Alliance, Women for Peace, the W. E. B. Du Bois Club, University Friends of SNCC, as well as against Arthur and Jackie Goldberg and Mario Savio. Movement leaders demanded nothing less than the dropping of all charges against every student and group. Five thousand people gathered at the steps to await Clark Kerr's decision. Joan

220

THE
PRIVATE
DEATH
OF
PUBLIC
DISCOURSE

---

*See Ivan Illich and Barry Sanders, *ABC: The Alphabetization of the Popular Mind* (San Francisco: North Point Press, 1988); and Barry Sanders, *A Is for Ox: Violence, Electronic Media, and the Silencing of the Written Word* (New York: Pantheon Books, 1994).

Baez opened the rally by leading the entire assembly in a resounding call and response. Heirich describes a different mood on that morning from previous rallies, a high-pitched fervor similar to that of those who had heard King's first speech before the bus boycott less than ten years earlier, a new, more deeply felt rhythm and cadence that suffused itself through the crowd:

There was an urgency in striking contrast to the pace of FSM rallies in the past. Previously some speakers may have been militant, and speaking styles varied widely, but there had been an element of rational discourse, of charm of expression, in most of the rallies. On December 2, this was gone. The tone, the rhythms, the tense, searing timber of voices were similar to those heard during an altar call in a major religious revival campaign. The crowd felt the tension.*

After Joan Baez sang, Mario Savio came to the front of the crowd and, at the climax of his speech, closed with an image that captured the vulnerability of the movement, of those who were the movement:

We're human beings. And that brings me to the second mode of civil disobedience. There is a time when the operation of the machine becomes so odious, makes you so sick at heart, that you can't take part; you can't even passively take part, and you've got to put your bodies upon the gears and upon the wheels, upon the levers, upon all the apparatus and you've got to make it stop. And you've got to indicate to the people who run it, to the people who own it, that unless you're free, the machines will be prevented from working at all.†

In the pitch of excitement, in the face of that huge crowd, Savio spoke from somewhere deep in his being. He spoke, but the layering of sentences, the steady push toward a climactic moment—to the image of the tender, fleshy body against the flinty edge of the machine—came from someone who had spent a good deal of time reading, in Savio's case, reading philosophical texts.

What Savio said, in the end, seems less important, somehow, than the fact that he spoke; that he could deliberately withdraw into himself and sound out his very own being in words. A happy coincidence, that Savio

---

*Heirich, *The Spiral of Conflict*, p. 271.
†Ibid, p. 272.

lived into his name—"the wise one" (El Sabio). In a most moving obituary, the writer Wendy Lesser, who heard Savio's early speeches only on video-tape, can still recall the poetic power of Savio's words:

He was the only political figure of my era for whom language truly mattered. He was the last American, perhaps, who believed that civil, expressive, precisely worded, emotionally truthful exhortation could bring about significant change. He was the only person I have ever seen or met who gave political speech the weight and subtlety of literature. The irony is that his power lay entirely in the spoken word, so that what he said on any given occasion could never quite be captured in print. His voice—the very sound of it, its accent and emphasis and pitch—was physically a part of the meaning of his words. And with his death on Nov. 6, that voice was silenced.*

With Savio in mind, I can envision only one way to get our lives back. I realize that people will not willingly or totally shake off their TVs, video games, and computers. But to experience the full power of literacy, to have it really take hold deep within us, we will have to shun at least some of technology's dominance over our daily existence. We have to make a small opening, a chance to re-embody literacy without the damaging side-effects of technology. The only way back to literacy for many of us these days—as strange as it sounds—lies in talking ourselves back to the foundations of lit-eracy, back to orality itself. This means speaking sentences we think up our-selves, in noisy conversation and discussion with others. It means listening to stories and conversation—truly listening—in silent, attentive ease. In the end, it means impromptu talk—speech pried loose from all program-ming—inspired talk, as Lesser says, "as if he were breathing thought through language."†

Twain had to create Jim to invigorate Huck. Ellison made clear the importance of blacks in maintaining linguistic vitality in America. One can-not write about this country—on any conceivable subject, I am con-vinced—without confronting issues of race. We must imagine some Other, some self, unfettered and uninhibited by technology—a self as stranger in

222

THE
PRIVATE
DEATH
OF
PUBLIC
DISCOURSE

---

*Wendy Lesser, "Speech with the Weight of Literature," *New York Times Book Review*, December 15, 1996, p. 43.
†Ibid.

our own lives—to reinvigorate our own daily language. Beyond that, however, we need to pull off the most compelling turn toward integration— *integration*, yet another seventeenth-century term, which means "putting parts together to form a whole"—and imagine ourselves, deeply imagine ourselves, as dropout, as homeless, as marginal, as Other. Having that alienated creature inside us, how then would we talk? How different, then, the compassion and concern? How different the sentences?

To reconstruct America, we need to think in Whitmanic terms of expanding the country, adding back to the roster of imaginable citizens the neglected and the abused. I believe we can make such an enumeration only through informed talk. Only reading and writing, those strangely isolating activities, can point us back toward community and civility again. Books of virtues or morals will not get us there. Such manuals run counter to the goal of creating civil and sincere human beings. They mask the emotions in much the way the same tools, books of manners, papered over emotions in the seventeenth century. Only one pursuit opens the way where articulate voices find mutual respect.

One more meaning of *meaning* remains. I have saved it for the last. In the range of definitions of *mean*, I have tried to trace the word's slow drift from the average—the middle—out to the edge: specifically, from a place of meaning to one of meanness. The word has yet another spatial dimension. From *medianus*—one of the word's Latin roots—derives the word *medial* (the middle) and another, more recent, and much more important definition in defining contemporary life, *medium*: "Any intervening substance through which a force acts on objects at a distance or through which impressions are conveyed to the senses." So, as the seventeenth century believed, air or ether served as media for transmitting light or sound.*

By the late nineteenth century, *medium* had come to refer to newspapers; and then, in the twentieth century, of course, to the various electronic vehicles of information. The most powerful, most ubiquitous of

---

*A medium, as clairvoyant, conducts the truth from one world—the beyond—to this one.

those electronic devices, the personal computer with all of its concomitant innovations—Internet, Web page, e-mail, and on and on—has proved to be most damaging to the overwhelming variety of everyday experiences. The majority of Americans watch the same programs, see the same images, hear the same sentences, ponder the same events—all from the same perspective. In that programmatic sense, then, the media make out of the tumult and abundance of experience a *medial*, or average, common, event. In the process, the media muffle voices. Thus, as the key electronic medium, the personal computer contributes to extreme behavior by moving people, metaphorically, into a straitened, barely tolerable middle.

In *The Road Ahead*, a reverie on how the electronic future will liberate every American, Bill Gates envisions a life totally in thrall to a fiber optics network:

224

THE ·
PRIVATE
DEATH
OF
PUBLIC
DISCOURSE

The day has almost arrived when you can easily conduct business, study, explore the world and its cultures, call up great entertainment, make friends, go to neighborly markets, and show pictures to your relatives, wherever they are— without leaving your desk or your armchair. Once this new era is in full swing, you won't leave your network connection behind at the office or in your classroom. Your connection will be more than an appliance you've bought or an object you carry. It will be your passport into a new, "mediated" way of life.

Firsthand experiences are unmediated. No one will take away from you in the name of progress the experience of lying on a beach, walking in the woods, shopping at a flea market, or breaking up at a comedy club. But firsthand experiences aren't always so rewarding. Waiting in line is a firsthand experience, but we have been trying to invent ways to avoid it ever since we first queued up.*

From this new, electronically inspired middle place, a person sitting behind a desk has only to manipulate the Microsoft program and, as John Seabrook, the media critic, says, "everything in your environment will be responsive to you and your needs." Seabrook goes on to characterize Gates as an American with a potent dream, "a dream of an entirely personal relationship to technology. His achievement has been to make the world better conform to the needs of a person working alone, rather than to create

---

*Bill Gates, *The Road Ahead* (New York: Viking Penguin, 1995), pp. 4–5.

spaces in which people coexist: he's not, at least instinctively, a 'network' man."*

That way, down the road to cyberspace, loneliness lies. The virtual world may promise wonderful benefits, and it may even deliver on some of them; but none of us will ever truly *meet* there. Neat and tidy a mediated life will surely be, but lovely—in that amorous sense of the word—it does not stand a chance of being. Only my face staring back at your face, only in moments when I can see your expressions, note your gestures and stance, the way my words embody themselves in the listening you—only then can I say we have discourse. In such a fleshy interchange, when I refer to *you*, I mean the transcendent you in which discourse speaks of something miraculous beyond speaker and listener.

In the eerie space separating person from person across the Internet, silence settles over every interaction like a pall, a silence that deadens by disregarding the spirit, by making impossible the key journey from meaning to meaningfulness. I can imagine another, more emphatic silence, the pregnant silence that the conjuring of words and ideas always requires. That kind of silence, so different from the spaces between electronic blips—the o's that separate the 1's in a binary system—is alphabetically constructed. It should not seem odd that the hope of reinstating noisy talk—the clamor of being—should lie in the depths of meditative silence.

The opposite of death is not life, but the *creation* of life—an emergence in which meaning continuously presents itself. It occurs deep in interior space, where, as Ivan Illich observes, we can experience "the silence of syntony; the silence in which we await the proper moment for the Word to be born into the world."† And we wait in silence, in anticipation of that most powerful emergency, to receive the Word back from Others.

---

*John Seabrook, "Gates at the Temple,"*New Yorker*, December 11, 1995, p. 78.

†Ivan Illich, *The Celebration of Awareness: A Call for Institutional Revolution* (New York: Doubleday, 1970), p. 34.

Albert, Judith Clavir, and Stewart Edward Albert, eds. *The Sixties Papers: Documents of a Rebellious Decade*. New York: Praeger Special Studies, 1984.

Allan, Jonathan S. "Fear of Viruses." *New York Times*, January 21, 1996, Sec. A, p. 15.

Arendt, Hannah. *The Human Condition*. Chicago: University of Chicago Press, 1958.

——. *Thinking*. Vol. 1 of *The Life of the Mind*. New York: Harcourt Brace Jovanovich, 1981.

Aries, Philippe. *Western Attitudes toward Death, from the Middle Ages to the Present*. Trans. Patricia M. Ranum. Baltimore: Johns Hopkins University Press, 1974.

——, and Georges Duby, eds. *A History of Private Life: Revelations of the Medieval World*. Trans. Arthur Goldhammer. Cambridge: Harvard University Press, 1988.

Auden, W. H. *W. H. Auden: Collected Poems*. New York: Random House, 1965.

Avorn, Jerry L. *Up against the Ivory Wall: A History of the Columbia Crisis*. New York: Atheneum Press, 1968.

Bachelard, Gaston. *The Poetics of Space*. Trans. Maria Jolas. Boston: Beacon Press, 1969.

Baigent, Michael, and Richard Leigh. *The Temple and the Lodge*. New York: Arcade Publishing, 1989.

Baida, Peter. *Poor Richard's Legacy: American Business Values from Benjamin Franklin to Donald Trump*. New York: William Morrow, 1990.

Bakhtin, Mikhail. *The Dialogic Imagination*. Trans. Caryl Emerson and Michael Holquist. Austin: University of Texas Press, 1981.

——, *Marxism and the Philosophy of Language*. Trans. Ladislav Matejka and I. R. Titunik. Cambridge: Harvard University Press, 1986.

Benedikt, Michael, ed. *The Prose Poem: An International Anthology*. New York: Dell Publishing, 1976.

Bercovitch, Sacvan. *The Puritan Origins of the American Self*. New Haven: Yale University Press, 1975.

Berman, Marshall. *All That Is Solid Melts into Air*. New York: Simon and Schuster, 1982.

Birkerts, Sven. "The Fate of the Book." *Antioch Review* 54, no. 3 (summer 1996): 261–72.

——, *The Gutenberg Elegies: The Fate of Reading in an Electronic Age*. Boston: Faber and Faber, 1994.

Bloom, Allan. *The Closing of the American Mind*. New York: Simon and Schuster, 1987.

Bloom, Harold. *The Western Canon: The Books and Schools of the Ages*. New York: Riverhead Books, 1994.

Bly, Robert. *American Poetry: Wildness and Domesticity*. New York: Harper and Row, 1990.

———. *Leaping Poetry: An Idea with Poems and Translations*. Boston: Beacon Press, 1975.

Boorstin, Daniel J. *The Image; or, Whatever Happened to the American Dream?* New York: Atheneum Press, 1962.

Bourdieu, Pierre. "The Social Space and the Genesis of Groups." *Theory and Society* 14 (1985): 723–44.

Branch, Taylor. *Parting the Waters: America in the King Years, 1954–63*. New York: Simon and Schuster, 1988.

Bremmer, Jan, and Herman Roodenburg, eds. *A Cultural History of Gesture*. Ithaca: Cornell University Press, 1991.

Camille, Michael. *Image on the Edge: The Margins of Medieval Art*. Cambridge: Harvard University Press, 1992.

Carruthers, Mary J. *The Book of Memory: A Study of Memory in Medieval Culture*. New York: Cambridge University Press, 1990.

Carson, Clayborne. *In Struggle: SNCC and the Black Awakening of the 1960s*. Cambridge: Harvard University Press, 1981.

Caute, David. *The Year of the Barricades: A Journey through 1968*. New York: Harper and Row, 1988.

Cixous, Helene. "Writing Blind." Trans. Eric Prenowitz. *TriQuarterly* 97 (fall 1996): 7–20.

Close, Ellis. *The Rage of a Privileged Class*. New York: Harper Collins, 1993.

Cmiel, Kenneth. *Democratic Eloquence: The Fight over Popular Speech in Nineteenth-Century America*. New York: William Morrow, 1990.

Colomina, Beatriz, ed. *Sexuality and Space*. Princeton: Princeton University Press, 1992.

Condland, Douglas Keith. *Feral Children and Clever Animals: Reflections on Human Nature*. New York: Oxford University Press, 1993.

Cook, Philip J., and Robert H. Frank. *The Winner-Take-All Society*. New York: Free Press, 1995.

Davidson, Cathy N., ed. *Reading in America: Literature and Social History*. Baltimore: Johns Hopkins University Press, 1989.

De Bastide, Jean-Françoise. *The Little House: An Architectural Seduction*. Trans. Rodolphe El-Khoury. Princeton: Princeton University Press, 1996.

Douglas, Mary, ed. *Essays in the Sociology of Perception*. London: Routledge and Kegan Paul, 1982.

Du Bois, W. E. B. *The Souls of Black Folk*. New York: Dodd Mead, 1961.

Elias, Norbert. *The History of Manners: The Civilizing Process*. New York: Pantheon Books, 1978.

Ellison, Ralph. *Going to the Territory*. New York: Vintage Books, 1987.

Emerson, Ralph Waldo. *Essays and Lectures*. Ed. Joel Porte. New York: Library Classics of the United States, 1983.

Engelhardt, Tom. *The End of Victory Culture: Cold War America and the Disillusioning of a Generation*. New York: Basic Books, 1995.

Erikson, Kai T. *The Wayward Puritans: A Study in the Sociology of Deviance*. New York: John Wiley and Sons, 1966.

Ezekial, Raphael S. *The Racist Mind: Portraits of Neo-Nazis and Klansmen*. New York: Viking Penguin, 1995.

Fish, Stanley, *There's No Such Thing as Free Speech: And It's a Good Thing Too*. New York: Oxford University Press, 1994.

Fishkin, Shelley Fisher. "Huck's Black Voice." *Wilson Quarterly* 20 (autumn 1996): 81–85.

——. *Was Huck Black? Mark Twain and African-American Voices*. New York: Oxford University Press, 1993.

Fiss, Owen. *The Irony of Free Speech*. Cambridge: Harvard University Press, 1996.

Ford, Richard. *Independence Day*. New York: Alfred A. Knopf, 1995.

Foucault, Michel. *Discipline and Punish*. Trans. Alan Sheridan. New York: Vintage Books, 1979.

——. *The Order of Things: An Archaeology of the Human Sciences*. New York: Random House, 1970.

——. *Power/Knowledge*. New York: Pantheon Books, 1980.

Fumento, Michael. "Politics and Church Burnings." *Commentary* 102, no. 4 (October 1996): 57–69.

Garreau, Joel. *Edge City: Life on the New Frontier*. New York: Doubleday, 1991.

Gass, William. *The World within the Word*. Boston: David Godine, 1979.

Gates, Henry Louis, Jr. *Loose Canons: Notes on the Culture Wars*. New York: Oxford University Press, 1992.

Giedion, Sigfried, S. *Space, Time, and Architecture: The Growth of a New Tradition*. Cambridge: Harvard University Press, 1954.

Ginsberg, Allen. *Empty Mirror*. New York: Corinth Books, 1961.

Gitlin, Todd. *The Sixties: Years of Hope, Days of Rage*. New York: Bantam Books, 1987.

——. *The Twilight of Common Dreams: Why America Is Wracked by Culture Wars*. New York: Henry Holt, 1995.

Goffman, Erving. *Interaction Ritual: Essays in Face-to-Face Behavior*. Chicago: Aldine Publishing, 1967.

Goleman, Daniel. *Emotional Intelligence*. New York: Bantam Books, 1996.

Graff, Gerald. *Beyond the Culture Wars: How Teaching the Conflicts Can Revitalize American Education*. New York: W. W. Norton, 1992.

Greenblatt, Stephen, and Giles Green, eds. *Redrawing the Boundaries: The Transformation of English and American Literary Studies*. New York: MLA of America, 1992.

Grudin, Robert. *On Dialogue: An Essay in Free Thought*. Boston: Houghton Mifflin, 1996.

Guillory, John. *Cultural Capital: The Problem of Literary Canon Formation*. Chicago: University of Chicago Press, 1993.

Gutman, Amy, and Dennis Thompson. *Democracy and Disagreement*. Cambridge: Harvard University Press, 1996.

Habermas, Jurgen. *Between Facts and Norms: Contributions to a Discourse Theory of Law and Democracy*. Trans. William Rehg. Cambridge: MIT Press, 1988.

———. *The Structural Transformation of the Public Sphere*. Trans. Thomas Berger. Cambridge: MIT Press, 1989.

Harrison, Bennett. *Lean and Mean: The Changing Landscape of Corporate Power in the Age of Flexibility*. New York: Basic Books, 1994.

Hasselbach, Ingo, with Tom Reiss. "How Nazis Are Made." *New Yorker*, January 8, 1996, pp. 36ff.

Havelock, Eric. *The Literate Revolution in Greece and Its Cultural Consequences*. Princeton: Princeton University Press, 1982.

Heirich, Max. *The Spiral of Conflict: Berkeley, 1964*. New York: Columbia University Press, 1971.

Herdman, John. *The Double in Nineteenth-Century Fiction*. New York: St. Martin's Press, 1991.

Joe Holley. "Who Was Burning the Black Churches?" *Columbia Journalism Review* 35, no. 3 (September–October 1996): 26–39.

Hunt, Lynn, ed. *The New Cultural History*. Berkeley: University of California Press, 1989.

Jaeger, Werner. *Paideia: The Ideals of Greek Culture*. Trans. Gilbert Highet. New York: Oxford University Press, 1939.

Jardine, Lisa. *Reading Shakespeare Historically*. London: Routledge, 1996.

Jarrell, Randall. *Poetry and the Age*. New York: Random House, 1953.

Judy, Ronald. *(Dis)Forming the American Canon: African-Arabic Slave Narratives and the Vernacular*. Minneapolis: University of Minnesota Press, 1993.

Kaplan, Justin. *Walt Whitman: A Life*. New York: Simon and Schuster, 1980.

Katsiaficas, George. *The Imagination of the New Left: A Global Analysis of 1968*. Boston: South End Press, 1987.

Kelly, Michael. "Playing with Fire." *New Yorker*, July 15, 1996, pp. 28–35.

Kern, Stephen. *The Culture of Time and Space, 1880–1918*. Cambridge: Harvard University Press, 1983.

King, Martin Luther, Jr. *Stride toward Freedom: The Montgomery Story*. New York: Harper and Row, 1958.

Kundera, Milan. "You're Not in Your Own House Here, My Dear Fellow." *New York Review of Books*, September 24, 1995, pp. 21ff.

———. "The Day Panurge No Longer Makes People Laugh." *Critical Quarterly* 38, no. 2 (1996): 33ff.

Kunen, James K. "Teaching Prisoners a Lesson." *New Yorker*, July 10, 1995, pp. 34ff.

Lakoff, George, and Mark Johnson. *Metaphors We Live By*. Chicago: University of Chicago Press, 1980.

Lasch, Christopher. *The Culture of Narcissism: American Life in an Age of Diminishing Expectations*. New York: W. W. Norton, 1978.

Le Doux, Joseph. *The Mysterious Underpinnings of Emotional Life*. New York: Simon and Schuster, 1997.

Lesser, Wendy. "Speech with the Weight of Literature." *New York Times Book Review*, December 15, 1996, p. 43.

Lefebvre, Henri. *The Production of Space*. Trans. Donald Nicholson-Smith. London: Basil Blackwell, 1991.

Lehman, David. *Signs of the Times: Deconstruction and the Fall of Paul de Man*. New York: Poseidon Press, 1991.

Leroi-Gourhan, Andre. *The Hunters of Prehistory*. Trans. Claire Jacobson. New York: Atheneum Press, 1983.

———. *An Introduction to Paleolithic Cave Drawing*. Trans. Sara Champion. New York: Cambridge University Press, 1982.

Levinas, Emmanuel. *Totality and Infinity: An Essay on Exteriority*. Trans. Alphonso Lingis. Pittsburgh: Duquesne University Press, 1969.

Levine, Lawrence W. *The Opening of the American Mind: Canons, Culture, and History*. Boston: Beacon Press, 1996.

Lewis, C. S. *Studies in Words*. New York: Cambridge University Press, 1967.

Lewis, Nigel. *The Book of Babel: Words and the Way We See Things*. Iowa City: University of Iowa Press, 1994.

Lhamon, W. T., Jr. *Deliberate Speed: The Origins of a Cultural Style in the American 1950s*. Washington, D.C. : Smithsonian Institution Press, 1990.

Lipking, Lawrence. "The Marginal Gloss." *Critical Inquiry* 3, no. 4 (summer 1977): 609–55.

Lipset, Seymour Martin, and Sheldon S. Wolin, eds. *The Berkeley Student Revolt: Facts and Interpretations*. Garden City, N. J.: Doubleday, 1965.

Locke, John. *The Educational Writings of John Locke*. Ed. James L. Axtell. London: Cambridge University Press, 1968.

———. *Essay Concerning Human Understanding*. New York: New American Library, 1974.

———. *Two Treatises of Government*. Ed. Mark Goldie. London: J. M. Dent, 1993.

Lyotard, Jean-François. *The Postmodern Condition: A Report on Knowledge*. Trans. Geoff Bennington and Brian Massumi. Minneapolis: University of Minnesota Press, 1984.

MacDonald, J. Fred. *One Nation under Television: The Rise and Decline of Network TV*. New York: Pantheon Books, 1990.

MacIntyre, Alasdair. *After Virtue*. Notre Dame: University of Notre Dame Press, 1981.

Mailer, Norman. *The White Negro: Superficial Reflections on the Hipster*. San Francisco: City Lights Books, 1957.

Manguel, Alberto. *A History of Reading*. New York: Viking Press, 1996.

Mayer, Martin. *About Television*. New York: Harper and Row, 1972.

Miles, Barry. *Ginsberg: A Biography*. New York: Simon and Schuster, 1984.

Mills, Nicolaus. *The Triumph of Meanness*. New York: Houghton Mifflin, 1997.

Miyoshi, Masao. "A Borderless World? From Colonialism to Transnationalism and the Decline of the Nation-State." *Critical Inquiry* 19, no. 4 (summer 1993): 726–51.

Moynihan, Daniel Patrick. *Miles to Go: A Personal History of Social Policy*. Cambridge: Harvard University Press, 1996.

Murray, Albert. *The Omni-Americans: New Perspectives on Black Experience and American Culture*. New York: Outerbridge and Dienstfrey, 1970.

Nocera, Joseph. "Getting Borked." *Gentleman's Quarterly*, Summer 1995, p. 18.

Oates, Joyce Carol. "I Had No Other Thrill or Happiness." *New York Review of Books*, March 24, 1994, 52–59.

Ong, Walter. *Orality and Literacy: The Technologizing of the Word*. London: Methuen, 1982.

Perlina, Nina. "Mikhail Bakhtin and Martin Buber: Problems of Dialogic Imagination." *Studies in Twentieth-Century Literature* 9, no. 1 (fall 1984): 13–28.

Perlstein, Steven. "No More Mr. Nice Guy." *Washington Post*, weekly edition, December 18–24, 1995, p. 11.

Philips, Adam. *On Kissing, Tickling, and Being Bored: Psychoanalytic Essays on the Unexamined Life*. Cambridge: Harvard University Press, 1993.

Piore, Michael J. *Beyond Individualism*. Cambridge: Harvard University Press, 1995.

Readings, Bill. *The University in Ruins*. Cambridge: Harvard University Press, 1996.

Ridgeway, James. *Blood in the Face: The Ku Klux Klan, Aryan Nations, Nazi Skinheads, and the Rise of a New White Culture*. New York: Thunder's Mouth Press, 1990.

Robbins, Bruce, ed. *The Phantom Public Sphere*. Minneapolis: University of Minnesota Press, 1993.

Robert, Jean. *Water Is a Commons*. Mexico City: Habitat International Coalition, 1994.

Robinson, Jo Ann Gibson. *The Montgomery Bus Boycott and the Women Who Started It: The Memoir of Jo Ann Gibson Robinson*. Edited and with a foreword by David J. Garrow. Knoxville: University of Tennessee Press, 1987.

Rosenbaum, David E. "In with the Idealogues, on with Deadlock." *New York Times*, January 21, 1996, Sec. A, p. 5.

Ross, Alex. "The Shock of the True: Crime and Why We Can't Stop Reading about It." *New Yorker*, August 19, 1996, pp. 70ff.

Ruspoli, Mario. *The Cave of Lascaux: The Final Photographs*. New York: Harry N. Abrams, 1987.

Rykwert, Joseph. *The Dancing Column: On Order in Architecture*. Cambridge: MIT Press, 1996.

Rymer, Russ. *Genie: An Abused Child's Flight from Silence*. New York: Harper Collins, 1993.

Sandel, Michael J. *Democracy's Discontents*. Cambridge: Harvard University Press, 1996.

Sanders, Barry. *A Is for Ox: Violence, Electronic Media, and the Silencing of the Written Word*. New York: Pantheon Books, 1994.

Sardello, Robert, ed. *What Makes a City: Growth and Undergrowth*. Dallas: Dallas Institute of Humanities and Culture Newsletter, 1985.

Sargent, Lyman Tower, ed. *Extremism in America*. New York: New York University Press, 1995.

Savageau, Cheryl. *Dirt Road Home*. Willimantic, Conn.: Curbstone Press, 1995.

Scruggs, Charles. *Sweet Home: Invisible Cities in the Afro-American Novel*. Baltimore: Johns Hopkins University Press, 1993.

Scull, Andrew, ed. *Madhouses, Mad-Doctors, and Madmen*. Philadelphia: University of Pennsylvania Press, 1981.

Shields, Rob. *Places on the Margin: Alternative Geographies of Modernity*. London: Routledge, 1991.

Shiva, Vandana. *Ecology and the Politics of Survival: Conflicts over Natural Resources in India*. Newbury Park, Calif.: Sage Publications, 1991.

Sobel, Dava. *Longitude: The True Story of a Lone Genius Who Solved the Greatest Scientific Problem of His Time*. New York: Penguin Books, 1996.

Sommer, Robert. *Personal Space: The Behavioral Basis of Design*. Englewood Cliffs, N. J.: Prentice-Hall, 1969.

Sontag, Susan. "AIDS as Metaphor." *New York Review of Books*, October 27, 1988, pp. 89–99.

———. *Illness as Metaphor*. New York: Farrar, Straus and Giroux, 1978.

Spock, Benjamin. *The Common Sense Book of Baby and Child Care*. New York: Duell, Sloan and Pearce, 1946.

———. *Decent and Indecent: Our Personal and Political Behavior*. New York: McCall, 1970.

———. *Raising Children in a Difficult Time: A Philosophy of Parental Leadership and High Ideals*. New York: W. W. Norton, 1974.

Stallybrass, Peter, and Allon White. *The Politics and Poetics of Transgression*. Ithaca: Cornell University Press, 1986.

Stearns, Carol Zisowitz, and Peter N. Stearns. *Anger: The Struggle for Emotional Control in America's History*. Chicago: University of Chicago Press, 1986.

Stein, Gertrude. *Narration: Four Lectures*. Chicago: University of Chicago Press, 1937.

Steiner, George. *No Passion Spent: Essays, 1978–1995*. New Haven: Yale University Press, 1996.

———. *Real Presences*. Chicago: University of Chicago Press, 1989.

Tafuri, Manfredo. *Theories and History of Architecture*. Trans. Giorgio Verrecchia. New York: Harper and Row, 1980.

Teresa of Avila. *Interior Castle*. Ed. E. Allison Peers. New York: Doubleday, 1989.

Thomas, Keith. *Man and the Natural World: A History of the Modern Sensibility*. New York: Pantheon Books, 1983.

Trento, Susan. *The Power House: Robert Keith Gray and the Selling of Access and Influence in Washington*. New York: St. Martin's Press, 1992.

Trilling, Diana. *We Must March My Darlings: A Critical Decade*. New York: Harcourt Brace Jovanovich, 1977.

Turner, Frederick Jackson. *The Frontier in American History*. New York: Henry Holt, 1928.

Valéry, Paul. *Selected Writings*. New York: New Directions Books, 1964.

Vitruvius, Pollio. *De architectura*. Edited by Frank Granger from Harleian Ms. 2767. Loeb Classical Library. London: Heinemann, 1931–34.

Von Feuerbach, Anselm. *Kasper Hauser: An Account of an Individual Life in a Dungeon Separated from All Communication with the World, from Early Childhood to about the Age of Seventeen*. London: Simpkin and Marshall, 1833.

Weber, Samuel. *Intuition and Interpretation*. Minneapolis: University of Minnesota Press, 1987.

Whitman, Walt. *Leaves of Grass*. Ed. Malcolm Cowley. New York: Viking Press, 1959.

Williams, Raymond. *The Country and the City*. London: Chatto and Windus, 1973.

———. *Keywords: A Vocabulary of Culture and Society*. New York: Oxford University Press, 1976.

Wills, Garry. *John Wayne's America: The Politics of Celebrity*. New York: Simon and Schuster, 1997.

Wilson, William Julius. *When Work Disappears: The World of the New Urban Poor*. New York: Alfred A. Knopf, 1996.

Woolf, Virginia. *A Room of One's Own*. New York: Harcourt, Brace, 1929.

Yudice, George. "Marginality and the Ethics of Survival." In *Universal Abandon? The Politics of Postmodernism*, ed. Andrew Ross. Minneapolis: University of Minnesota Press, 1988.

Zerubavel, Eviator. *The Fine Line: Making Distinctions in Everyday Life*. Chicago: University of Chicago Press, 1991.

Zevi, Bruno. *Architecture as Space: How to Look at Architecture*. Trans. Milton Gendel. New York: Horizon Press, 1957.

Zinn, Howard. *SNCC: The New Abolitionists*. New York: Alfred A. Knopf, 1965.

INDEX